MARXIST HUMANISM AND PRAXIS

Edited, with translations, by

Gerson S. Sher

Published by Prometheus Books
1203 Kensington Avenue, Buffalo, New York 14215

Library of Congress Catalog Number: 77-26377
ISBN 0-87975-097-9

Printed in the United States of America

Contents

Introduction

This volume presents a collection of essays by the principal members of a group of Yugoslav philosophers who have perhaps become best known in the international context by the name of their now defunct journal, *Praxis*. As philosophers, they have made vital contributions to the theory of Marxist humanism, provoking widespread debate about the essential humanist dimension of Marx's thought, the points of convergence and divergence of Marxism with other philosophical persuasions, and the nature of philosophical discourse. As members of their own society, they have drawn attention to the extent to which "official" Marxism, as represented by the regime's ideology, has been divested of its humanist thrust and critical cutting edge through association with the institutions of social power, and for this many of them have had to pay dearly. Though widely respected in the world philosophical community, in Yugoslavia several members of the *Praxis* group are barred from teaching, making public appearances, publishing, or responding to scurrilous attacks in the press; their journal *Praxis*, once a lively Yugoslav and international forum for discussion of the issues of Marxist humanism and of the ambitious Yugoslav experiment in workers' self-management, has been silenced.[1] While the repression of the *Praxis* group may not be the most serious instance of intellectual persecution in

Eastern Europe today in terms of physical hardship or imprisonment, it is certainly among the most tragic.

Praxis was a natural outgrowth of the Yugoslav Revolution, a unique series of events that began by embracing the principles of Stalinism and that culminated by just as passionately advocating the revolutionary principle of socialist humanism. It was the great theoretical accomplishment of *Praxis* to elaborate a systematic philosophical basis for that principle in an equally revolutionary reinterpretation of Marx himself, a reinterpretation based firmly upon the premise that Marxism is first and foremost a philosophy of *man*. But the conclusions ultimately reached by that reinterpretation, as well as the internal logic of the process of reinterpretation itself, were such that the *Praxis* enterprise was virtually destined to result in a more or less fundamental confrontation with the authorities, if not, perhaps, in a total rupture.

Why this was so can be seen from a brief sketch of the premises of *Praxis* theory. Underlying the humanist interpretation of Marxism is a radically dynamic view of man and his relation to nature, history, and society. It is a view of man that stands in direct contrast to that of the orthodox Marxist school, for which man is merely a passive creature of objective forces—"laws of movement" of nature, history, and society—which exist externally and independently of him. Man is a being of praxis, of practical activity which seeks to challenge, destroy, and transcend the limitations that everyday existence places upon his ability to develop as a free, creative being. Yet because this practical activity transpires in a world of objects and symbols and must ultimately assume objective form, it is capable of becoming alienated from its source. Thus man comes to confront the product of his activity as an estranged and hostile force that is the agent of his enslavement rather than of his liberation. By the same token, it is the consciousness of this very state of alienation that provides man with the impulse for new acts of praxis. This interaction between praxis and alienation so characteristic of all human activity, not the general properties of matter or movement in some metaphysical sense, is the source of the revolutionary dialectic.

Just as Marxist humanism stresses the dynamic side of human nature, it presupposes a dynamic role for theory as well. And while the *Praxis* Marxists may have devoted the greater part of their philosophical oeuvre to elaborating a profoundly humanist vision of man, perhaps their most important theoretical and indeed practical contribution lies in their view of theory itself. Theory—or, more broadly, consciousness—emerges not merely as a passive reflection of objective reality, but instead as the product of man's creative confrontation with reality, which itself must be understood not as that which is merely given in the present but as a sum of historically conditioned possibilities. Indeed one of the most vital tasks of consciousness is to identify those possibilities by penetrating and exposing the mystifications of ideology and by recognizing alienation in all its forms. Consciousness—or, more accurately, radical, *critical* consciousness—thus becomes the touchstone of all praxis, from the microlevel of man's daily interaction with the world to the macrolevel of the transformation of political structures and social systems. What is at issue, then, is not merely the status of Lenin's mechanistic reflection theory or even of the orthodox Marxist thesis of the relationship of base to superstructure, but the very ability of Marxism to remain a potent tool for the critical examination of reality in the postrevolutionary era. With Marx himself, the *Praxis* Marxists stressed at the very outset their commitment to a "critique of all existing conditions," which must, in Marx's words, be "ruthless in two senses: The criticism must not be afraid of its own conclusions, nor of conflict with the powers that be."[2]

The *Praxis* Marxists took this challenge literally. Their commitment to radical criticism led them not only to reject the dogmas of dialectical materialism in the name of a humanist philosophy of man more faithful to Marx's original meaning, but also to defy authoritative interpretations of existing social and political reality, to subject contemporary incarnations of socialist practice to unremitting criticism, and to undertake the unwelcome task of reminding political leaders of how far their efforts had strayed from originally charted ideals. To be sure, this course involved taking certain risks. Not least of these was the risk of running afoul of those in authority, of ruffling the feathers of this or that politician who might find cause to take exception to their barbs, or of exacerbating controversy when it was politically more convenient to stifle it. Yet the fact that they were willing to take these risks itself signified a basic level of trust on their part toward the political system. For the "Yugoslav path" was to have represented a radically new departure in the history of socialism, a decisive rejection of the Soviet authoritarian model and a bold experiment in truly democratic socialism characterized by workers' self-management, economic rationality, and a relaxation of Party control in the area of culture. In order to ensure that the new democratic forms generated in the course of the experiment were not to degenerate into new forms of alienated authority and repression, the *Praxis* Marxists came to believe that criticism—persistent, incisive, uncensored, philosophically grounded, theoretically sound Marxist criticism—was a vital component of that sustained effort at social transformation. In his essay on "Authority and Authoritarian Thinking" in this volume, Ljubomir Tadić expresses this idea in the following way: "The principal difference between socialism and every form of authoritarian thought is best expressed in the difference between the status of the *citizen* and that of the *subject*. For only the citizen is a being with the 'gift' of free speech. The mentality of the subject, in contrast, is distinguished by *silence* and respect toward higher authority." Indeed in their constantly recurring emphasis on the supreme importance of the freedom of criticism to the goal of democratic socialism, the *Praxis* Marxists have made an important contribution to democratic theory in general in an age when the dominant forms of "socialism" and "democracy" cast ominous shadows on the prospects of a humane and truly democratic world order.

The journal *Praxis*, on the pages of which many of the contributions to this volume appeared for the first time, was in fact nothing less than a bold attempt to institutionalize theoretical criticism informed by Marxist-humanist philosophy as an integral part of the Yugoslav experiment. And for over a decade, from 1964 to 1975, the *Praxis* Marxists were unprecedently successful in this effort. To appreciate the significance of their accomplishment it is necessary to view it in the broader context of East European development since World War II. Nowhere else in Eastern Europe has there arisen such a sustained, public, animated, unfettered, and candid dialogue concerning the founding principles of the society, the sociopolitical and cultural forms that have evolved under communist rule, and the nature of political authority. Nowhere else has such debate, even when it has surfaced no matter how briefly, been accorded the degree of acceptance and even legitimacy that it earned in Yugoslavia, and nowhere else did it attract such broad international interest among Marxists of all persuasions, socialists, humanists, social scientists and philosophers, students, and many others—not excluding the official custodians of truth of the communist one-party states. That all this occurred within the theoretical framework of a humanist interpretation of Marxist theory testifies to the elasticity and depth of an intellectual structure that is capable of recognizing, criticizing, and rectifying its own failures. That all this occurred in Yugoslavia, moreover, testifies not only to the extraordinary elasticity and resilience of that remarkable country and its political structure, but also, in the wake of the forceful termination of the *Praxis* experiment, to the gradual loss of some of those very qualities that have hitherto made the Yugoslav experiment a unique and bold adventure in democratic socialism.

The essays gathered in this volume are but a meager representation of the writings of members of the *Praxis* group. As suggested by the title of the leading essay by Gajo Petrović, *Praxis*'s primary spokesman and coeditor-in-chief throughout its often stormy existence, the general theme of these contributions is the relationship between philosophy and politics in socialism. What are the boundaries and areas of overlap between them? Must philosophy in a socialist society necessarily be the handmaiden of politics, and if not, must it necessarily be cast in the role of antagonist? To what extent, moreover, can socialist political life be governed by philosophical principles if, as Marx put it, the realization of philosophy implies that the philosophical must become worldly, and the world philosophical? The answers offered by the *Praxis* Marxists may largely be informed by their own personal experiences and aspirations, but they are of an intrinsic value that is not exhausted by considerations of time and place alone.

The structure of the collection follows a distinction made by Petrović early in his opening essay among socialism as a social order, socialism as a movement, and socialism as instrumental theory—or, what is often the same thing, as ideology. A final section is devoted to a theoretical discussion of the question of socialism and human rights, a term which has entered popular parlance of late but which, as its uneven history in the worlds of both academic philosophy and everyday practice has suggested, may be in need of serious critical analysis. As for the scope of essays represented here, the editor takes full responsibility for any shortcoming that may result from the relatively narrow thematic focus in the limited space available. It would require more than one volume to do justice to the dizzyingly broad spectrum of *Praxis* theory.

With the exception of the essays by Petrović, Vranicki, and Stojanović, which are reproduced here from earlier English translations by permission of their publishers, the contributions to this volume appear here in English for the first time, and some of them for the first time in any foreign language. In translating these essays, I have taken the liberty of providing references to all works cited in English-language editions when available for the reader's convenience.

Gerson S. Sher
Reston, Virginia

NOTES

1. For an account of the *Praxis* experience, see my *Praxis and Marxist Criticism and Dissent in Socialist Yugoslavia* (Bloomington: Indiana University Press, 1977).
2. Karl Marx to Arnold Ruge, September 1843, in Robert C. Tucker (ed.), *The Marx-Engels Reader* (New York: Norton, 1972), p. 8.

Part 1

PHILOSOPHY AND PRAXIS

Philosophy and Politics in Socialism

Gajo Petrović

We live in a time when even children all over the world know something about socialism, and theoreticians have written mountains of books and articles on the "topic." Nevertheless, it would be wrong to think that the question of what socialism means and what its prospects are has been "solved" and is therefore out of date. Indeed, at a time when among socialists (or those who declare themselves to be socialists) there are dozens, and even hundreds, of different interpretations of socialism, and many of these interpretations are backed not only by single lonely thinkers or groups of thinkers, but also by strong social groups, organizations, and institutions, sometimes even by dominant national forces, or whole states (this is why people sometimes talk of a "Chinese," "Yugoslav," "Italian," "Cuban," "Algerian," "Indian," "Burmese," etc., conception of socialism), it would be ridiculous to assume that the question has been solved. Similarly, at a time when the prospects of mankind as a whole are neither clear nor certain (because the very existence of the human race has become endangered), it would be naïve to assume that the prospects of socialism are quite clear and certain.

What holds for the general question of the meaning and prospects of socialism largely holds also for the subject, "Philosophy and Politics in Socialism." This subject is by no means new; it can be found as far back as Plato. But it is still not out of date, although, it seems, there is more "agreement" here than there is in the general question about the meaning of socialism. In a great number of socialist countries the relationship between politics and philosophy is very similar: philosophy performs the function of a servant of politics. Even in those socialist countries where this relationship does not exist, there are influential groups and individuals who long to create such a relationship and from time to time try to establish it. Karl Marx never depicted the relationship between philosophy and politics in socialism in such a way, and this leads us to ask: Is there something wrong with Marx; or is something wrong with the relationship between philosophy and politics in socialism, and with that socialism where such a relationship exists? This question can be approached in different ways. Why not approach it by asking first what socialism is?

The term "socialism" has been used so far for three different areas. It has been used as a name: 1.) for a certain social order that should arise, or is already arising, as a negation of capitalism; 2.) for the political movement fighting for the realization of socialism in the first sense; and 3.) for the theory that establishes the possibility and shows ways and means for furthering socialism in the second sense and for achieving socialism in the first sense. In this essay we will discuss socialism in the first of these three meanings. We believe, however, that much of what holds good for socialism as a social order also holds good for socialism as a political movement and for socialism as a theory. The relation between philosophy and politics in socialism as a social order is certainly not independent of the relationship between the two that exists or existed in socialism as a theory and in socialism as a social movement. It is also clear that by determining the field of application of the concept, the question about its content is not yet solved. Different interpretations are still possible.

In the conception of socialism that was canonized by Stalin and that is still widespread in some socialist countries, the term denotes the "lower phase of communism," which comes after the "period of the dictatorship of the proletariat" and before the "upper phase of communism." According to this conceptual and terminological scheme, we have the following sequence of social orders: capitalism, dictatorship of the proletariat, the lower phase of communism (socialism), the upper phase of communism (true communism). According to the proponents of the scheme, the period of the dictatorship of the proletariat lasted in the Soviet Union up to the proclamation of the Stalin Constitution; after the Stalin Constitution the period of socialism or the lower phase of communism began; and today, after the building of socialism has been completed, there is already a transition from socialism to communism.

I think that this scheme is defective for a number of reasons. Before criticizing it, however, I would like to make clear that this favorite Stalinistic scheme is not an arbitrary Stalinistic invention; it has its root in Marx. In his *Critique of the Gotha Program* Marx speaks of the two phases of communism, although he does not terminologically fix them as "socialism" and "communism." In the same work he also refers to "the period of the revolutionary transformation of the one into the other" (of the capitalist society into communist), as something that differs from both capitalism and communism, some third thing to which "there corresponds . . . also a political transition period in which the state can be nothing but *the revolutionary dictatorship of the proletariat.*"[1]

In connection with the conception of the transition period as a period of the dictatorship of the proletariat, which differs essentially from both capitalism and socialism, it is necessary to remark, first, that this is a very dangerous theory, which can be used, and actually has been used, for antisocialist purposes. If the transition period is neither capitalism nor socialism, if it has some properties of its own that distinguish it essentially from both capitalism and socialism, then it is possible to maintain that, although the developed capitalist society is characterized by political democracy, and although the developed socialist order will be democratic, the transition period from capitalism to socialism—that is, from bourgeois democracy to socialist democracy—need not be democratic. Moreover, it may even be maintained that inhumanity, unfreedom, and violence make the best, or the only possible, "dialectical" road to socialism; that they are those dialectical means that lead to their opposite—to the true democracy, freedom, and humaneness of the socialist society. Of course, when we say that it is possible to maintain this in the framework of the theory regarding the dictatorship of the proletariat as a special transitory period, it does not mean that this *must* be maintained, that such an interpretation necessarily follows from the essence of the theory. But one must not overlook the fact that this is not only one among many possible interpretations, but is *the* interpretation that was promoted by Stalinism, in deeds as well as words. If Marx could have foreseen such an interpretation of his theory, he would perhaps never have formulated it, not even in the passing way in which he did in the *Critique of the Gotha Program*. He would probably have adhered to another version of his theory about the transitory period, which excludes the above-mentioned Stalinistic interpretation. This is the version according to which the transitory period is characterized not only by the dictatorship of the proletariat but also by communism and socialism. In order to make this theory clearer, we must for the moment leave aside the question of the transitory period and consider more carefully the theory of the two phases of communism.

On the basis of what Marx says in the *Critique of the Gotha Program*, one might get the impression that he distinguished the two phases of communism according to the ruling principle of distribution, ascribing the principle of distribution according to work to the first phase, and the principle of distribution according to needs to the second phase. In the lower phase of communism, according to Marx, "the individual producer receives back from society—after the deductions have been made—exactly what he gives to it,"[2] whereas in the upper phase of communism the society will be able to inscribe on its banners: "From each according to his ability, to each according to his needs!"[3] Marx stressed that society will be able to proclaim the principle of distribution according to needs only when certain conditions have been fulfilled, namely, "after the enslaving subordination of the individual to the division of labor, and therewith also the antithesis between mental and physical labor, has vanished; after labor has become not only a means of life but life's prime want; after the productive forces have also increased with the all-around development of the individual, and all the springs of cooperative wealth flow more abundantly."[4] But this enumeration of the conditions for distribution according to labor does not exclude the view that this principle is the essential characteristic of the higher phase of communism. As if he himself felt that he might be misunderstood, Marx expressly warned: "Quite apart from the analysis so far given, it was in general a mistake to make a fuss about so-called *distribution* and put the principal stress on it. Any distribution whatever of the means of consumption is only a consequence of the distribution of the conditions of production themselves. The latter distribution, however, is a feature of the mode of production itself. ... Vulgar socialism (and from it in turn a section of democracy) has taken over from the bourgeois economists the consideration and treatment of distribution as independent of the mode of production and hence the presentation of socialism as turning principally on distribution."[5] Thus, after having seemingly attributed the decisive part in distinguishing the two phases of communism to differences in distribution, Marx criticized those who believe that socialism turns on distribution and asserted that this view had been inherited from the bourgeois economists. Such a criticism is in accordance with Marx's basic view that production is more important than distribution and that forms of distribution are dependent on forms of production.

One could ask whether one should not distinguish the "lower" and the "higher" phase of communism according to the forms of economic production. A positive answer to this question would not be in the spirit of Marx, however. According to Marx, in an epoch of human history, the epoch of alienated class society, man really was an economic animal; his whole life was, in the last analysis, determined by the sphere of economic production. When we speak of that epoch, it is justifiable to distinguish different stages of development primarily according to the ruling mode of production. But the society that has to arise as a negation of capitalism has to be, according to Marx, not merely a negation of the capitalistic economic order; it must also negate the relationship between the "spheres," which was characteristic of class society; it must abolish not only the primacy of the economic sphere, but also the split of man into mutually estranged spheres. Accordingly, the criterion for distinguishing phases in that society cannot be the difference in the mode of economic production, it must be much more complex.

If we look at the familiar distinction between the lower and the higher phase of communism from the point of view of content, we see that not only the Stalinists, but even Marx himself, did not succeed in clarifying it. The lack of clarity is not only in content, it is also in terminology. Marx did not call the two phases "socialism" and "communism." These names were fixed later. Despite that, many Marxists still accept not only this distinction, which really is derived from Marx (although it does not agree with some of his fundamental views), but also the terminology, which is not his. This terminology as such is not "false," but it is not adequate for distinguishing the main phases of the communist society. Although the Stalinistic conception of socialism and communism has already been criticized, the terminology it used has remained untouched. The view that socialism is a finished social system essentially different from communism has been criticized, as has the view that inhumanity is allowed in socialism as a means for achieving humaneness in communism. But none of the critics, as far as I know, have called into question either the division of the development of communist society into two phases or the terminological fixation of the two phases as "socialism" (the "lower" phase) and "communism" (the "higher" phase).

The texts of Marx speak in favor of regarding socialism as a higher phase compared with communism. The etymology of the words also supports such a terminology. "Communism" (compared with *communis*—common) suggests a society in which means of production are common, and "socialism" (corresponding to *socius*—comrade) points to a society in which a man is comrade to another man. And the second is certainly higher and more difficult to achieve than the first.

That Marx really considered socialism "higher" than communism can be shown by help of a text that is well known and often quoted, but inadequately interpreted, because Marx is still much read through Stalinistic glasses. Marx writes: "*Atheism*, as a denial of this unreality, is no longer meaningful, for atheism is a *negation of God* and seeks to assert by this negation the *existence of man*. Socialism no longer requires such a mediation; it begins from the *theoretical* and *practical sense consciousness* of man and nature as essential beings; it is positive human *self-consciousness*, no longer a self-consciousness mediated through the negation of religion; just as the *real life* of man is the positive reality of man no longer mediated through the negation of private property, through communism."[6] As we see, communism for Marx is that mediation ("roundabout method") through which private property is abolished, and real life is the positive reality of man no longer mediated through that abolishment. In other words, communism is the "lower" phase, and real life is the "higher" phase. The relationship between "atheism" and "socialism" is analogous to this relationship between "communism" and "real life." Atheism is the affirmation of the existence of man through the negation of God. Socialism on the contrary needs no mediator. It is positive human self-consciousness, which is not mediated by the abolishment of religion. Consequently, whereas communism is the humane society mediated through the abolition of private property, socialism is an aspect of that higher form of society, which is immediately humane. Socialism is not that society as a whole, it is merely an aspect of "real life," its self-consciousness. Of course, if Marx regarded communism as the "lower" phase and socialism as one aspect of the "higher" phase (its self-consciousness), this does not mean that we must accept his terminology and his view (because this is not merely a terminology). But is it not of vital importance for mankind today to distinguish between the social condition in which private property is abolished (communism), and the humane community of men in which a man is a *socius* to another man (socialism, or, more adequately, humanism)?

In discussions of socialism and communism, the question is often asked whether socialism or communism represents the final goal, the end of human history; and Marxists and Marxologists answer unanimously that, of course, it does not. When uninformed people ask what then has to follow after communism, the experts explain patronizingly that it is a scholastic question that goes too far into the future. It is clear that communism will not last forever, and that something will happen after it, but what is going to happen we do not and cannot know. So if a "scholastic" calls attention to the fact that Marx sometimes spoke of communism as a "solved puzzle of history" and sometimes stated that "communism as such is not an aim of human development" but only a "necessary form and an *energetic* principle of the nearest future," he will get the explanation that this is "dialectics." If we study Marx more attentively, however, we will see that "dialectics" in the sense of simultaneous assertion of contradictory theses was not allied to him. We will also discover that Marx clearly answered the "scholastic" question: What is going to happen after communism? He wrote: "In the same way, atheism as the annulment of God is the emergence of theoretical humanism, and communism as the annulment of private property is the vindication of real human life as man's property. The latter is also the emergence of practical humanism, for atheism is humanism mediated to itself by the annulment of religion, while communism is humanism mediated to itself by the annulment of private property. It is only by the supersession of this mediation (which is, however, a necessary pre-condition) that self-originating *positive* humanism can appear."[7]

Consequently, according to Marx, communism is in essence the emergence of humanism; but in contradistinction to atheism, which is the emergence of theoretical humanism, it is the emergence of practical humanism. As the emergence of humanism, it cannot be essentially different or contrary to humanism; it already is humanism, but a humanism mediated through the abolishment of private property. Only through and after this mediation can the positive humanism emerge, a humanism that begins positively from itself. This positive humanism has no reason to call itself "communism," because this name suggests that we have to do with a community that emerged as a negation of the society based on private property.

When he insists that communism is a mediated humanism, Marx does not want to say that communism is not humanism at all. On the contrary, he remarks: "But atheism and communism are not flight or abstraction from, or loss of, the objective world which men have created by the objectification of their faculties. They are not an impoverished return to unnatural, primitive simplicity. They are rather the first real emergence, the genuine actualization, of man's nature as something real."[8]

In this way Marx does not advocate the replacement of capitalistic society through another form of class society, or through another form of the self-alienated society in which the economic sphere would still dominate; he advocates an essentially different, *humanistic* society. And communist society is humanistic society in the process of emergence. *Communism*, in fact, is the *"transitory period" from capitalism (and class society in general) to humanism,* but this does not mean that it is somewhere in the middle between capitalism and humanism. Communism is communism to the extent to which it is humanism. And socialism is one of the aspects of the humanistic society, because in the society in which man really *is* man, man is a comrade to other men too.

What is the more precise meaning of communism conceived as the emerging of humanism? In his "Private Property and Communism" (a well-known fragment in the *Economic and Philosophical Manuscripts*)[9] Marx writes in a detailed way about communism and its three main phases. It seems to me that the division into three phases is not essential. What is much more important is what Marx has to say generally on communism. And he speaks on communism in general, even when he is concerned with the description of a single phase. Thus, in connection with the first two phases, he writes: "In both forms communism is already aware of being the reintegration of man, his return to himself, the supersession of man's self-alienation. But since it has not yet grasped the positive nature of private property, or the *human* nature of needs, it is still captured and contaminated by private property. It has well understood the concept, but not the essence."[10]

In this way Marx clearly states the humanistic essence of communism: the abolition of man's self-alienation, the reintegration, or return of man to himself. Discussing the "third phase," he specifies this explanation when he maintains that religion, family, the state, morals, science, art, etc., are merely special modes of production, and that "the positive supersession of *private property*, as the appropriation of *human* life, is therefore the *positive* supersession of all alienation, and the return of man from religion, the family, the state, etc., to his *human*, i.e., *social*, life."[11]

If one wished to summarize Marx's answer to the question of what communism and humanism are, one could say that they are the appropriation of man's life through the abolishment of man's self-alienation, especially through the abolishment of man's split into separate spheres that stand in relationships of external determination. Communism is, accordingly, not simply a new socioeconomic formation, it is the abolishment of the primacy of the economic criteria in distinguishing human communities.

This conception of communism, socialism and humanism requires a determined relationship between philosophy and politics in a society that is communist, socialist, or humanist (the three are not identical, but they are not essentially different, because, as has already been said, communism is the merging of humanism and socialism, one aspect of communism and humanism).

I shall not try to give here a precise definition of either philosophy or politics. It is well known that the different definitions of philosophy are legion, and controversy about which is best will probably never end. I have explained my own viewpoint on the essence of philosophy elsewhere in this volume, and it is not necessary to repeat it here. I will merely mention again I do not regard philosophy as a branch of either science or art, that I consider it a separate form of mental activity through which a man not only discovers his own essence and his place in the world, his capabilities for changing the world and for enriching his own nature, but also stimulates the deed of transforming the world, and participates in it in a creative way.

It is also well known that there are a lot of different definitions of politics, from narrow ones, which treat politics as an activity of ruling the state, to wider ones, which regard politics as a way of administrating society as a whole, to those that identify politics with every directed human activity, or with the way of life of a people. I cannot enter into the controversy about the best definition of politics here. I will mention only that in this context I do not mean by politics either every directed human activity or merely the activity of ruling the state. Under politics I mean here every activity of administrating social life, whether this is done through the state or through a stateless form.

Despite the fact that philosophy and politics have always been and still are different, they have always had certain common characteristics. Both philosophy and politics have been so far special activities, parallel to many other activities (economic, artistic, scientific, religious, legal, etc.), clearly separated from the rest and from one another, but connected through the external relationships of mutual influencing and conditioning. Both activities have also been bound up with special social groups—politicians and philosophers. Although other people have taken part in both politics and philosophy (there is almost no one who has no interest at all in politics, or without at least an "amateurish" philosophy), and although the participation of "masses," especially in politics, may attain a very high degree of intensity (for example, in revolutions), these activities have always been performed and furthered mainly by a narrow circle of people, politicians and philosophers. Although many philosophers and politicians throughout history have been at the same time slave owners, landlords, capitalists, merchants, lawyers, etc., with the development of class society the tendency to professionalize both activities, to turn both philosophers and politicians into special social strata, which by performing these activities make their living, secure their means for life, has increased. A bureaucratic, or, in Marx's words, "rough and thoughtless communism," does not oppose this tendency, it sometimes even brings it to the absurd by transforming politicians into politicants and philosophers into schoolmen. The originality of such a communism is that it "dialectically" abolishes the opposition between the two strata by transforming one ("philosophers") into the servant of the other ("politicians").

But if this happens in fact, must it necessarily happen? Does such a relationship follow from the essence of communism, philosophy and politics? Or does from the essence of these phenomena follow quite another relationship, which is, in turn, not merely an ideal project or a powerless wish, but a real possibility and the already existing tendency of historical development, albeit a possibility that cannot be realized without our active engagement?

What, accordingly, could and should happen to philosophy and politics under communism and humanism? In accordance with the sketched conception of communism, philosophy in communism and humanism should disappear as a special activity separated from all others. But it should remain and develop as the critical thought of man about himself, as a self-reflection that penetrates the whole of his life, as a coordinating force of his whole activity, as a form through which he achieves the wholeness of his personality. Philosophy should also cease to be a professional duty or privilege of a special social stratum. This does not mean that all people can or must become great philosophers, but it does mean that philosophy must break its narrow limits, that it must turn to the essential human questions of its time and develop through broad, free, and equal discussion among all those who think about these questions.

In communism and humanism, politics should develop in a similar direction. It should disappear as a special activity exercised by a privileged stratum and determined primarily through the economic interests of social classes (and of that stratum). It should be transformed into an activity that is not a privilege of professional politicians, but through which the social community as a whole, on the basis of critical reflection about its problems, solves the important questions of its life.

Consequently, if questioned about the relationship of philosophy and politics in communism (socialism, humanism), my answer would be that philosophy as man's critical self-reflection should direct the whole of his activity, including his political activity. But I do not think that political acts could or should be prescribed by any philosophy or by a philosophical forum. These should come about by a democratic, free decision of all those interested.

If one depicts in this way, on the one hand, what the relationship between philosophy and politics has been up to now, and, on the other hand, what their relationship should be in socialism, one might ask what roads, if any, lead to the realization of such a relationship. In answer it should be remarked, first, that such a relationship cannot be established if we first start going in the opposite direction, i.e., if we "temporarily" employ philosophy as the handmaid of politics and instead of developing democratic forms of government strengthen bureaucratic ones. Without awaiting the "right time" for the development of the humanistic essence of communism (for those who wait for it the right time never seems to have come), we must today, and now, try to realize the maximum of what according to our beliefs it could and should be.

Without passively waiting for the "future," philosophy must make the real world, including politics, the object of its criticism. In answering the question whether one should discuss politics in a philosophical way in newspapers, the young Marx replied that newspapers have not only the right but also the obligation to write about political questions and that philosophy, as the "wisdom of the world," must care for the state as the "kingdom" of this world. "The question is here not whether one should philosophize about the state, the question is whether one should philosophize about the state well or badly, philosophically or unphilosophically, in a prejudiced way or without prejudices, with consciousness or without consciousness, consequentially or unconsequentially, quite rationally or semirationally."[12]

Philosophy must make the real world, including its politics, the subject of criticism. But this is not enough. Philosophy must also break the limits of discussion within a narrow circle of professional philosophers; it must turn itself to nonphilosophers, not only to scientists, artists, politicians, but to all those who think about the living problems of our time.

In order to establish the described relationship between philosophy and politics, politics must also develop in a given direction. It must more and more become the concern and work of the whole community. It must also become more and more the function of critical thought and discussion, not of accidental or arbitrary decision. Developing in this direction, philosophy and politics can free themselves from being separated "sectors" or "spheres" of a split social life, and fulfill themselves and develop as essential "aspects" or "moments" of the whole man.

On such a road various obstacles may arise. This may occur partly because the bearers of the process of superseding philosophy and politics can be only philosophers and politicians, and that only insofar as they are able to raise themselves above the egoistic interests of their own social strata can they look from the standpoint of the whole of mankind and of that social class that can today be the bearer of the social transformation, i.e., the working class.

Although both professional philosophers and professional politicians are interested in retaining the social privileges of their strata, and this (not insurmountably) can obstruct them in taking a revolutionary standpoint, there is a considerable difference between philosophers and politicians as social strata. The difference is not only in the kind or quantity of social privileges, although this difference can be fairly large and easily observable. There is an even greater importance in the following fundamental asymmetry: in order to make the activity of ruling society common, the stratum of politicians that has ruled so far must restrict its activity. In order that all may be able to rule, those who have ruled so far must rule less. In order that all can think critically about fundamental problems of contemporary man and world, however, no philosopher ought to renounce his right and duty to think critically. The "space" for that is wide enough for all. On the contrary, the greater the number of those who think and discuss philosophical questions is, the more stimulating the atmosphere for philosophical thought will be, and the greater the possibility for every individual to develop his own philosophical thinking to the maximum.

The asymmetry in the social being of politicians and philosophers may result in certain misunderstandings between the members of the two strata in the beginning of the construction of communism and humanism. It may happen, for example, that some politicians who are not able to raise themselves to the universal social standpoint, and who strive to keep their privileged position as social rulers together with the corresponding material privileges, may regard philosophy directed against all privileges as a danger to themselves. Such politicians will have an entirely negative attitude toward philosophy and philosophers, but they will avoid an open discussion of controversial questions, and they will try to represent the defense of their material interests and privileges as a defense of socialism against "nonsocialist" strivings.

Such conflicts and tensions can be avoided or solved in different ways. One way would be to liquidate philosophy or to transform it into a subservient handmaid of politics. In some socialist countries this has largely succeeded. In others (primarily in Yugoslavia) such a danger does not exist. But where there are no real conditions for transforming philosophy into the servant of politics, there may be the danger that politicians will try, by surrendering a part (more accurately, a small particle) of their power to "corrupt" philosophers, to divide their power over all society with philosophers and scientists (although, of course, not equally). This is the most dangerous trap philosophers in socialism have to avoid. It is the duty of philosopher-Marxists to develop a critical consciousness toward themselves as a special social stratum, toward politicians, and toward anybody else who may try or wish to maintain or to achieve a privileged position in society. In these efforts philosopher-Marxists can find their best allies among those politician-Marxists who do not confine themselves to the standpoint of their own social stratum, but take the standpoint of society as a whole.

NOTES

1. Marx, Engels, *Basic Writings on Politics and Philosophy*, p. 127.
2. *Ibid.*, pp. 117–18.
3. *Ibid.*, p. 119.
4. Marx, Engels, *Basic Writings on Politics and Philosophy*, p. 119.
5. *Ibid.*, p. 120.
6. Cf. Fromm, *Marx's Concept of Man*, p. 140.
7. Fromm, *Marx's Concept of Man*, pp. 188-89.
8. *Ibid.*, p. 189.
9. *Ibid.*, pp. 123–40.
10. *Ibid.*, p. 127.
11. *Ibid.*, p. 128.
12. Marx, Engels, *Werke*, bd. I, s. 100–101.

Reason and Historical Praxis

Mihailo Marković

I

There are at least three different reasons for which most contemporary philosophers either proclaim themselves incompetent and powerless to have a significant effect on the course of events in their societies or, more dogmatically, declare that the making of the future is not the concern of philosophy.

The first such reason is that philosophy has, in principle, nothing to do with actual history. Its task is, according to analytical philosophy, to clarify general concepts and remove puzzles generated by the improper use of language. Another school, phenomenology, claims the function of philosophy to be the rigorous description of timeless essences. Even many Marxists, with all their apparent interest in the creation of a new future society, leave it to politicians to take care of this while comfortably devoting themselves to the study of the general laws of the world and waging war against rival ideologies.

A second reason for this reluctance to pass any judgment about the future is methodological. It is true that some classical philosophers have considered the issue of the perfect, rational, just society a legitimate philosophical problem. However, the utopian visions that emerged as the products of such undertakings could not satisfy the validation criteria of modern philosophy. As nonlogical statements, lacking adequate empirical support, they could be neither verified nor falsified. As something not yet given, they could not be the subject matter of phenomenological description. As free exploration of ideal possibilities they could not be derived from existing "scientific laws."

A third reason for believing that philosophy has neither the power nor responsibility for the shaping of actual historical process is the strict division of labor and separation of roles in the entire sphere of culture that condemns philosophy to intangible, abstract generality. Even when the issue of the "good society" has been discussed and a normative, ethical consciousness conceptualized, it has been presented as transcendental and ahistorical. The issues of the good society were quite outside the scope of such *philosophia perrenis.*

II

All these arguments stem from a narrow, static conception of philosophy, a rigid division of labor within the realm of theory, and a cleavage between theory and action.

Philosophy is inherently more historical than is commonly recognized. Philosophical categories and principles may refer to certain structures of the world and the human mind which are extremely stable and of lasting, universal importance. But they are also human symbolic forms, created within specific cultural traditions. There is no reason to consider them timeless or eternal or a priori with respect to all human experience, because there is no way to disentangle the objective external regularity from the subjective human form of experiencing, conceptualizing, and imaginatively exploring that regularity at any given historical moment.

Philosophy could become much more historical if it would consciously accept responsibility for critical study of the basic structure of actual historical process, for building up an epochal critical self-consciousness. Nowadays the term "philosophy of history" encompasses only one of the disciplines of philosophy, dealing with either the methodology of historical research or the analysis of concepts used in the language of history—which is important, but too restrictive. The crucial problems are substantive rather than methodological: What happens to human beings in history? What is the nature of their relationships, their communities, the quality of their life at a specific stage of historical development? To what extent do they manage to realize their basic capacities and needs under given social arrangements? Where are they going? What are they striving for? What are the essential limitations of their condition in the present? What are their opti-

mal possibilities in the future? Asking such questions is perfectly legitimate and indeed indispensible for rational beings who have the
chance to make their own history consciously. On the other hand,
when such questions are neither asked nor answered, history becomes
mindless and anarchic, a playground of uncontrollable blind forces.
But asking them is quite risky. Sooner or later it leads to sharp conflict
with the ideology of the status quo and the formidable powers behind
it. The philosopher is tolerated while he is absorbed in abstruse logical
and methodological issues, and he is tolerated because he is regarded
as a harmless creature, a nonentity. The philosopher is praised and
celebrated when he assumes the role of an apologist of the past history
of the establishment—and that is where the spiritual life of quite a few
official Marxists has concluded: in efforts to demonstrate that whatever their Party did in the past was necessary, rational, and progressive. But when the philosopher asks those tough questions about the
deeper human meaning behind the successes of technology and improvements of material well-being, about the senseless waste of human and natural resources, about crippled existences, unnecessary
suffering, ignorance and boredom, about still widespread material and
spiritual misery, about the destruction of communal solidarity, about
the possibilities and ways of transcending the human condition—then
he becomes dangerous, subversive. Surely he is dangerous for the
existing power because he sees beyond it, demystifies it, undermines
its most reliable weapon for manipulating people and ruling comfortably—its ideology.

III

A critical theory of the present and vision of the future might, but need
not necessarily, be utopian. Even the utopian philosophy of history
does not deserve to be underestimated. True, it is speculative and
metaphysical, more a product of fantasy than of knowledge, more an
expression of hope and faith than of carefully studied historical potential and human needs. It disregards existing economic, political, and
cultural constraints; it explores possibilities which might be desirable
but which are clearly not feasible in the given historical situation.
Utopian visions are indeed sometimes responsible for diverting social
energy from historically possible tasks to romantic adventures doomed
to failure.

In spite of all this, the utopian and eschatological philosophy of
history cannot be brushed aside as a worthless, marginal product of
intellectual life. Utopian thought is the repository of genuine and universal human aspirations, such as justice, freedom, communal solidarity, power over nature, and creativity. While it is true that too often it
gives birth to illusory expectations which culminate in tragic frustra-

tion, it is also true that some of the most important breakthroughs in history would hardly have been possible without certain utopian illusions, without idealizations of great historical initiatives. What would have been the outcome of the American Revolution without the utopian faith of hundreds of thousands of rebels that, with their victory, all those freedoms and inalienable human rights which were so beautifully stated in the Declaration of Independence would be fully and immediately realized? The great social energies required to bring about great historical changes and to clear the ground for freer and more rapid development can be set in motion only by great, exciting, passionately advocated, more or less utopian ideas, not by balanced, sober, realistic accounts of the true measure of achievement that is feasible under the circumstances. For not only do such "realistic" accounts consider merely *given* social forces and fail to create *new* ones; there is also no guarantee that they accurately estimate even existing forces. What is the real mood of the people, what are their hidden, latent dispositions to endure, to conform, or to resist and rebel—these cannot always be derived from their overt behavior with complete reliability. Furthermore, no matter how much they might be enslaved, programmed, and predictable, human beings are potentially free and able to act in utterly surprising ways. Therefore, we cannot always be sure what the realm of real historical possibilities is, and we can be wrong about the a priori estimated boundaries of that realm. Consequently, what we might "realistically" estimate to be historically impossible, a "mere utopian dream," may eventually come true, because human conduct may turn out to be much more imaginative, creative, perseverant, unselfish, and courageous than we might reasonably expect on the basis of all available evidence from the past.

IV

For all these reasons, the utopian philosophy of history cannot simply be written off. But it can be transcended. Its basic theoretical limitations are the excessive abstractness of its projections; the absence of any mediation between the unique, present historical situation and a universal vision of the distant future; and a simplistic view of historical determination.

A critical theory of history will preserve the utopian general tendency to go beyond given historical reality, to assume a negative attitude toward irrational and inhumane social structures in the present. But far from simply condemning the present and offering an essentially different vision of the future, it will embark on a concrete interdisciplinary study of the given historical situation—its crucial problems, its economic, political, and cultural constraints, and the existing and possible social forces. Such a critical theory will no longer be pure philosophy, and yet its theoretical ground would be constituted by a philosophical study of human being, its basic capacities and needs, and its potential for development.

Only a critical theory that is much richer and more concrete than the articulation of utopias is able to *mediate* between the singular present situation and a general future horizon of the whole epoch. It will be able to indicate specific types of transitional and intermediary phases of the process; it will be able to point to the practical steps which are necessary in each phase to reach the envisaged objectives.

But nothing is certain and nothing is guaranteed in the whole process. Various alternatives remain open all the time. Most utopias assume a conception of historical determination which is quite obsolete nowadays. There is no linear logic or dialectic of history, no *eshaton* which will inevitably be reached sooner or later. On the other hand, the historical process is also not so open that one can completely disregard things that happened in the past, the way our ancestors molded their natural and social surroundings and themselves. Habits and products of the past are very real constraints, excluding many ideal, conceivable possibilities, making only a limited set of them likely to occur. But within this limited framework we are free to produce our future history, and we are able to increase our freedom by raising the level of our knowledge, by critically examining and transcending our past conduct, by making bold choices, by avoiding fruitless, wasteful frictions, and by coordinating the activity of all those who share some basic commitments.

This last point is of crucial importance for understanding how lonely, socially isolated philosophers can effectively contribute to the conscious making of history. They overcome their loneliness and isolation when they happen to raise precisely those general issues which translate into articulated theoretical terms the actually experienced grievances, sufferings, and needs of large, powerful (actually or potentially) social groups. Philosophy begins to live when its universal ethical and political ideals become a practical standpoint for a vivid, forceful critque of the narrowness, irrationality, and inhumanity of actual arrangements in one's own society. The secret of the practical relevance of philosophy is in the meeting of vaguely felt, inarticulated popular needs with elaborate theoretical projects derived from the immensely rich world of culture and ultimately from the accumulated universal experience of thousands of preceding generations.

Without philosophically grounded theory, practical engagement remains shallow, short-lived, and inspired only by the meager experience of one generation in one country or one part of the world during a brief interval of time. Theory is necessary to mediate between this limited particular experience and the comprehensive universal experience of humankind. The greater the crisis of society and the greater the urgency of radical global solutions of existing problems, the greater the objective need for philosophical guidance.

V

One of the clearest examples of how philosophy can affect actual history by offering a general orientation to great social movements is the case of the bourgeois democratic revolutions. These are unthinkable without the political philosophy of Montesquieu, Locke, Rousseau, Voltaire, and Jefferson. It is true that the ideas of popular sovereignty, of liberty and equality before the law, of the separation of civil and political society, of the legally grounded order of political authority derived from election and consent, of the separation of powers, of inalienable civil rights—including the right of private property—that these ideas articulated the needs of a new social arrangement in the making and expressed the vital interests of both the rising bourgeoisie and the entire *tiers* ëtat. But conversely, too, the fact is that those ideas, once formulated by philosophers, gave clarity, rational justification, durability, and deep conviction to vaguely felt drives, bringing forth enormous new forces. Most importantly of all, those ideas expressed the optimal historical possibilities of the epoch; without them, without the liberal political culture and democratic mass movements inspired by them, capitalism would have emerged in a *different,* authoritarian, populist form—as the twentieth-century examples of fascism, Peronism, and de Gaullism clearly illustrate.

The roots of liberal philosophy are the entire great tradition of humanism, in which since early Stoic philoscphy the ideals of freedom and equality were asserted time and again; two centuries of battle against scholastic ideology and every other form of dogmatism and obscurantism; a strong emphasis on experience and action as sources of knowledge since Bacon; the affirmation of subjectivity since Descartes; the detailed elaboration of an exact, calculable rationality in Descartes, Spinoza, Leibnitz, etc. Liberal political philosophy was an essential part of a new coherent philosophical spirit, and in each phase of its emergence one could demonstrate feedback and interdetermination between this new epochal spirit and the new needs of the growing *tiers* ëtat.

VI

Another example is Marx's philosophy. Its starting point is the revolt against the irrationality and inhumanity of established bourgeois society. It begins by taking up the incompletely fulfilled Enlightenment program of universal human emancipation, brotherhood, and equality.

It develops by giving a concrete economic and political interpretation of Hegel's metaphysical idea of alienation. The subject of alienation is man and his activity, his labor, rather than the mystical absolute spirit. And alienation does not consist of mere objectification in nature (because all work is indeed objectification of human projects) but in the fact that human work is not what it could be; it is condemned to be crippled, wasted, reduced to repetitive, mechanical drudgery in the historical conditions of bourgeois society. The project of communism appears at first as the *philosophical solution* of the problem of economic, political, and religious alienation. Only in 1843, when Marx sought to identify the social force capable of practically bringing this solution to life, did he come to the conclusion that only the working class can be such a force. The crucial point is that the bearer of this great historical mission was not supposed to be the empirically given proletariat, but rather the philosophically enlightened proletariat—which has become aware of what revolutionary philosophy asserted to be its potential and its mission. This revolution is impossible without philosophy: "The *head* of this emancipation is *philosophy*, its *heart* is the *proletariat*. Philosophy can only be realized by the abolition of the proletariat, and the proletariat can only be abolished by the realization of philosophy" (Marx in the *Contribution to the Critique of Hegel's 'Philosophy of Right': Introduction*). It is true that the working class movement already existed in 1843 when Marx wrote these lines. But Marx's idea of revolution as universal human emancipation was not and could not have been derived from the existing communist movement, which was rather confused about both its ultimate goals and the means adequate to reach them. Marx's idea of communist revolution was, on the one hand, a radical consequence of certain fundamental assumptions of the preceding bourgeois revolution: the principle of popular sovereignty, the idea that each individual should be the master over the result of his or her work, and the idea that people have the right to overthrow a government which pursues its own particular interests rather than the general interests of the whole community. On the other hand, Marx's idea of revolution was derived from Hegel's concept of transcendence (*Aufhebung*), only it was applied to socioeconomic formulations rather than to philosophical categories. To *transcend,* i.e., to *revolutionize* a socioeconomic formation, meant (1) to abolish its essential structural limitations; (2) to preserve all those institutions and past achievements that are necessary for further development; and (3) to lift the whole society to a higher, more progressive level. Clearly the ideas of "essential limitation," "development," and "progress" presupposed more basic anthropological assumptions about human nature and universal human needs and capacities, specifically human creative activity—*praxis,* assumptions which were explicitly stated *at the beginning* of Marx's theoretical development and were never abandoned (as any careful reader of the *Grundrisse* and *Capital* can ascertain).

Once Marx's critical theory of history was formulated, it became the most important single factor of subsequent socialist revolutionary movements, even in countries where historical conditions were not ripe for a strong labor movement, let alone a socialist revolution—for example, in Russia, China, and Yugoslavia. More conclusive confirmation can hardly be given for Marx's dictum that all revolutions are born in the heads of philosophers. To be sure, in all those cases philosophy was a necessary but not sufficient condition. There must have been strong social forces whose interests at least partly coincided with theoretically formulated objectives. And there must have been skillful leadership which was able to translate abstract theory into emotionally appealing symbols of an action program capable of mobilizing and organizing different social groups into a coherent, effective movement.

VII

The crucial problem is not the ineffectivenes of philosophical thought but rather the loss of original meaning in the process of reinterpretation and adaptation to all kinds of historical conditions for which it is not meant. It is in the very nature of philosophy that it cannot be simply applied: each step in its practical application will represent either creative transcendence or deformation and vulgarization. The tragedy of revolutionary philosophical thought is that too often, in the hands of victors and bearers of a new political authority, it becomes suitably adapted and transformed into a new official ideology, into a rationalization and apology of a new social hierarchy. Neither liberalism nor Marxism were able to escape this destiny.

No theory is safeguarded against this specific form of alienation: loss of control over the products of our own intellectual activity and the emergence of practical consequences that betray our original intentions. And yet a clear awareness of the problem is the starting point of its solution.

Philosophy, and science in general, could begin to develop an articulated critical perception of its own use and misuse, of its overall effect on human lives, a kind of philosophical "praxeology." True, this is to a considerable extent the sphere of the irrational, of passions and interests; this is an "external" question (in Carnap's terminology). But "the irrational" can become a subject of rational study at a meta-level; a rational will can oppose the irrationality of behavior. Also a question that is external at a certain level of theory building becomes internal at a higher level, following the expansion of our universe of theoretical interest.

The general problem is this: if we treat action-oriented philosophy as a symbolic activity which can be translated into overt practical activity according to certain general principles, then how are those principles to be established in such a way as to minimize the possibilities of degenerate interpretations and applications which betray the original purpose? Thus, if it is the initial intention of an action-oriented philosophy to bring about a more rational society and to create room for the free and creative development of each individual, then instances of its degenerate interpretation and application would include its use to encourage irrational, reckless adventures, to legitimize clearly abortive undertakings attempted under adverse conditions, to justify a demand for the unquestioned loyalty and obedience to whatever is presented as *the Cause,* and so forth.

In order to prevent the degeneration of an initially rational theory and to secure its adequate translation into rational practical activity we must be able to spell out the inner structure of rational behavior in both cases, when we create theory and when we use it. Degeneration is precisely the situation when theory building follows certain rational rules and theory use does not. The former rules are already known to a considerable extent: they are the subject matter of general methodology or inquiry. The question is then: are not these rules special cases of a general pattern of rational human behavior, of *praxis?* Is it not possible to generalize them and thus get the rational rules of theory use?

Here I shall only indicate how this can be done.

(1) One of the basic rules of theory building is *consistency,* in the sense of an absence of contradiction among (actually known and derivable) statements of the theory. An analogous rule of theory use would be consistency between statements and actions. One would have to live one's philosophy, one's critical social theory. Practical actions would have to be undertaken under the assumption that the theoretical statements are true. Once it becomes clear that this is no longer possible (because the statements could have after all been wrong and misleading), the theory would have to be revised and generalized, or abandoned.

(2) Another basic methodological rule is antidogmatism, permanent *openness to critical reexamination.* No proposition can be accepted on the basis of authority and as the mere expression of faith or hope. It has to be both supported by theoretical general arguments and confirmed by empirical evidence. Actions, similarly, cannot be rationally undertaken and justified by reference to authority, tradition, or institution. All practical activity, including that of the leaders—and especially that of the leaders—must be open to challenge and criticism. Its ultimate resort in attempts at justification must have a universal character, just as in theory building. Here, confirming evidence will be sought in practical experience, and supporting arguments will be de-

rived from principles expressing basic human needs and rights. In both there are elements of universal, transcultural validity.

Other instances of analogous rational rules in theory building and theory use may be briefly mentioned: (3) In the same way in which identical criteria of truth must hold for both a theory as a whole and any of its parts, so identical criteria of validation are necessary for ends and means, for long-range and short-range projects of social change. No imaginative theory can justify experimental sloppiness; no noble ends can justify corrupt, immoral means. (4) An old theory incompatible with new facts need not be, and in most cases cannot be, simply rejected; it will be superseded and remain a special case within a new, more general theory, still being correct under certain specific conditions. In the same way, an old social system, when it is no longer able to solve new historical problems, will not be destroyed but transcended. Its basic structural limitations will be abolished, but quite a few institutions and achievements will be incorporated within the new system.

A philosophical praxeology that would demand as much rationality, consistency, critical spirit, openness, clarity, and transcultural solidarity in the practical use of theories as in their building might alert us to the dangers of abuse and help to preserve original purposes.

VIII

What are the prospects for a new world? Whatever deserves to be regarded as a truly new world will probably emerge in a plurality of shapes. There is nothing in the stars nor in the laws of history that strictly determines the outcome of human creativity. But the framework of possibilities among which to choose differs from country to country, depending on the already attained level of material and cultural development and on the specific subjective habits of different social groups formed during preceding historical periods.

If we now ask about the future of the liberal industrialized Western societies, provided that we are reasonably well acquainted with the past and the present, we first need to consider several methods of social change.

While the method of utopian projection may always contribute to the exploration of ideal possibilities, its defects are even more serious in the present-day West than elsewhere. It is not likely to generate any significantly strong new subjective forces for at least two reasons. First, a high level of affluence generates a conformist political culture. Any radical, emotionally loaded new ideas are received with skepticism and rejected by the wealthy silent majority. Second, utopian visions of the just society are compromised because of their association with less developed authoritarian and bureaucratic postrevolutionary societies in the East.

Another method is pragmatic: the gradual discovery and creation of the future by trial and error. In this case nothing can be said about the future a priori, nothing in the existing basic structure can be challenged. In this manner one avoids heavy risks and unnecessary destruction, but one also surrenders one's power to create essentially new and more rational social arrangements.

This method can be improved if politics is enlightened by positive science. In contrast to crude pragmatism, here politics accepts a certain amount of guidance from economics, political science, ecology, and the technical and other sciences. Knowledge produced by these sciences is *positive* when it assumes the necessity of a given social framework and does not challenge it. But it may promptly indicate important specific problems within the system and urge rational modifications. A series of limited reforms may reduce but not remove a significantly high level of waste in human and natural resources and suffering by underprivileged minorities.

Western liberal societies live today with a false dilemma. The only alternatives seem to be, on the one hand, a utopia of equality which can only be attained by violence and destruction and which too often culminates in a bureaucratic despotism and, on the other hand, an unjust wasteful reality which nevertheless offers, at least, a reasonable level of stability, security, and civil liberty.

But a third alternative is historically possible and indeed optimal: a series of substantive reforms implemented in a peaceful, continuous manner but as a whole transcending the basic social framework of liberal capitalism and bringing to life a more just political and economic participatory democracy. The theoretical ground of such revolutionary reformism is a philosophical and scientific critique of the given society. The method of this critique is the opening and radical solution of the essential problems of the given society. Each essential problem represents a certain incompatibility between defining the structural characteristics of liberal capitalism and certain basic needs of human beings to survive, to develop, and genuinely to belong to a social community. To solve such problems radically means to reorganize social institutions and structures and to make them fit these needs.

IX

Five crucial problems deserve to be singled out: privatization, bureaucratization, material and spiritual poverty, alienated labor, and ecological degradation.

(1) Among the strongest human needs is the need to belong to a community, to share common values with other members of a community, and to live in solidarity with them and rationally to coordinate individual activities of general social concern. These needs cannot be fulfilled in liberal capitalism. Its economic arrangements make per-

manent competition and conflict indispensable and push individuals toward increasing privatization. As a surrogate, illusory communities are formed on the basis of shared religious faith and "national interest," and ultimately on the basis of fear of death and fear of enemies. With the decline of religion and disillusionment with aggressive patriotism, disintegrative forces tend to prevail over integrative ones. A drastic recent example is the actual or imminent economic breakdown of the great American cities and the exodus into suburbs which do not satisfy even the minimal conditions to be considered communities.

The problem appears unsolvable, and it is accordingly believed that the only alternatives are corporate capitalism or the state-owned, state-controlled economy. But there is a third alternative that has already been tested in practice with very positive results, even in the U.S.A. The solution is a policy of strong social support for public economic enterprises and associations, owned and managed by the workers and employees themselves independently of either corporate capital or the state. Only when aggressive competition, insecurity, envy, and hatred are eliminated from the economic sphere can real communal life be brought into existence in the sphere of politics and culture.

(2) There is a universal human capacity and need to participate in social decision making. This need is increasingly strong in all liberal Western countries, especially in Scandinavia and Western Europe. It cannot, however, be fulfilled under the conditions of representative democracy. It is true that in this initial form of democracy, civil liberties are better protected than in any other existing political structure. On the other hand, the growing role of the state in the economy and public welfare has resulted in a rapidly growing bureaucracy, the abuse of power, and corruption. At precisely the same time as better material conditions of life, more leisure, higher quality of education, and a higher level of political culture have enabled millions of citizens to participate meaningfully and rationally in social decision making, the natural tendency of further democratization has been obstructed by the gigantic bureaucratic machinery residing in the state, the political parties, and the enterprises. The problem again looks unsolvable while it is believed that there are only three alternatives: (1) a laissez faire system in which economic coordination and public welfare are completely outside the political sphere; (2) statist, total control over all social processes; or (3) bureaucratic control within the framework of a multiparty parliamentary system. But there is a fourth alternative: building up a network of self-governing bodies composed of elected, nonprofessional delegates of the people, subject to recall and rotation, at all levels of social organization—in the communities and enterprises, at the level of regions and entire branches of socioeconomic

activity, and at the level of whole society. These bodies, councils and assemblies, would assume responsibility for policy making and overall control in all those—and only those—functions where coordination and rational direction are indispensable. They would assign definite technical tasks to experts and administrators but would retain full power over them and would remain the supreme organs of public authority in their particular fields or territories.

The basic differences between *representative* and *participatory* democracy are: *first,* an incomparably higher degree of active participation of an increasing number of citizens in the latter and, *second,* a profound change in the character and role of political parties. Parties, themselves hierarchical and more or less bureaucratic organizations, appear in the role of mediators between the people and the government in representative democracy. In the classical form of representative democracy in Great Britain (less so in the U.S.A.), members of Parliament and of the government, once elected, owe their loyalty to their party rather than to their electorate. In participatory democracy members of self-governing bodies, whatever political organization they might belong to, are directly responsible to those who delegated their power to them. Parties are no longer ruling organizations but, at best, political organizations that articulate programs, raise people's political consciousness, try to mobilize them for specific goals, and help to select the best candidates.

Under these conditions professional politics is no longer needed and bureaucracy loses its *raison d'être* and disappears as a ruling stratum.

(3) Poverty, once a necessary consequence of low labor productivity, is becoming an anachronism in the wealthy societies of Western Europe and North America. With a $6,000 to $7,000 average national income per capita, it has for the first time in history become possible to satisfy each individual's elementary needs (for food, housing, basic education, health protection, etc.). In some Northern European countries, especially Sweden, the problem has been solved. In other equally wealthy countries like the U.S.A. there is still about one-fifth of the population that lives under conditions of both material and spiritual misery: inadequately fed, poorly housed in slums, often permanently unemployed, without health protection, without satisfactory education, without almost any culture, and socially discriminated against, especially when they belong to racial minorities. The problem cannot be solved within classical laissez faire capitalism, which needs a segment of unemployed and poor population in order to improve its bargaining position against organized labor. The solution offered by the present American variant of welfare capitalism is partial and inadequate; it involves the humiliation of being unwanted and thrown out of

any useful work, and it also involves the wasteful and corrupt bureaucratic treatment of welfare programs—which generate considerable resistance to the very idea of social care of the weak, old, and sick.

A genuine solution is possible in a system based upon communal solidarity (rather than privatization) in which organs of self-management would distribute the total amount of socially necessary work among all members of society and secure for each individual a minimum level of income sufficient to cover all basic material and cultural needs.

(4) There is a universal human capacity and need to act freely, spontaneously, imaginatively, to engage in *praxis*. Modern industrial production, with its extreme specialization and mechanization, destroyed at the outset every trace of creativity which still remained in the work of the artisan. Now, at a much higher level of productivity, it opens up new possibilities of freer organization of work, of beautification of the industrial milieu, of increasing worker participation, and, above all, of substantially reducing the number of obligatory working hours and creating a sufficient amount of leisure. With better education, this leisure time could be used for creative activities, play, communal engagement, and greater participation in the political process.

Most of these possibilities are being wasted. The system is geared toward expansion of output and increase of corporate power, not toward improvement of the quality of each person's active life. Consequently, increased productivity is used to increase consumption, not to liberate time and to offer each individual substantially more culture and opportunity for *praxis*. This solution is irrational because, on the one hand, it leads to increasingly wasteful production, and on the other hand it blocks the potential human development of both those workers who must waste their lives in unnecessarily long hours of stupefying work and those who are thrown out of the production process and offered compensation for nonwork.

The rational solution is obviously full employment, decreased working hours, the reduction of waste in production and consumption, and transferring funds from compensation for nonwork to education for creative work.

(5) A system which rests on the need constantly to expand material production and to encourage wasteful consumption is incompatible with the overriding need to use natural resources wisely and to preserve a balanced, healthy natural environment. At the same time as we know how scarce and irrevocably limited certain natural energies are, an entire industry is working hard to create artificial needs and to increase the consumption of those very scarce natural resources. No system can survive for long in such a state of affairs. The only rational solution, quite compatible with solutions of other problems, seems to be to stop the unnecessary depletion of our natural resources, to elim-

inate consumerism, to give all individuals an opportunity to develop higher-level needs that do not require the accumulation of material goods, and to allow a natural transition from excessive comfort to culture, communal engagements, *praxis*.

In different societies these problems will be solved in different order, in different degrees, with different speed, in more or less peaceful or violent ways, and with more or less ingenuity and fantasy. If they are not solved at all, the old story will be repeated once again. One more civilization will go down the drain forever.

Only a philosophically grounded social theory can see beyond immediate practical problems and provide an epochal critical consciousness that would both alert us to the dangers of degradation and direct us to look for creative and rational long-range solutions. Such a theory will not always reach the majority of people, no matter how loudly it speaks. It will not always mobilize sufficient social energy significantly to accelerate historical progress and radically to reshape existing social forms. But the least it can do is to exert pressure in the proper direction within an otherwise spontaneous development pushed by necessity. There is always a more enlightened part of the ruling class which realizes that certain urgent problems have to be solved even at the price of sacrificing certain existing institutions in order to preserve other, more basic ones. And there is always a chance that reforms meant to be conservative would generate new forces that would carry the process of social change beyond its initial limited intention.

Reason is powerful even when it is not an overwhelming immediate material force. In the struggle of existing irrational material forces it can often manage to give that struggle a rational sense of direction.

Part 2

SOCIALISM AS
A SOCIAL SYSTEM

Socialism and the
Problem of Alienation*

Predrag Vranicki

I

The phenomenon of alienation is very complex and has not been suffi-
ciently studied. Philosophical and sociological analysis must still face
up to a number of problems, viz., what the concept of alienation encompasses, what the dynamics of alienation have been in the course of
history, the functions of identical forms of alienation in different eras,
whether alienation is overcome by a continuous and unilateral process,
etc. Leaving aside all of these issues for the moment, I feel compelled to
stress one factor that I consider essential to the concept of alienation
encompasses, what the dynamics of alienation have been in the course of
history, the functions of identical forms of alienation: While all of
human history and all historical creations (the state, culture, religion,
etc.) are man's work and the expression of man's own potentialities and
powers, man has been capable of existing only by separating these

powers from himself and by finding these same powers counterposed to himself as specific material, social or ideological forces.

So long as man's own work continues to exist as something external to him (the political sphere, religion, the market, money, etc.) and to oppose itself to him in the form of a superior authority, we will encounter the phenomenon of alienation. Man's world up to now has always been a world divided against itself—a world in which man, the creator of history, has been largely powerless, disfranchised, and debased in historical terms. History is a constant tyranny over man to this day.

However, every form of alienation is distinguished by a specific historical content and function, for which reason different forms of alienation cannot all be evaluated in the same way. Furthermore, every form of alienation identified thus far has been superseded by some other form of alienation. A particular "alienational situation" becomes intolerable only when new opportunities arise for the development of human forces and relationships. Regardless of the fact that human progress has always taken place within the confines of various forms of alienation, some forms of alienation have been more permissive than others toward the development of man as a "polyvalent" being and the further generation of the richness of the human being, and have abolished the various social restrictions interfering with man's freer historical movement.

Hence, certain forms of alienation have been of historically progressive significance under certain historical circumstances. When new historical prospects open up in the course of this development for the liberation of man from some forms of alienation, the old forms of alienation become intolerable. Some of these forms will disappear in the course of this process (e.g., slavery and various forms of ideological alienation).

The historical process thus far has consisted just as much of a process of the creation of various forms of alienation as of a process of de-alienation. This process is in evidence, among other ways, in the increasing emphasis given to man himself and in the increasing preponderence ascribed to human rather than "transhuman" political forces. The processes of de-alienation will be all the more powerful when this orientation of man toward "man proper" and man's creativeness, become primary and essential factors, and when people so associated come to regulate their relationships with each other and with nature in this way.

Alienated historical situations have not only presupposed man's division against himself but have also been essentially characterized by the isolation of man from man by virtue of racial, national, class, or other hostilities. These antagonisms have dragged contemporary man to the brink of disaster. Only the terrifying prospect of self-destruction has begun to have some effect in the sense of overcoming all the narrow-minded and anachronistic consequences of the contemporary alienated world.

The essential import of socialism derives from just such a historical legacy as this and from the specific historical structure known as bour-geois society. This is not the place to analyze all the grand accomplish-ments of bourgeois society, the achievements that are so significant an accretion to human creativity. Likewise, there is no room here to analyze all the limitations of bourgeois society. Such analysis has been performed often enough, sometimes well and sometimes not so well, from the time of Marx to our own day. To understand the founda-tions and historical traditions from which contemporary socialism springs, however, we must take note of at least those characteristics by which bourgeois society no longer corresponds to contemporary human requirements and potentialities.

Bourgeois society has carried the development of man to unheard-of heights, but only by transforming man within the framework of the wage-labor relationship into a component part of an omnipotent piece of machinery. The classic society of commodity production has con-verted everything into a commodity, into a thing. The worker in such a society sells his ability to work just as everybody else sells whatever is at his disposal—a commodity, his mind, his ideas, a trade, his body, or his talent. Relationships have clearly been deprived of the funda-mental characteristics of humanity if the entire society amounts to a relationship of buying and selling, if man has become a statistical cipher, and if man is regarded as though he were part of a mechanism. A man who in ordinary life has become no more than a commodity producing other commodities and part of a value-producing mecha-nism can with equal ease become part of a mechanism which sees an enemy in another man or nation.

This alienation of contemporary man's everyday life is the founda-tion and source for all the other forms of his alienated condition. Just as the owners of commodities and the entire technocratic mechanism counterpose themselves to him as forces controlling his work and very existence, so also do the commodities which he produces counterpose themselves to him as either a power or a challenge. The *fetishism of commodities* has long been a familiar phenomenon, along with a num-ber of its consequences. Even if the most recent contemporary pro-cesses of bourgeois society succeed, through scientific and statistical organizational arrangements, in modifying the extreme consequences of the market mechanism, the commodity is acquiring increasingly magical power. Man comes to believe that the possession of certain commodities alters his qualities as a man and that wealth in commodities can be identified with enrichment as a human being. Man becomes wholly oriented in the direction of this externality, and thus impoverishes himself.

The "thingification" of man, as one of the essential forms of man's alienation in bourgeois society, also dehumanizes a number of his other relationships. If the politico-technocratic mechanism relates to man as to a thing, man's active role will then be confined to the pursuit of well-being or political voting, and man will eventually relate to another man as toward a thing. The extreme and drastic forms of inhumanity that have come to light in the past thirty years are no more than the consequences of a more fundamental constellation.

The polyvalence of the human being in the midst of this extremely thingified and compartmentalized relationship becomes so distorted that the very process of work itself proves unbearable. All the efforts on the part of psychologists and sociologists to solve this impersonal situation for modern man, whatever improvements may have taken place, have ended in failure. Any such efforts are nothing more than serviceable palliatives, for the problem is not primarily psychological or technological, but rather a matter of the philosophy of history.

Man may be more or less aware of his alienated condition, but the end result is the division of his personality against itself and the formation of the *homo duplex*. As a man, he does not feel himself to be part of the broader community. As an official being, he does not feel himself to be a man. And this characteristic feature of the alienated man, so long familiar, has consequences of the most tragic kind in the field of human relationships.

II

If the contemporary society of private ownership and wage-labor relationships can be characterized in terms of the aforementioned factors—and the history of the last few centuries has confirmed this to be the case on innumerable occasions (e.g., wars, economic crises, concentration camps, gas chambers, etc.)—then the struggle to overcome such a state of affairs as this is surely the struggle for socialism as well.

At one time, at least in general terms, the problem of socialism was phrased more simply and appeared less complicated. Today, after many experiences, not devoid of tragedy, the problem of socialism must be considered primarily within these philosophico-sociological horizons. The revolution and revolutionary authority have often been regarded as sufficient guarantees that man would be liberated not only from the hired-labor relationship but also from all other forms of alienation. The problem of alienation thus becomes "superfluous." For example, the concept of alienation did not crop up at all in theoretical discussions during the decades of Stalinism. Even today, many theoreticians of socialism consider alienation to be incompatible with socialism, as though socialism were immune by nature to this disease.

Historical experiences offer an entirely different picture, for they have served to shatter numerous illusions and myths, especially those of the Stalinist era.

Stalinism failed to grasp that the time to put the revolution into effect is after the revolution has taken place, insofar as it exists at all. Only then such social forms of relationships as will lead to the constant liberation of man and to the creation of a new historical personality can be created on a permanent basis. In a word, the fundamental principles of philosophical and humanistic thought must be implanted in the deepest possible way. To be sure, socialism, to reach this goal, must continue on the basis of a number of alienated forms that cannot be immediately abolished or leaped over (state, classes, party, nations, bureaucracy, religion, commodity production, the market, etc.). Such is the case despite the fact that these forms in genuine socialist development must acquire other symbols and meanings and play a new role, as we shall see.

By virtue of their very existence, however, certain aspects of these alienated forms can (but need not) manifest themselves in the most negative fashion. So long as man under whatever system (socialism included) generates, senses, and experiences his powers as a set of factors apart from himself, the possibility will exist for such factors to act toward him as a superior authority and to obstruct historical creations that deserve to be measured against the level of contemporary human development.

Therefore, contrary to the thesis of the superfluity of the problem of alienation under socialism, we must advance the thesis in the most decisive manner possible that the problem of alienation is the central problem of socialism.

This problem could not have been the central problem of bourgeois society for the simple reason that the basic historical task of bourgeois society was never, nor is it now, to liberate man from all the forms of his alienation. Bourgeois society accomplished its historical task by superseding feudal forms of dependence and subordination and by evolving certain limited forms of democratization in the realm of economic democracy. To the extent to which there is a tendency within bourgeois society to overcome certain of the negative consequences of bourgeois private ownership, the classic bourgeois order is going to give way to statist tendencies; yet bourgeois society did not and could not have the historical duty of abolishing economic and political, and hence ideological, *authority*. The basic task of bourgeois society was to make this authority function and not to abolish it, to solidify the position of the ruling class and not to eliminate it, and to separate authority from the people and not to transform the people into an "authority."

Bourgeois society is a political society par excellence in the sense that "political" is a synonym for the authority of a particular group of people over another.

Hence, socialism cannot be based on those categories which are essential to bourgeois society. Since the task of socialism is to overcome those forms of human existence which create the alienated man, the dissolution of the alienated forms of man's social life becomes the central problem of socialism.

If the problem of socialism is not comprehended in these terms, the end result may be the evolution of political forms into paroxysms of dehumanization.

Stalinism is a typical instance of failure to consider the essential problems of socialism. Historically, Stalinism meant that the various forms of human alienation inherited directly from the former class societies were relied upon and strengthened. Instead of putting its trust in man—the historical creator of social life itself—Stalinism offered the major role in the formation and development of the community to the state and to various "transmission belts."

Having lost sight, on the intellectual horizon, of the true import of the socialist transformation, i.e., the gradual effort to abolish the system of political society and hence the forms of economic and political alienation, Stalinism based the evolution of this political society on extremes of power. The omnipotence of the political apparatus of the state was necessarily accompanied by the universal powerlessness of the individual, the human being, the personality—precisely the objects of the import of this radical historical endeavor.

Man as producer finds himself again in the alienated position of hired labor if he has been wholly deprived of participation in the management of production and in the distribution of the resultant product under such a system, which consists not only of total state planning but also of the disposal of surplus value by the state. The only difference in this instance is that capitalist monopoly has been supplanted by the universal monopoly of the state. The Marxist idea of planned production as opposed to the haphazardness of the capitalist market has been transformed into its own contradiction. Man as producer, not having become himself the planner, has become part of a plan, i.e., "planned out." We need not waste many words about the fact that numerous other characteristics of alienated labor have also manifested themselves in the process.

Instead of superseding the hired-labor relationship that is the fundamental characteristic from which all the other deformations of bourgeois political society originate, socialism in its Stalinist phase of development evolved new forms of this very relationship. The problem of economic and thereby political alienation, far from ceasing to exist, has thus become socialism's real and vital problem.

Very understandably, the historical illusion that socialism has been accomplished as the first phase of communism on the basis of such a relationship has given rise to a variety of other myths and obfuscations. We should not forget the truism that obfuscation is one of the fundamental forms of ideological alienation. Like every other form of alienation, of course, this form should not be comprehended in unhistoric and abstract terms. During certain periods of primitive awareness and a low level of social development, man has been able to advance only with the help of such alienated forms of consciousness. Man's very existence often depended on them. However, though mankind was capable at one time of progressing with this type of ideological consciousness, the contemporary evolution of man and his high level of development in knowledge and philosophy are incompatible with such a structure. This is especially true of a socialist evolution, in which man's relationships toward man, society, and nature should become more lucid, more rational, and more comprehensible. Man in socialist society must become increasingly aware of himself as the sole creator of his life and his destiny.

One of the myths already mentioned is that of the socialist state as the fundamental driving force and lever behind socialist advancement. Since the state consists primarily of a particular apparatus, this attitude has inevitably exalted the political sphere. The worker, instead of being recognized as the basic actor in this new historical transformation, has again found himself opposed by an institution which is essentially inaccessible to him and which has been managing all spheres of his life. Thus the foundation for the development of the bureaucracy and of all bureaucratic pretensions and mystifications has been created. It is but a step from this myth—that the problem of freedom has been solved by abolishing the bourgeois state—to the concurrent myth that a working-class state cannot generate a force which under certain circumstances dominates the working class, and espouses the primitive cult of the personality. The realm of state arbitration thus comes to encompass not only political and economic processes and relationships but also all others—scientific, philosophical, and artistic. Whereas philosophy and science at one time had been the ancillaries of theology, in this case all these spheres became the ancillaries of politics.

The cult of personality and all the other alienated forms are therefore not just accidents of circumstance but rather expressions of a definite structure that rests on a concept of socialism as the absorption of all spheres of social life into the state.[1] This concept reached a culminating point in Stalinist theory and practice in the thesis of "completed socialism" once state ownership and arbitration came to predominate in society.[2]

This ideological fascination with bureaucracy and technocracy established an extremely alienated theoretical credo. A number of facts were lost sight of in the process. First, to give such great power to political institutions necessarily meant to diminish in practice the real freedom of the workers and the intellectuals. Second, the import of socialism cannot consist of the evolution of the alienated forms of bourgeois society to still greater power. Third, the dissolution of these alienated forms necessarily presupposes the creation of new relationships that will supersede all the forms of authority and force inherited by socialism. Fourth, socialism is a development of these new relationships which enable the workingman to have an increasing influence on the direction and organization of his own life.

The thesis of "completed socialism" is consequently a *contradictio in adjecto,* for anything involved in a constant transformation process can never be completed. It is impossible to build on the old political forms (state, party, bureaucracy) due to the reasons mentioned, but it is also impossible to build on new forms, for the old ones cannot be abolished all at once. In other words, socialism is the initial phase of communism during which these contradictory processes evolve, while the predominance of new forms of a specifically communist nature will mean that the first phase has been overcome.

III

The problem of alienation is thus of vital and historical importance to socialism, not only because practical experience has shown that many deforming aspects of alienation are possible under socialism, but also because socialism must continue on the basis of various social forms which in themselves represent forms of alienation. Furthermore, as we shall see, the very level of economic and cultural development in contemporary society generates various other forms of alienation which socialism cannot get rid of all at once. The entry of socialism on the world stage is not the appearance of some magic wand to convert all evils into good and to resolve all human problems in the twinkling of an eye.

If our desire is to contribute more fully to human liberation, i.e., to the overcoming of various forms of alienation, then socialism must place its fundamental stress on man, and the free personality must be considered a prerequisite to social freedom, in theory and in practice. This means the permanent creation of those relations which will enable the workingman to govern himself and his work process in economics, culture, education, and all other sectors of his social life. The opposite of the absolutization of the political factor is to strengthen the power of the entire community rather than just the political segment thereof. Another aspect of this social management (in the form of workers' councils and various other councils) is for the state to wither away and die out as a power over man.[3]

We dare not close our eyes to these facts, or to the fact that socialism is not a magical leap from an alienated to a de-alienated society; to the contrary, it is a new historical process which also contains certain alienated forms; nor can one ignore the fact that its historical import and mission is precisely the conquest, not the increase, of alienation.

In terms of the contemporary level of human development, regardless of specific countries, socialism is also a hierarchical society. In view of this circumstance, and of the forms in which socialism evolves, bureaucracy is a constant accompaniment to socialism. Particular hierarchies in all spheres of life invariably endeavor to make themselves as independent as possible in relation to the lower levels. This again means that the tendency to create new forms of alienation is a permanent process that socialism must thwart and overcome. Socialism is thus a process in which the evolution of forms of self-management permeates and opposes statist and bureaucratic tendencies. What is involved is not a linear process devoid of conflict, but rather a genuinely dialectical and contradictory process. *In other words, the political forms in which socialism evolves are essentially particular forms of alienation and are wholly positive and historically progressive only if they tend to dissolve themselves.*

However paradoxical it may seem, the socialist forces accomplish the process of de-alienation precisely by means of different forms of alienation, alongside de-alienated forms. This is a unique, wholly new, original, and profoundly humane process and historical task of its own kind. While every authority in the past had endeavored to make itself absolute and eternal, socialist forces use their power to eliminate themselves.[4]

Socialism from this philosophico-sociological standpoint is a process by which the previous forms of human alienation are to be overcome.

Socialism has emerged thus far in the less developed countries, and therefore increases in production and industrial development have appeared to be its prime tasks. This is just one aspect of the problems of these countries, an everyday concern and reality, without whose solution higher forms of human relationships cannot evolve. Yet this problem is not in itself a specifically *socialist* one, since increases in production are likewise the problem of capitalism. The vital problem of socialism is to be found in the realm of social relationships.

Without wishing to underestimate the significance of economic and cultural factors, I must conclude that such measures (rising production, industrial development) fail to strike their historical target unless accompanied by profound social transformation in the sense of self-management by man himself.

In view of the complexity of the domestic and international situations during the initial phases of development, however, even these forms of self-management are not by themselves absolute despite their essentially de-alienated structure. In the same way as political forms tend in themselves to develop into bureaucracy and to dominate politically, various forms of particularism and localism (which are also forms of alienation) may develop in the same way in the field of self-management. The activities of the most progressive forces of socialism to overcome both bureaucracy and localism, along with all the other deformations, are of such great importance for precisely this reason. Such is indeed the fundamental import of the endeavors of the socialist and communist parties and leagues, wherever they happen to exist.

Alienation inevitably persists under socialism in other areas of social life which are generally similar in contemporary developed societies. Socialism has not as yet abolished the production of commodities, hence the market, money, or any of the fetishes which inevitably appear at this level of economic and cultural development of mankind. Regardless of the possibility of much stronger intervention on the part of the socialist state of society itself to prevent the occurrence of the various deformations originating from such a pattern, the occult power of the market and of money, and the hierarchy of status, are bound to have an alienating effect on the unstable structure of contemporary man. Egocentricity, the division of the personality into an official and a private component, and various other resultant moral aberrations are nothing more than manifestations of human alienation, even under socialism. The *homo duplex*, that characteristic phenomenon of contemporary civilization, has not disappeared as a problem under socialism. The effect of the external, the superficial, and the ephemeral in the form of the living standard, prestige, or only shallow amusement is at work in the period of socialism. The structure and physiognomy of contemporary man is still primitive in many respects, burdened with a variety of negative characteristics inherited from the past, and hence quite unstable. Many people run away from themselves after having failed to find genuine contentment within themselves or in their creative relationship to socialism. Such people find their vital contentment outside themselves in the external and the incidental, rather than in the essential problems of their own personalities and communities.

Another problem of socialism is modern industrial production, which has led to extremes of specialization and the division of labor, thus alienating workers from their jobs, which are monotonous, uncreative, and boring. Under socialism as elsewhere, of course, various palliatives will naturally be used to alleviate the situation. However, the historical solution is not to be found in any such palliatives, but rather in those measures which characterize socialism as a new historical form of the social organization of labor, i.e., of social relationships generally. The abolishment of those relationships in which the worker is cut off from participation in the entire organization of labor, production, planning, and the distribution of surplus labor is the *conditio sine qua non* to any solution of this fundamental problem of contemporary civilization. But self-management on the part of the workingman begins as a process of abolishing the wage-labor relationship, that alienated relationship in which man is no more than a means. The whole hierarchy of values shifts with the transformation of the workingman from a tool into an active factor in society.

But this factor alone is not sufficient to solve the entire problem. With the ever-growing process of creating a society in which the center is man's self-government, with the ever-increasing abandonment of the political forms of his existence, the structure of productive forces, including man himself, must be changed simultaneously. The perspectives which are opened up by automation and the other achievements of modern science, along with the drastic shortening of the working day and, eventually, the abolition of the present division of labor into physical and mental, will extend the range of human freedom simultaneously with the transformations of social relationships.

However, there is still another prerequisite to be met if this "free time" is to be used creatively. A new, "polycultural," critical, and historically responsible personality is needed, a personality requiring no intermediaries or alienated forms to sense a unity with history, a personality with horizons not confined to family or tribe or nation. Therefore this entire transformation period of socialism is the period of developing a new personality which will, in its entirety, become conscious of history as its personal creation, so that there will be no need for the idea of transcendence in order to explain its own existence and its own purpose.

Summing up, we may state again that alienation is not the problem of bourgeois society, because that society may itself exist as an alienated society. Alienation becomes the central problem of socialism, since socialism may exist and develop only under the condition that it overcomes and eliminates alienation.

NOTES

1. By "state" we are naturally referring in the Marxian sense primarily to a particular organizational arrangement and apparatus serving a given class or group in its exercise of authority over another. Aside from this, the concept of the state encompasses a number of other constituent parts.

2. I have given a critique of this thesis of "completed socialism" in my dissertation on "Marginalia on Humanism" in the collection entitled *Socijalizam i humanizam* (*Socialism and Humanism*; Zagreb: Naprijed Publishing House, 1963).

3. These forms of management are known as "social self-management" in Yugoslav terminology and display a variety of specific features characteristic of Yugoslav society. The frequency of the disputes over the problem of the "withering away" of the state only serves to show that the essence of the problem is not understood. The state is capable of "withering away" in connection with a number of extremely significant functions in the field of economics or culture, leading to the elimination of certain forms of alienation. At the same time, however, no socialist society can weaken or abolish its armed forces so long as international antagonisms have not been resolved. Socialism is therefore in the vanguard of the struggle for coexistence and general disarmament, for to supersede this historical anachronism (the existence of armies) would mean that man had made a great stride forward in his development.

4. I might point out that socialism in Yugoslavia has developed in precisely this way and that a great deal of historical experience has already been accumulated on the basis of workers' and social self-management.

The Statist Myth
of Socialism

Svetozar Stojanović

I

Our century abounds in ideological-political myths. The most prominent of them—the myth above myths of our age—is the statist myth of socialism. With the degeneration of the October Revolution a new exploitative class system was created, a system which stubbornly tries to pass itself off as socialism. Unfortunately, almost everyone believes in the socialist identity of Stalinist society.

The ideologues of "socialist" statism announced long ago that their society had completed the construction of socialism and had begun the construction of communism. They operate on the assumption that the construction of communism can be based upon an omnipotent state. Thus, in addition to the statist myth of socialism, there is also the statist myth of communism. Marxists may argue over adequate interpretations of Marx's conception of the socialist state, but *statist communism*, even at first glance, is completely absurd to anyone who knows anything about the authentic Marx.

In this chapter I shall suggest an outline for a theory of statism as a new form of class society. There have generally been few *ideas* in contemporary social science which have not had their roots in the past. The idea of a new form of class society after capitalism originated with Jan Waclaw Machajski. In *The Evolution of Social Democracy* (1899), he claimed that after the socialist revolution the intelligentsia would become the new ruling class. In a letter written in 1930, Khristian Rakovsky contended that a new ruling class was already being created in the U.S.S.R. Anton Ciliga expressed a similar opinion in his *Au Pays du grande mensonge* (In the Land of the Big Lie), published in Paris in 1937. Toward the end of the 1930s there was a long discussion in the press of the Fourth International on the nature of the Stalinist system; some discussants put forth the view that this was a new form of class society. In 1939, in his *La Bureaucratisation du monde* (The Bureaucratization of the World), Bruno Rizzi called this society "bureaucratic collectivism."

Another tradition—the theory of *managerial* society—was formulated by James Burnham in *The Managerial Revolution* (New York, 1941). The conception which I advocate here shares nothing substantive with the idea of managerial revolution and managerial society.[1]

1. Burnham generally does not use the categories of statism and the statist class. The difference here is not only terminological. His managerial class is not the same as the statist class which I suggest. The statist class is composed of the entire state apparatus, having transformed itself from the representative of the working class into the collective owner of the means of production. Burnham's managerial class is composed of state economic functionaries. He explicitly excludes state political functionaries from its membership and therefore rejects, also explicitly, theories of bureaucratic society, including Rizzi's theory of bureaucratic collectivism.

2. For Burnham the October Revolution was a managerial revolution, while for me it was a socialist revolution par excellence, although a new form of class, statist society was born with Stalinism. Burnham considered the establishment of managerial society not only a real process, but also a *necessary* one. He went so far as to assert that in the 1960s the managerial transformation of the world would near completion. For me, again, the degeneration of the socialist revolution is not at all inevitable. Two possibilities are being laid bare as a consequence of the crisis of capitalism: statism and socialism. This is now the principal dilemma of our epoch.

3. Burnham asserted that the U.S.S.R., Germany, and Italy most closely approximated the model of managerial society, while the process of "managerization" was perceptible in other countries as well, including the United States. He held the principal managerial ideologies to be

Leninism-Stalinism, fascism, nazism, and the ideology of the New Deal. Of course, it would not occur to me to lump all these countries and ideologies together. For me Leninism is a socialist revolutionary ideology, while for Burnham it is an ideology of the managerial revolution.

4. On the basis of his theory Burnham made several other mistaken judgments and predictions: that World War II was the first great managerial struggle; that it would yield the formation of three managerial superpowers, the core of which would be composed of Germany, Japan, and the United States; that the U.S.S.R. would decompose into two parts, western and eastern, and that the former would be part of the superpower centered upon Germany, while the latter would be part of the superpower centered upon Japan; and that there would be no other independent countries.

It is well known that after 1948 a critical examination and interpretation of Stalinism began to develop in Yugoslavia. The limitations of this process of reinterpretation have, among other things, influenced me to propose an outline of a theory of statist society. In one view, Stalinism is a form of state capitalism;[2] this was the officially accepted view in Yugoslavia during the struggle with the Cominform. But, the difference between state capitalism and the Stalinist system is rather obvious, as in the latter there are no capitalists nor does capital exist as a social relation. In another view (one which currently reigns in Yugoslavia and to which we shall return later), Stalinism is *bureaucratic socialist* society. While I am rather indebted to this tradition, I must say that it was precisely its difficulties which above all prompted me to follow the argument to its logical conclusion—to my position on statist society.

2

Marx expected the socialist revolution to occur in the wealthiest capitalist countries. But Lenin rejected this assumption in both the theoretical and practical-political senses; indeed, historical practice has proved him right insofar as socialist revolutions have actually taken place in the undeveloped rather than the developed countries. On the other hand, those who found in Marx's assumption a more hidden, indirect sense of foreboding and caution were not far from the truth, either.

The absence of a large, developed industrial proletariat was one of the decisive causes of the statist perversion of the socialist revolution. Moreover, the small proletariat which did exist was decimated in the revolutionary struggle. We shall cite only some of the other extremely unfavorable factors in this respect: the feudal-capitalistic economic and social legacy of Russia, the atmosphere bred by a tradition of political absolutism and a low standard of education and culture, the world war, the obstinate counterrevolution and foreign intervention which devastated the land, the absence of effective support from the workers' movements of the developed countries, and the prolonged hostile encirclement. In such conditions the tendency toward statism was all the stronger and its victory all the more certain. Nevertheless, it cannot be said that the struggle for socialism was doomed in advance to failure. There is no "iron law" of revolutionary degeneration.[3] The triumph of the statist tendency, which as a rule has a great deal of vigor and endurance, can be prevented by persistent struggle on the part of the revolutionary forces.

But let us go half a century into the past. In Russia the revolutionary party had to take it largely upon itself to accomplish the mission of a yet undeveloped industrial proletariat. After the seizure and consolidation of power, it found itself confronted with a choice: either to develop the social self-government of the soviets of workers', soldiers', and peasants' deputies, or to base the entire system permanently and exclusively upon the state-party apparatus. It must be kept in mind that the idea of socialist self-government—based upon workers' self-management—was only theoretically sketched out in Marx's analysis of the Paris Commune and in Lenin's *State and Revolution*. Exactly how a socialist economy was going to look in practice was left quite vague. And to a certain extent this difficulty as well contributed to the victory of the statist tendency.

There is still research on this process which remains to be done. Perhaps we ought to turn our attention all the way back to the first confrontations within the Bolshevik Party after it had come to power. One of the turning points was apparently the conflict with the so-called "Workers' Opposition." Fifty years after the October Revolution, Marxists have yet to examine and evaluate Lenin's role in this conflict in all its dimensions with a sufficient degree of impartiality. Lenin was obviously torn between the ideas on self-management he expressed in *State and Revolution* (for the sake of which he had so fiercely attacked growing bureaucratism and had demanded workers' control), and the unquestionable need for the state to introduce order by means of force and to organize social life out of the chaos born of counterrevolution, poverty, and famine. After Lenin's death the emphasis shifted increasingly, both in theory and in practice, from society to the state. State socialism gradually developed into statism.

Although it had originated as a distinctly antistatist theory, Marxism has been perverted into the ideological basis of statism. The period of statist modification and adaptation of Marxism culminated at the Eighteenth Congress of the C.P.S.U.(b), at which Stalin openly prescribed the position that the state would grow stronger in socialism.

Some parallels can be drawn between the fates of bourgeois democratic and socialist revolutions. Both were born of hope in the definitive realization of equality. In the case of the former, the bourgeoisie gradually emerged from the ranks of the broad people's masses (the Third Estate). A parallel differentiation of society unfolded after the October Revolution. Expropriated feudal and bourgeois property gradually was transformed into the foundation of statist ownership, while the working class and the laboring masses became the object of a new form of exploitation.

3

Many severe critics of Stalinism, including the majority of ·Yugoslav Marxists, are prisoners of the *"socialist"* ideology of statism. Instead of recognizing Stalinism as a new form of class society, they claim that it is state socialism, albeit bureaucratized.

Upon seizing power the revolutionary movement nationalizes the means of production and the management both of production and of all social life. To be sure, this *state socialism*, a stage through which all socialist revolutions have passed or are still passing, is a very elementary form of socialism. One can speak of mature socialism only insofar as state property is transcended by social property, and state management by social self-government. For Marx, mature socialism is a society composed of associations of free producers who consciously work according to a common and rational plan. In it the working class develops its own powers of self-management and simultaneously stimulates the development of universal and integral social self-government.

So long as the new apparatus represents the interests of the working class and the laboring masses as a whole, Marxists can consider the system built upon these foundations to be socialist (more specifically, state socialist). However, it is well known that the state apparatus, from its very inception, has a second tendency as well—to emancipate itself from society, to become its master and to give the pursuit of its own interests priority over all others. When this indeed does happen, in my opinion, it is no longer possible to speak of *state socialism,* but only of *statism.* Of course, this does not mean that in statism there are not certain elements of socialism; these may even be important elements of socialism. But only the dominant characteristics of the system as a whole are at issue here.

It is theoretically insupportable to include those two essentially different systems under the heading of a single concept—that of socialism. After all, even those theorists who do so implicitly acknowledge unresolvable difficulties, for they find it necessary to draw a distinction between *revolutionary* and *bureaucratized* state socialism. But can both one and the other really remain defined as socialism without sacrificing theoretical coherence? What is there that revolutionary state socialism and this bureaucratized system have so essentially in common that we might be able to classify the latter as state socialism as well? The characteristics ascribed to this bureaucratic society by the theorists whom we are presently criticizing are diametrically opposed to those which they themselves include in their definition of revolutionary state socialism. Can we say that two entities are of the same type when their properties are not only different but mutually opposed?

The theorists under discussion nevertheless assert that these systems do have one important feature in common: *state ownership* of the means of production and of the products of labor. But this phrase covers two completely different notions which are not made explicit.

When we speak of state ownership *in socialism,* in terms of original Marxism we mean that the state represents and ensures the interests of the working class and the laboring masses; it is this idea which the theorists whom we have been discussing here include, with good reason, in their definition of revolutionary state socialism. Thus, state ownership simultaneously represents an initial and indirect form of social ownership. But this can hardly be said of the Stalinist system, in which the bureaucratic state is the master of society, disposing of ownership sovereignly and in its own interests. Such state ownership is *collective ownership on the part of the state apparatus.* The theory under criticism here would dispute this assertion, but at the same time would have to admit that state ownership in a bureaucratic system is not even indirectly social ownership. It would turn out that the means of production and the products of labor are neither the property of any social group (nor products of the state apparatus), nor indirectly the property of society. But whose property are they then? No one's!

History has in fact obliged Marxists to introduce into their earlier differentiation of socialism and communism a division within socialism itself, between state and self-governing socialism. Consequently the picture of the so-called transitional period has been further complicated. Not only is socialism the transitional period between capitalism and communism, but state socialism *may* be the transitional phase leading to self-governing socialism. But it does not have to be, as it can also degenerate into a new form of class society—statism. If the revolutionary movement is not aware that state socialism is only an elementary form of socialism, then the most probable outcome will be statism.

The view that *pure* state socialism—where all social life is centered exclusively upon the ruling party and the state, and where not even elementary workers' self-management is an objective possibility—is *inevitable* has gained great currency. But I think that we might speak more accurately about *choice* of such a path. And the choice does not necessarily depend exclusively upon objective conditions. The claim that pure state socialism is objectively necessary is most often a rationalization for the weaknesses of the ruling party. The party comes to power holding certain conceptions about the new society; these conceptions, as well, play a great role here. The weakness of Marxist theory in this respect is apparent. The most there is to rely upon in the classics of Marxism is a mere *sketch* of socialism, which itself was from the very first the subject of interpretive debate. Thus, in the absence of a clear conception of the new society, the communist party has always come to power with the idea that state socialism is the paradigm of socialism.

Nor has the history of the Yugoslav revolution offered adequate proof that the period of pure state socialism prior to the introduction of workers' self-management in Yugoslavia was inevitable. What is there to be said against the *opposite* thesis that it was possible to begin true socialization *concurrently* with nationalization? We can speak of "inevitability" here only if we include among the decisive factors the conception of the new society with which the Communist Party of Yugoslavia came to power. But this is something completely different from what the theorists whom we have been criticizing have in mind. Even if the Party did have other ideas, they say, it would not have been able to realize them because of objective conditions. But surely conditions were more difficult between 1945 and 1948 than during the period of the most severe Stalinist offensive against Yugoslavia when the first workers' councils were created. The struggle with the Cominform compelled the Party to reconsider and alter its conception of internal development. By that time the state socialist system had already begun to show symptoms of statist degeneration.

Marx's categorization of socioeconomic systems long ago lost its ability to cover certain new cases, and not only those under discussion here. There are many more countries, especially those that have been recently decolonized, whose systems are also based upon state ownership and central state planning, but which few Marxists would be prepared to call socialist. Why, indeed, should such societies be called socialist only because their ruling circles do so? In such instances certain theorists seek their "salvation" in the designation "noncapitalist countries"! Would it not be more acceptable to broaden Marx's categorization by introducing the category of statism? Of course, this type of statism is quite different from the statism which arose as a consequence of the degeneration of the October Revolution.

Many theorists, especially Marxists, are quite happy to use this category, but only in a milder sense than the one I have suggested. They use the term to apply to the strengthening of the state in contemporary society, whether capitalist or socialist. Thus they are theoretically powerless when the statist tendency takes such full control as to necessitate speaking about a changed, essentially new system. Even classical Marxism recognized the ever-present possibility that the state apparatus might emancipate itself from social classes. Marx warned of the danger that the revolutionary state might become alienated from the proletariat and finally turn against it. It is precisely this, in the opinion of many Marxists, which constitutes the principal danger confronting the socialist revolution. Yet historical events have even surpassed Marx's forebodings.

Thus we must follow our line of argument to its conclusion and create a category to cover the transformation of the state apparatus into a ruling class, and accordingly for a new type of class system. It need not puzzle us in the least that it was usually only a part of the ruling class which directly participated in the governing of society in the past, and that in contrast, the ruling class and the state apparatus in statist society are identical.

In the case of the statism which developed in the wake of the degeneration of the socialist revolution, the state apparatus completely coalesced with those of the communist party and the other political organizations constituting its transmission mechanisms. As the *collective* owner of the means of production, this apparatus employs the labor force and exploits it. The personal share of each representative of the ruling class in the distribution of surplus value is proportional to his position in the state hierarchy. With respect to the statist class, as well, we must speak in the true Marxist spirit of the prospects for expropriating the expropriators and for socializing the means of production.

4

The Stalinist system possesses all the essential properties of statism. Stalinists equate the state with society in every respect, even with reference to ownership of the means of production and management of production.

Some critics of Stalinism are not able to see through the socialist mystification of statist property because they adhere to the practice of connecting the concept of ruling class ownership with *private* ownership of the means of production.[4] But according to this logic, the church hierarchy was not part of the feudal ruling class since its members did not privately own the means of production, nor did their children (!) inherit any property.

In statist society, as has been stated already, the ruling class is the *collective* owner of the means of production. The share of surplus value appropriated by its members is defined by their position in the state hierarchy. Actually, the nature and degree of their participation in *all* decisions about production and the distribution of surplus value is defined in this manner. One peculiarity of the statist class is that its economic power derives from its political power, while the opposite is true of the bourgeoisie. We must admit that Marxist theory has not left enough latitude for this type of political determinism.

Since members of the ruling class, as individuals, cannot dispose of the means of production, many people suppose that the means of production are not the property of the state apparatus. The observation that nepotism plays no significant role in the rejuvenation of the statist class, in contrast to other ruling classes in history, adds to this impression. Yet the state apparatus does, in fact, control production and dispose of surplus value (primarily in its own interest), and it is therefore de facto the owner of the means of production, regardless of any formal legal decrees to the contrary. We need not puzzle over the concept of *collective class ownership,* for it has not been unknown in history—I again cite the example of feudal church ownership.

One would have to have a vivid imagination indeed to believe that the proletariat is the ruling class in the Stalinist system. This ideological myth derives its strength from the fact that an occasional worker does enter the state apparatus. Do not such workers, it may be asked, represent above all the interests of the working class? But first, we may note that there are fewer workers than is usually supposed and that the further the revolution recedes into the past the fewer workers there are relative to other groups. Moreover, it doesn't occur to anyone to deny that the bourgeoisie is the ruling class in a capitalist society solely on the grounds that an occasional worker breaks into its ranks, albeit less frequently than he penetrates the Stalinist state apparatus. The bourgeoisie renews itself as a class primarily by means of inheritance, while this does not play a significant role in the case of the statist class. As it came into being as a consequence of the degeneration of the revolutionary state apparatus, it is natural for the statist class to recruit workers in a deliberate manner. It thus reaffirms its status as the representative of the working class. But it is naïve to believe that these workers retain the same attitudes and interests permanently. A "Marxist" who does so must also hold that one's consciousness is determined primarily by his past, and not by his present social existence! Finally, it must also be noted that the social origin of members of a given social group is not one of Marx's criteria for identification of the ruling class.

Short of irony or cynicism, there is no sense in which the working class in the Stalinist system may be called the ruling class, not even in the most liberal sense of the term. The working class is completely subjugated and severely exploited. Not only is it barred from controlling production and making decisions concerning the distribution of surplus value (either directly or indirectly); it does not even possess certain rights that it has realized in capitalism—the rights to choose one's employer and to negotiate over working conditions and wage levels. In this respect we might draw an analogy between Stalinism and feudalism: in Stalinism, in addition to the reification of the labor force, even the workers themselves are reified to a significant degree.

Independent organizations that might really represent the rights of the proletariat are unknown in Stalinism. Nominal workers' organizations do exist, but in practice are nationalized and transformed into transmission belts of the statist class. Work is done not only under economic pressure but under strong noneconomic pressure as well. As for the peasantry, it becomes part of the proletariat in fully developed statism through nationalization of land holdings and control of agriculture; as such, it is employed by the ruling class.

Some analysts and critics prefer to speak of a ruling *caste* rather than of a ruling class. But this is really an overly free use of an otherwise quite precise sociological concept. A caste is an exclusive sociological grouping based upon inheritance. Surely the ruling statist group does not have these characteristics.

Many Marxists apply only the mildest analytical-critical term to this group, calling it a social *stratum*. But this procedure only plays into the hands of the ideological mystification of the ruling class. In state socialism one can indeed talk meaningfully about the working class and the stratum of its representatives, the state officials. But in Stalinist society, where there are concentrations of political and economic power, wealth, and social prestige on the one hand, and subjugation and exploitation on the other, the real relations between the ruling group and the proletariat can only be seen in terms of the following categorical symmetry: statist class—working class.

The statist class "adheres" firmly to Marxism (adapted, of course, to meet the circumstances) as its ideology. It uses the Marxist interpretation of socialism as the stage of preparation for classless society in order to lower an ideological veil over class reality. When the Constitution of the U.S.S.R. was proclaimed in 1937, Stalin declared that the exploiting class had disappeared forever—and this at the very time that the new ruling class was passing through an intensive formative period. This is hardly unusual:

> For each new class which puts itself in the place of one ruling class before it, is compelled, merely in order to carry through its aim, to represent its interest as the common interest of all the members of society . . . ; it will give its ideas the form of universality, and represent them as the only rational, universally valid ones.[5]

The statist class modestly legitimizes itself as the representative of the class which it actually exploits.

As difficult as it is for a Marxist to concede the possibility of a socialist revolution degenerating into a new form of class, exploitative society, it is even harder for him to admit that it has actually happened. He thinks that his admission would dim the further prospects of socialism. The accurate observation that strong, although suppressed elements of socialism do exist in Stalinist society, above all in the working class, only reinforces his emotive resistence. The degree of violence which Stalinism had to employ attests to the strength of the socialist resistence to statist decadence. Still, we ought not confuse the existence of forces that resist the establishment of a socioeconomic system, or that hope to change it, with the nature of the system itself.

We shall call the Stalinist type of statism *oligarchic*. The monopoly of the ruling class—economic, political, cultural, moral—is direct and full. In addition to the conditions enumerated earlier in this chapter, another role in the construction of this type of statism was played by the model of the ruling Stalinist party. *Permanently* based upon the principles of strict centralism, hierarchy, and the absolute monopolization of social life, the party naturally aspired to fashion the entire social system in its own image.

5

In order to avoid any misunderstanding and at the same time to neutralize another possible objection to my thesis, I wish to emphasize that we may appreciate the progressiveness of statism over the capitalism of tsarist Russia without any sense of discomfort. The October Revolution did indeed run out of steam after a while. Nevertheless, statism did produce a great deal of progress in Russia. Our concern here is with a completely ascendant ruling class.

The U.S.S.R. has been transformed from backward Russia into one of two economic, political, cultural, and military superpowers of the world. Its share in world industry has grown from 3 percent to 20 percent, and its gross product is more than half that of the United States. While Russia's population was among the most illiterate and uneducated in the world, the U.S.S.R. today ranks among the highest both in its level of literacy and in the number of personnel working in the cultural, artistic, technical, and medical fields. Its free child care and medical and social care, as well as schooling, are among the best in the world. In no other country has the emancipation of women proceeded with such speed. The above evidence is usually justly supplemented by citing the fact that the U.S.S.R. played the greatest role in defeating nazism in World War II.

However, even given the great progress made by the U.S.S.R., it does not at all follow that Stalinism was justified. The correct question does not involve how much progress there was, but whether there was an optimum degree of progress. Would there have been less progress or more had the Stalinist path not been chosen? Obviously any answer to this question can only be hypothetical.

How does this progress look as viewed from the other side? The final balance also includes: the millions of victims of Stalinism; the annihilation of the commanding cadres of the Red Army and the real unpreparedness of the U.S.S.R. to defend itself, for which it had to pay with an inordinate amount of human death and material destruction; the disarray of the communist parties unable to organize resistance to nazism and thus help Russia; an agriculture ruined by a bloody period of collectivization from which it did not recover for a long time; the excessively low level of social science and philosophy; the stagnation of individual arts, also due to their vulgar politicization; and finally, the subordination of the international communist movement to the Stalinist party with serious consequences, especially for the internal development of the Eastern European countries. The conclusion to be drawn from all this is that the U.S.S.R. would have been stronger in a political, cultural, and moral sense had the forces of Stalinism not triumphed.

But Stalinism is usually justified not only by pointing to the progress it achieved, but also by asserting that it was *necessary*.[6] Stalin himself endeavored time and again to explain his policies by citing the situation of the U.S.S.R. Thus in 1939 he subjected to criticism this famous thought of Engels:

> The first act by virtue of which the state really constitutes itself the representative of the whole society—the taking possession of the means of production in the name of society—that is, at the same time, its last independent act as a state. State interference in social relations becomes, in one domain after another, superfluous, and then dies out of itself.[7]

In his report to the Eighteenth Party Congress in 1939, Stalin said:

> Is this proposition of Engels's correct? Yes, it is correct, but only on one of two conditions: (1) *if* we study the socialist state only from the angle of the internal development of the country, abstracting ourselves in advance from the international factor, isolating, for the convenience of investigation, the country and the state from the international situation: or (2) *if* we assume that socialism is already victorious in all countries, or in the majority

of countries, that a socialist encirclement exists instead of a capitalist encirclement, that there is no more danger in foreign attack, and that there is no more need to strengthen the army and the state. Well, but what if socialism has been victorious only in one country, and if, in view of this, it is quite impossible to abstract oneself from international conditions—what then? Engels's formula does not furnish an answer to this question. As a matter of fact, Engels did not set himself this question, and therefore could not have given an answer to it. Engels proceeds from the assumption that socialism has already been victorious in all countries, or in a majority of countries, more or less simultaneously. Consequently, Engels is not here investigating any specific socialist state of any particular country, but the development of the socialist state in general, on the assumption that socialism has been victorious in a majority of countries—according to the formula: "Assuming that socialism is victorious in a majority of countries, what changes must the proletarian, socialist state undergo?"[8]

Further:

And the functions of our socialist state changed accordingly. The function of military suppression inside the country ceased, died away; for exploitation had been abolished, there were no more exploiters left, and so there was no one to suppress. In place of this function of suppression the state acquired the function of protecting socialist property from thieves and pilferers of the people's property. The function of defending the country from foreign attack fully remained . . . as did the punitive organs and the intelligence service, which are indispensable for the detection and punishment of the spies, assassins, and wreckers sent into our country by foreign espionage services. The function of economic organization and cultural education by the state organs also remained, and was developed to the full. Now the main task of our state inside the country is the work of peaceful economic organization and cultural education.[9]

The sophistry in this line of argument was recognized long ago. Stalin sought to prove that the Soviet state would not wither away in any of its functions (1. defense of the order from external and internal enemies; 2. economic organization; 3. cultural and educational organization) and therefore referred to the existence of a capitalist encirclement. But capitalist encirclement is reason to retain only the first function, not any of the others. Does it really follow from the premise that the U.S.S.R. was at the time the only socialist country in the world and that it was menaced by the capitalist countries that the strengthening of the state (instead of the development of social self-government) in economics, education, and culture was necessary?

It is interesting that some of the most serious students of Stalinism who are not Stalinists support the view that Stalinism was necessary. Isaac Deutscher, in his famous three-volume biographical study of Trotsky, asserts that Stalinism was necessary in order to overcome the resistance of the masses to industrialization. Nationalized property had to be protected—even from the working class—by all means available. Stalin, through his dictatorship, was the bearer of harsh historical necessity. When industrialization was completed, despotism necessarily came into conflict with the new economic level which demanded democratization. It is striking how Deutscher *inversely* applied Marx's thesis on the *necessity* of socialism and socialist democracy in highly developed countries. According to Deutscher, socialist revolution in undeveloped countries *inevitably* leads to a Stalinist or similar type of dictatorship.

The problem of the historical necessity of Stalinism demands more detailed consideration. Here I can only point to some conceptual confusions and outline the direction in which one ought to look for the answer.

Adherents of the view that Stalinism was necessary see Stalinism as the sole possibility under the given conditions. They fail to take account of the human factor in explaining the historical process, which to them seems to be but a series of events upon which people can have no significant impact. In their view, only one real possibility confronted the Bolsheviks—precisely that possibility which the Stalinists recognized and confirmed. It would not have been objectively possible in the conditions which reigned at the time for the dominant (Stalinist) forces to select another path of social development, and any attempt to burden them with the responsibility for what happened is senseless. The only "guilty" party was the objective situation.

The initial premise itself of this line of reasoning is fallacious. After the October Revolution there were two possibilities (excepting victory of the classic counterrevolution). The first possibility was the total and permanent nationalization of all social life, simultaneously with the alienation of the state from society. The second possibility was the further strengthening of the influence of the working class and of all the working people upon the state, and the development of social self- government. A critic of the thesis of the necessity of Stalinism can acknowledge that in the conditions of the times this second possibility had fewer real prospects. Nor is he bothered by the assertion that in those conditions the development of social self-government based upon workers' self-management (a condition for the victory of the second possibility) would most likely have been fairly slow. It is enough for him to say that this path was a real possibility. In fact, it was not only a possibility, but a strong tendency as well. Evidence of this was the existence of soviets of workers, peasants, and soldiers at all levels of social organization. The dilemma which we are discussing here evoked bitter discussion and struggle within the Party. The Stalinists knew very well that the path opposite to the one they advocated was a real possibility and they, therefore, used a great deal of guile and brutality in the struggle with their opponents.

At the crossroads described here the decisive role was played by the Stalinist group, which was strong enough to impose its conceptions upon the rest of the Party. Thus we can justly hold the Stalinists to have been responsible. The assertion that Stalinism was objectively necessary is acceptable only if this subjective factor is taken into account as one of the decisive factors. But this is merely an ex post facto explanation which does not deny the existence of various possibilities, conceptions, and their bearers but which on the basis of an evaluation of the real forces at the time merely draws a conclusion about the necessity of the corresponding outcomes of struggles among them. No one can have anthing against *this,* essentially trivial, thesis about the necessity of Stalinism. However, in the previous pages we have been challenging another thesis that is much more ambitious, incorrect, and dangerous.

6

In proposing a supplement to Marx's typology of socioeconomic systems I have, of course, maintained his classificatory principle, i.e., the basic type of relations of production. Human society is still centered upon the process of material production, and the mode of production, today as in the past, decisively influences the totality of social relations. As long as this is the case, Marx's classificatory principle will remain fundamental. Moreover, it has the added advantage that, in the case of statism, this principle makes it possible to destroy the statist myth of socialism.

We have already discussed the gain rendered to Marxism by the addition of the category of statism. Are there any other advantages? Marxists often stop dead in their tracks with bewilderment before the worst aspects of Stalinism, asking themselves how such practices are possible in socialism. A satisfactory answer, however, cannot be reached so long as the question is incorrectly posed. We must first ask whether Stalinism is socialism at all.[10] Unfortunately, some radical critics of Stalinism answer that what we are looking at is, for instance, "completely degenerated socialism." But if an entity degenerates completely, is it not something other than what it had been?

I believe that the theoretical solution I have proposed has other advantages. Without it certain significant aspects of social reality remain poorly articulated or even completely unnoticed. We have already seen that social stratification and social conflict appear in a completely different light when the concept of the ruling statist class is applied. This demythologization could enable the working class to grasp the essence of its position and to take an adequate practical and political stance toward the statist system.

Primitive-politocratic statism in the U.S.S.R., which reached its crisis long ago because it represented a serious fetter on further social development (primarily on economic development), is gradually being transformed into technocratic statism. The core of the statist class will be increasingly composed of technocratic elements. Closely bound to this phenomenon is the economic reform of statism, over which an ideological battle is being conducted at the present. Indeed, Saint-Simon, rather than Marx, would seem to be the ideological precursor of this movement toward technocratic statism.

Social systems do not follow one another in a *necessary* and *unilinear* pattern. Those who retain such a conception of socioeconomic formations are powerless when confronted by historical reality, and they often solve pseudoproblems. For the sake of illustration, I shall direct the reader to a by now famous question: how do some countries "skip over" individual historical stages? Of course, historical events only "skip over" theoretical schema, not over themselves. There is no strict scheme in history on the basis of which one system necessarily replaces another.

We have mainly discussed here that type of statism which resulted from the degeneration of state socialism. Earlier it was suggested that other varieties of statism can develop in certain decolonized societies. There is also the possibility that individual state-capitalist systems may also be transformed gradually into statist systems. In countries with a developed bourgeois-democratic tradition—a multiparty system, political liberalism, parliamentarism—statism would most likely retain the forms and achievements of bourgeois political democracy. It is precisely such statism in the form of the "welfare state" which is the programmatic ideal of present-day social democracy.

Today the thesis of the convergence[11] of two systems—capitalist and socialist—is gaining ever greater currency. It seems to me that one can basically speak only of the tendency for state capitalism and statism to converge, through the broadening of state property, planning, and social services in the case of the former, and through the rehabilitation of market economy, limited decentralization, and a certain degree of political liberalization in the case of the latter.

Historical experience since the time of Marx has shown that there are two possibilities and tendencies inherent in capitalism, i.e., statist and socialist, and not only one as he had thought. As the epochal dilemma—capitalism or socialism—gradually recedes into the background, we are increasingly compelled to recognize the new epochal dilemma: statism or socialism.

The hundred-fiftieth anniversary of Marx's birth came at a time of revolutionary stirrings in Vietnam, Czechoslovakia, and France. By invoking the name of Marx in such diverse conditions, the forces of revolution have once again confirmed that he remains the greatest social thinker of our epoch. Historical events in these countries present us with three kinds of problems: (1) socialist revolutions in undeveloped countries, (2) socialist revolutions in countries which declare that they are socialist, and (3) socialist revolutions in highly developed capitalist countries.

Marxists have widely debated the prospects for socialism in the modern world. Why do we return to the same theme now? Primarily because of the events in Czechoslovakia and France. A country which people classify as socialist recently introduced *revolutionary* measures. Five other "socialist" countries carried out aggression against it in order to frustrate these changes. On the other hand, in a wealthy capitalist country, in May of the same year, events reached such a point that many described the situation as *revolutionary*. An editorial in the May-June 1968 issue of Sartre's journal *Les Temps modernes* opened with these ecstatic words: "Let us recognize that socialist revolution is not impossible in a country of Western Europe; perhaps it is possible even in two or three as well"!

Marxism is a revolutionary idea; it must therefore come face to face with this new situation. And it is a situation which both evokes angry despair among Marxists and arouses their greatest hopes.

7

Beginning with the bloody collectivization of the peasantry in the U.S.S.R. at the end of the 1920s, through the mass extermination of Communists in the 1930s, the Stalinist offensive against Yugoslavia from 1948 on, the military intervention in Hungary in 1956, and concluding with the occupation of Czechoslovakia—and we only cite a few examples—Marxists have despairingly asked themselves the same question time and again: How is all this possible in *socialism*? But as the question is incorrectly formulated, no satisfactory answer can be given. We must liberate ourselves from the theoretical framework surrounding this question and simply ask: How is all this possible?

"Socialism" in which debureaucratization and democratization, economic decentralization, the elimination of political terror and censorship, the introduction of workers' self-management, the attainment of national sovereignty, and so on—in which all this represents counterrevolution, can hardly be called socialism in Marx's sense of the term. Nevertheless, many people are still trying to convince the *Stalinist oligarchy* that its aggression against Czechoslovakia dealt a serious blow to the cause of *socialism* and are naïvely awaiting some positive results.

The case of Czechoslovakia has put all Marxists up against the wall. They must either unmask the statist myth of socialism or whirl helplessly within the circle of questions of how this is possible in socialism. If they opt for the second alternative, they still concede implicitly that socialism is at fault for the Czech case as well. With the aggression against Czechoslovakia the last socialist veil fell from the face of the oligarchic-statist system. Palliative explanations will no longer suffice.

The understated formula about the "crisis of socialism" lost its persuasiveness long ago, for we are talking about a system which normally and regularly generates such "crises." Nor can we speak any longer of "socialism with severe deformations," since these deformations are so numerous and of such a nature that they have introduced a new quality—statism.

A third commonly employed theoretical crutch has to do with "abuses" in socialism. But there is a limit to the accumulation of abuses beyond which the character of the entity which is being abused changes. Thus it is high time that we resolve to speak no more of abuses, but rather of the *systematic* use of social means for the achievement of unsocialist goals. Unless this is understood, dedication to socialist goals and belief in their attainability leads to their fetishization and becomes transformed into the last defense of a perverted, alienated consciousness of social reality. As if proclaimed goals have the magical power to give a socialist character to the reality that invokes them, even though it does not itself have such a character! At the same time, this fetishization of socialist goals is a fetishization of the revolutionary past as well: Love for the October Revolution becomes an opiate which prevents Marxists from seeing the present as it really is.

The militarist element in the Stalinist oligarchy is now threatening to turn the scales in its favor over the politicratic and technocratic elements. Of course, this sort of naked, brutal, and arrogant power would not cease to pose as the vehicle of socialism, truth and morality. When as proof of its *socialist* progress the U.S.S.R.'s position as a *superpower* is cited, then an essentially unsocialist criterion of "socialism" is being manifested.

Must we remind ourselves that historical experience knows of few examples of similar physical might which have not ended in aggressiveness? The fact that in 1948 Stalin did not carry out aggression against Yugoslavia but rather made use of political, economic, diplomatic, and military pressure is of no consequence for the present situation. He was so boundlessly sure of himself that at first glance it did not even occur to him that he would have to take military action if he were going to change the situation in Yugoslavia. When he came to his senses later on, it was already too late, since (among other factors) Yugoslavia had broken the economic blockade, while Stalin was afraid of an eventual military clash with the West which at the time was immeasurably superior to the U.S.S.R. in the field of nuclear armament.

The nonaligned orientation of a country such as Yugoslavia ought to be *permanent*—not only out of a desire to contribute thereby to peace and coexistence, but also for the sake of preserving socialist elements within its internal system. At the same time that illusions about the nature of the U.S.S.R. were renewed, the forces in our country who wanted Yugoslavia de facto to abandon its nonaligned posture began to gain strength.

Just as American imperialism tries to hide behind liberal phraseology ("the free world" and "democracy") when it intervenes in places like Vietnam and the Dominican Republic, so the Stalinist oligarchy invokes the principle of "proletarian internationalism" to the same end. However, the mask of "fraternal help" was too thin to conceal nationalist hegemony. Therefore, the Stalinist ideologues were compelled to resort to the thesis of "limited sovereignty," to which, of course, they added Marxist rhetoric about the "socialist community of states." Only the most incorrigible of Stalinists in the communist movement can believe the mystification of the "higher interests of socialism" and "the hard reasons" which "the Stalinists surely had" when they had decided upon such a serious step as "preventive intervention" in Czechoslovakia. From 1948 to the present there has been more than enough occasion to see through this sort of mystification.

Stalinism imposed upon Czechoslovakia an alien economic-political system of an incomparably lower level than that which would have grown organically out of that country's rich leftist tradition. Rapid de-Stalinization had begun in Czechoslovakia after the January 1968 Plenum of the Communist Party. Revolutionary pressure from below combined with significant changes of personnel at the summit of the state and party. Great prospects were created for the victory of real socialism. Abstracting from the international position of Czechoslovakia and Yugoslavia, the *objective* conditions for socialism were much more favorable in the former than in the latter. Czechoslovakia is a developed industrial country with a great culture and a strong democratic tradition with which its people desired to establish creative-critical continuity. For a short time an enviable level of political democracy was realized: freedom of criticism, of the press, of assembly; legal security of citizens, and so on. The intelligentsia had begun to play the role which naturally falls to it in the course of the revolutionary process. The action program of the Communist Party had anticipated the introduction of self-management and economic reform as basic demands with respect to the relations of production.

The occupation of Czechoslovakia will render the struggle of Western communist parties for a so-called democratic path to socialism much more difficult, for that country might well have served as a model of socialism for the developed countries. Although many Western communist parties unambiguously condemned the aggression, the electoral bodies in those countries will be less inclined in their direction. But that is not the only reason. The intervention of one side can serve as an excuse for the other side to intervene militarily whenever some communist party or other wants to come to power.

Before the "Prague Spring," Yugoslavia had a "monopoly" on socialist avant-gardism in Europe, as a result of which she had allowed herself to be lulled to sleep with self-satisfaction. From January to August 1968, Czechoslovakia had opened the possibility not only of closer cooperation, but also of competition with Yugoslavia in the initiation of revolutionary change.

The Stalinist military intervention was not so much the consequence of Czech desire for national liberation (there was no intervention in Rumania) as it was the result of *internal* revolutionary changes. This was final confirmation that in the U.S.S.R. de-Stalinization was seen only as the elimination of the "cult of personality" and the worst aspects of the criminal Stalinist state. In this respect even Khrushchev was too radical, as his subsequent departure from power has shown.

Under the pretense of preventing a bourgeois counterrevolution, the Stalinist oligarchy carried out a statist *counterrevolutionary* intervention in Czechoslovakia. On this occasion the internal system of the U.S.S.R. was manifested as well in its relations with the other countries of Eastern Europe. A small degree of relaxation in discipline within the Warsaw bloc was not essentially disturbing the U.S.S.R.'s dominant position in defining the external policy and internal arrangement of the countries of the bloc. The Stalinist oligarchy does not even permit different paths to statism, much less to socialism. The extent to which expedient fallacies about the nature of Stalinism are still held is best demonstrated by the complete astonishment experienced by Marxists when Czechoslovakia was occupied.

As after the October Revolution centers of revolutionary actions multiplied, so in the Stalinized communist movement monocentrism, hegemonism, and an attempt to impose upon all a single model of "socialism" has developed. The dissolution of the Third International was simply a diplomatic gesture of good will by Stalin toward the Western allies. Although a formal international Stalinist organization was no longer necessary to realize hegemonistic goals, a "small international," in the form of the Cominform, was created after the war. Ever since the dissolution of the Cominform, international consultative meetings of communist parties have served hegemonistic goals. But along with these developments, from 1948 onward individual countries and parties gradually began to free themselves: first Yugoslavia, then China along with an entire group of parties, and finally a great number of Western communist parties.

After relations between the U.S.S.R. and Yugoslavia had been normalized, there was a periodic renewal of Soviet pressure, for instance, upon the adoption of the 1957 Program of the League of Communists of Yugoslavia.[12] Earlier, in 1956, an attempt at revolution in Hungary had been smothered in blood, and the revolutionary stirrings which had begun in Poland were gradually frustrated. The entire communist movement was not long to express its approval of the military intervention in Hungary—as if it had escaped everyone's notice that the events in that country had started with socialist changes, and that the elements of bourgeois counterrevolution began to acquire strength only after foreign and domestic Stalinists had frustrated the opening to the Left. But even if this were not the case, how could communists approve an intervention in a country's internal affairs? Did they not thereby, although perhaps unintentionally, give a green light to future interventions?

The aggression against Czechoslovakia accelerated the process of differentiation within the communist movement. If no strict line is drawn between socialism and statism, then there is no way to explain the ever-deepening rifts among communist parties. It is evident that the title "communist" is claimed by extremely different, even oppositely oriented, parties. Some of them have lost the right to call themselves communist in the Marxist sense; an adequate name for them would be "statist parties." Severe conflicts have arisen between such parties representing, on the one hand, primitive-politocratic statism, and on the other, modern-technocratic statism.

Hope of socialist changes in the U.S.S.R. in the *long* run can be based upon the following factors: Statism, having carried out rapid industrialization, has thereby created a mass industrial proletariat to serve as its own "gravedigger." As we have seen, history already knows of attempts of the Eastern European working class to create its own organs of self-management. In this connection we should also count on the boomerang effect of the Marxist self-rationalization of statism. True Marxism, with its revolutionary-humanist program, the core of which is a plea for free association of the producers, will exert strong pressure in the direction of socialist change.

The Stalinist party has not seen fit to strike self-management totally from its program, but "merely" to postpone it to the communist future. But this postponement cannot go on indefinitely without irrevocably forfeiting the Marxist and communist ideological legitimacy which the statist party has gone to such lengths to establish. Fifty

years after the revolution the working class has still not won the right
to participate in the management of the enterprise, although it has
already won this right in some capitalist countries. Statism has provided the opportunity for mass education and has created an extremely
large intelligentsia. It can be assumed that one part of it will help the
masses to penetrate the ideological veil of statism and to shatter the
information vacuum into which that system has cast them.

8

Marx's thesis about proletarian revolution has suffered an amazing
fate. While Marx believed in the possibility of socialist revolution *foremost* in the most highly developed capitalist countries, many of his
adherents today see prospects for revolution only in the impoverished
part of the world. In the past orthodox Marxists denied the possibility
of revolution prior to the full development of capitalism, and now many
Marxists do not believe that revolution will come even when capitalism has reached this stage. Many draw the line dividing evolution
from revolution between the developed and undeveloped parts of the
world.

As a consequence of the modernization of capitalism in the West
many communist parties in that part of the world have *expressis verbis*
abandoned all hope in revolution. *In this respect* there is no difference
between them and the social democratic parties. They have also oriented themselves toward coalition with other leftist parties in order to
gain votes in the electoral bodies.

Chinese ultraleftism only *appears* to be preserving the revolutionary Marxist tradition, since it implicitly proceeds from the judgment
that the Western proletariat has become part of the bourgeoisie. Thus
Chinese politicians and theorists no longer see any real prospects for
socialist revolution in the conflict between wage labor and capital; they
look rather to the contradiction between the developed and undeveloped parts of the world, obviously projecting their revolutionary experience onto the rest of the world. The strategic base of the Chinese
revolution was the countryside, whence the ring was gradually closed
around Chiang Kai-shek's cities. By analogy with that situation, the
Chinese leaders seek the vehicle of revolution in the rural masses of
the undeveloped world, which they see as gradually surrounding the
imperialist stronghold of the developed countries. And now they annex
the U.S.S.R. as well to that stronghold.

Like all true dogmatists, the Chinese leaders are attempting to
universalize the classic model of revolution—armed struggle. Sensing
that it has no real prospects in the West, they seek to save it in the
form of people's wars of liberation in the undeveloped countries, demanding that these wars encircle the developed countries, which con-

stitute the core of class society. Obviously the Chinese theory of revolution does not respond to the real situation and needs of the workers' movement in the West, and this is why it has not found any real response there. The most that the Communist Party of China has achieved there is to create miniature pro-Chinese parties or factions.

Some Marxists, among them Marcuse, interpret the contradiction between the undeveloped and developed countries in a different way. In their view, the Viétnamese revolution and counterrevolution, for example, is a contradiction within the framework of the American capitalist system, not external to it. But this hardly seems the way to reconcile the Chinese view with the classical Marxist conception, according to which the internal class contradictions of capitalism are the basic source of socialist revolution.

The Cuban revolution is now theatened by the temptation which neither the Soviet nor Chinese revolutions were able to overcome. Of course, it is a smaller country—and its pretensions are more modest. The Cuban model of the revolutionary guerilla war must, according to Castro, Guevara, and Debray, be universally valid *for Latin America.* Many leftists, especially those who feel that other forms of revolution have a chance in that part of the world, have opposed this position, which they see as promoting Cuban ambitions, and the situation has become one of mutual accusations of pseudoadventurism on the one hand and of opportunistic reformism on the other. There are some who assert that the Cuban case cannot be repeated because the United States will not permit itself to be caught napping again. Others respond to them that Vietnam proves that even the greatest military power in the world *cannot* effectively employ its *entire* technical potential against the people's guerillas, nor can it crush them. At any rate, says Castro, "the obligation of every revolutionary is to make a revolution."

Guevara is the heroic personification of that pledge. His entire life and his death demonstrated his indomitable conviction that a revolutionary situation may not merely be created, but that it can be forced into existence. His revolutionary romanticism represents an extreme view of the relationship between revolutionary will and social reality. How pitiful, in comparison with Guevara, is the opposite point of view, which deludes itself into believing that undershooting revolutionary prospects is always better than overshooting them! Actually, only in action is it possible to discover the real possibilities inherent in any situation with complete accuracy. Castro's and Guevara's movement in Cuba was based on this principle of revolutionary activism, while the Communist Party was against their revolutionary "adventurism," believing that it had recognized a priori the entire range of possibilities.

The Communist Party of France recently behaved in a similar manner. In the name of realism it tried to amortize the revolutionary spontaneity of the students and workers! How and why did the actions of the students and workers in France—this "broadening of the realm of the possible" (Sartre)—remain outside of the perspective of a party which has pretensions to political avant-gardism?

9

The French working class did not attempt to seize state power in May 1968; even less so did its organizations. An attack on the centers of state power would certainly have led to civil war in France. Only a class under the pressure of great material need would take such a risk, and then only if it were to judge the existing system to be weak. The readiness to destroy the pillars of state power depends not only upon one's attitude toward it, but also upon an evaluation of its strength. The French ruling class was in a position to use brutal force against anyone who might try to shatter its power. Even were this not the case, any such move would most likely have evoked an international bourgeois intervention.

The possibility of civil war, with all its human and material losses, exists only on the margins of consciousness of the Western Workers. Their disposition to use violence has disappeared in the measure to which these countries are developed with respect to their standard of living, their level of cultural and political democracy, and the mentality that goes with it. Only under *special* conditions would this possibility again become real. Nevertheless, it is hard to deny that in 1968 the French working class demonstrated its revolutionary spirit in another form: millions of strikers quickly "occupied" all the institutions of production and culture. The working class demonstrated its spontaneous and mass revolutionary spirit, while the Communist Party did everything it could to undercut the "management" (*gestionaire*) dimension of the general strike, and attempted to turn it into a classical syndicalist strike.

This case highlights the necessity of a careful examination of the relationship between spontaneity and organization in the revolutionary process. The French events proved that a small and almost completely unorganized group can fulfill the role of the revolutionary detonator. Yet this fact escaped the unprepared theorists and politicians of the Left, as they had become accustomed to await such initiatives from above, from the Party, and they were consequently taken quite by surprise. This underestimation of revolutionary spontaneity and its potential was illustrated in yet another way: previously, whenever mention was made of the workers' *movement*, it was generally the workers' *organization* which one had in mind. May 1968 in France struck down the assumption that in capitalism the working class is well integrated.

Not long before the May events, the Communist Party of France declared itself in favor of the so-called peaceful path to socialism, and in May did everything in its power to preserve its democratic reputation. It fell into a false dilemma, thinking that the alternatives were either civil war or parliamentary struggle. The general strike, however, with its "management" dimension, was neither one nor the other. Otherwise a fierce critic of bourgeois democracy, the P.C.F. now became the prisoner of its rules and procedures. It rightly estimated that a struggle for the introduction of the dictatorship of the proletariat would lead to the catastrophic adventurism of civil war. This realism of the Communist Party, however, also had a second, unrealistic side: It did not see that there were still prospects for revolution, albeit for revolution in another form.

The workers' factory "occupation" had the goal of introducing self-management, or at least participation in self-management. It was neither an attempt to introduce the dictatorship of the proletariat, nor a "democratic" action in the classical sense of the word. It had certain characteristics of both; i.e., the attempt to *exact* acknowledgement of their right to participation or even to self-management but *in a peaceful manner*. Thus the eventual use of violence was abandoned to the ruling class. Yet this kind of negation of democracy is at the same time democratic in a more profound sense. That is to say, *bourgeois* democracy excludes democracy from the basic cells of everyday life. The "management" strike is democratic in the sense that the working people attempt thereby to gain control over these very groups and institutions of their everyday life.

The parliamentary Left is overly oriented toward the state and has not worked out a strategy of struggle for workers' participation and workers' self-management. Participation or self-management in the base would create a dualism in the capitalist system. Revolutionary changes at the higher levels of government would have greater prospects after the introduction and broadening of this dualism. In Sartre's editorial of *Les Temps modernes* referred to above, it was justly asserted that the outcome of the French events would have most probably been different had a strong *revolutionary* party existed. Such a party would have reinforced and organized the strikers to elect organs of self- management and to return to work in the "occupied" factories and institutions under their leadership.

If it may be presumed that the Left will win at the polls at some future date, it is hard to see how it could take charge of power and retain it without relying upon participation or self-management in the base. The French events have proved that there is no sharp boundary between the workers' syndicalist and political pretensions, since the general strike had at once both a classical syndicalist and political-"management" character.

What we have yet to discover is what can inspire people to take revolutionary action in the most highly developed capitalist countries. It is generally recognized that there is a close correlation between the readiness of the people for revolution and the conditions in which they live. The Western working class does not live in material poverty, and thus does not feel that revolution is a pressing need, nor is it disposed to risk what it already has for the sake of revolution. One need not accept the exaggerations of the theories of "the affluent society" and "the consumer society" in order to see that the proletariat in the West is no longer a class which has nothing to lose but its chains.

Many communist parties used to see material impoverishment as a *necessary* condition for socialist revolution. They thought that unless the proletariat is pauperized, all hope in its revolutionary potential must be abandoned. Thus they had long—altogether too long—attempted to preserve at all costs the old, by now mythological vision of an impoverished proletariat in the West. In order to retain this picture, communist theorists had to introduce new concepts, one of which is the notion of a "workers' aristocracy." But something could be achieved by use of this concept only in Lenin's day and for a while after that. Today a great part of the Western working class—in certain countries the majority of the working class—is "aristocratized."

The existence of political democracy in the West reinforces man's general desire to participate in the management of institutions and groups in which he lives and works daily. This demand, of course, has neither the force nor the spontaneity with which the desire for the procurement of one's material existence is expressed. In a case in which the material situation does not motivate people to revolution, it is the consciousness of their entire social situation which becomes the primary factor. After all, individual Marxists have long been insisting that the working class was for Marx the quintessence of total poverty (and not only material poverty), and that the key to understanding changes in its revolutionary motivation must be sought in this idea.

The growth of the intelligentsia and of its theoretical and ideological work in the Western revolutionary movement must also be seen in this light.[13] The worker spontaneously expresses his revolutionary spirit in conditions of *material* poverty. But *understanding* of the total social situation and of human perspectives must mediate between *human* poverty (as distinguished from *material* poverty) and the revolutionary spirit. Thus the role of the intelligentsia as the *primary and necessary* ally of the proletariat is all the more significant. (It is evident from this how shortsighted the thesis of the end of both revolutionary and other ideology has been.) Yet although the revolt of the intelligentsia itself is not without revolutionary significance, the intelligentsia is not the basic revolutionary subject of the modern world. One might more aptly speak of a broadening of the classical revolutionary subject. After all, a great part of the intelligentsia is also composed of wage laborers. Disenchanted in the working class which they had formerly fetishized, some theorists now fetishize the revolutionary potential of the intelligentsia. Yet while the French events showed that part of the intelligentsia, especially intellectual youth, can act as the revolutionary detonator, they also confirmed that no one can take the place of the working class in its revolutionary role. The socialist transformation of the class mode of production is not feasible without the participation of the proletariat as the primary producing class.[14] "The new working class," the class of the future as a consequence of the penetration of automation, is composed of technicians, supervisors, engineers, and researchers, however, and not only of the classical manual producers. Thus the sharp boundary between the working class and a good part of the intelligentsia is being destroyed. If "the new working class" is an increasingly significant and powerful part of the working class, then profound changes in the way in which that class expresses its revolutionary nature should not surprise us in the least.

The French workers did not occupy the factories only in order to negotiate questions of distribution; they were interested in questions of management, as well. Redistribution of power, and not only redistribution of wealth, entered into their demands. De Gaulle himself admitted that the question was not exclusively one of the level of wages, the length of the working day, and improvement of the conditions of labor, but that it was also one of the desire of the workers for self-determination. He understood that capitalism can save itself only through concessions—through worker participation in the management of the enterprise. Why was the Left so reluctant to accept these concessions and then later raise new and greater demands? Participation could hurt the workers' movement only if it were to exult that it had thereby achieved its goal.

The struggle of the working class for participation in capitalism will have, in turn, a great impact upon the outcome of the epochal dilemma—statism or socialism—in these countries. Whether or not the workers' political organizations will alienate themselves from the workers or simply be the executors of the workers' will depends largely upon the workers' position in the management of the enterprise at the moment when their organizations take power.

In almost all revolutionary movements in capitalism the workers' aspiration to self-management has been expressed. Nor was 1968 the first time that French workers had "seized" the factories. But the most recent wave of "seizures" has struck down the thesis that workers are interested in self-management only when they live in material poverty. And the view that the capitalist system of production is socially the most efficient was once again shattered. It would be difficult indeed to call a system "efficient" that had provoked a revolt of so many millions of workers!

In order to understand the events in France from a theoretical standpoint, we need not change Marx's definition of "revolution," but only his vision of the course of socialist revolution. Revolution must be seen as a process of radical transformation of a socioeconomic totality, and above all of its mode of production, which most powerfully defines the nature of the whole. In this respect it is no longer important in which order or by which means this process unfolds. Marx expected that political revolution would be the first step, from which other radical changes would follow. The course of socialist revolutions in the past has confirmed the belief held by Marxists in this order of events. Since in France there was no chance for the people to take over state power, the Old Left saw no prospects for any radical changes whatsoever. All indications are that in the West political revolution will be merely the finale to a prolonged process of social revolution. In this sense the socialist revolution will bear a greater resemblance to bourgeois-democratic revolutions than to the socialist revolutions of the past. We must also note that previous revolutions have been connected with violence, but in the future, neither will the term "violent revolution" be redundant, nor will "peaceful revolution" be a contradiction in terms.

As distinct from the majority of the Old Left, the New Left in the West does not limit its political arsenal to bourgeois-democratic means. This is why Marcuse, of all the contemporary Marxists, suits it so well. Che Guevara is the idol of the young, rather than some leftist who is competing for power or who has already achieved power; this in itself demonstrates the attitude with which the New Left regards the Old Left. Of course, the Old Left retaliates, attacking the new Left for anarchism, extremism, adventurism, revolutionary impatience, and the like. Insofar as they have replaced impatience with indifference, many old leftists, among them many communists, find themselves speaking the same language as the "bourgeois opposition" more often than the language of the new generation of leftists.

Nevertheless, when we talk about the New Left, we must take care, as a new version of the Old Left—Trotskyism, Maoism, and so forth—is also called the New Left. It is particularly important to determine why Maoism today appeals to some young people in the West. It seems that it appeals to them, for one thing, because of its asceticism, as well as because of its struggle to instill moral values in its adherents, and finally because of the participation which it demands of the broad masses. But asceticism can seem appealing only if one views it from the safe distance of "consumer society." Some young leftists overlook the fact that the Maoist system of moral values excludes, as a mere "trifle," freedom of personality, and that the great, "spontaneous" mass movements in China have obscured the manipulators of these very movements.

The New Left is a welcome phenomenon because it will reinforce the differentiation of the entire Left wing of the contemporary political scene. In an analogy to the former split between communists and social democrats, now a new differentiation between the revolutionary and the opportunistic Left has come into sight even *within* existing leftist parties. A great portion of the Old Left has become harmless to capitalism, and in statism has been transformed into the ruling and conservative Right. The Left-oriented younger generation must penetrate the leftist parties and try to revolutionize them. This, in my opinion, is a more hopeful path than simply to create completely new organizations.

Unfortunately, the New Left has an aversion to any durable form of organization, though it has shown an extraordinary sense for quick and spontaneous organization. While the organization of the Old Left suffers from petrifaction, the New Left is threatened by the danger of fetishizing revolutionary spontaneity.

Socialism is one of those great humanist conceptions which, in the process of their realization, suffer heavy setbacks but which nevertheless persistently come back to life. The current generation of leftists does not suffer from the illusions about Stalinism which was characteristic of the prewar Left and of its pupils. In its most recent actions the Stalinist oligarchy has done everything in its power to reinforce the immunity of youth to its "socialist" mythology. Fortunately the New Left is not prepared to identify socialism with the reality of any single country, considering it a "shining beacon" to the rest of the world. Although a great part of the Old Left—in the form of Stalinism and lowly social-democratic opportunism—has more than once drowned the ideals of socialism, these ideals still shine from the depths and magnetically attract a new generation of adherents, both in capitalism and in statism.

NOTES

1. In his article "Kritika teorijske misli o strukturi socijalističkog društva" ("A Critique of Theoretical Thought about the Structure of Socialist Society") (*Socijalizam* 11/ 1967), Miroslav Pečujlić asserted that in my article, "The Statist Myth of Socialism" (*Praxis*, Edition Internationale, 2/1967), where I first put forth my views on statism, I had merely borrowed Burnham's idea. I subsequently replied to him (in *Socijalizam* 1-2/1968) in an article entitled "Još jedanput o etatističkom mitu socijalizma" ("Once More on the Statist Myth of Socialism"). Therefore, I will only briefly recapitulate here the most important theoretical differences between Burnham's theory and my theoretical outline of statist society.

2. A group of Marxists in the West as well, including Erich Fromm and Herbert Marcuse, recognize that the Stalinist system is exploitative, and justly do not want to call it socialist. But since Marxist theory in its inertia only has places for either capitalism or socialism in its portrayal of contemporary society, they find the solution in the notion of state capitalism.

3. Robert Michels explicitly applied his "iron law of oligarchy" to the socialist movement: "The socialists may conquer, but not socialism, which would perish in the moment of its adherents' triumph." *Political Parties: A Sociological Study of the Oligarchic Tendencies of Modern Democracy* (Glencoe, Ill., 1915, 1949), p. 391.

4. See, for instance, the previously mentioned article by Miroslav Pečujlić: "Only the fusion of two great systems—private control over the conditions of labor and family inheritance—creates class structure" (p. 1402).

5. Marx, *The German Ideology*, pp. 40-41.

6. Even if this were correct, of course, it would not follow that Stalinism is a form of socialism.

7. Frederick Engels, *Herr Eugen Dühring's Revolution in Science (Anti-Dühring)* (New York, 1939), p. 307.

8. Joseph Stalin, "Report to the Eighteenth Party Congress," *Selected Writings* (New York, 1942), p. 471.

9. Stalin, "Report to the Eighteenth Party Congress," p. 474.

10. Many critics rightly reject the "cult of personality" explanation and seek the root of the problem in the nature of the Stalinist social system, but fail to make this final step. A myth has even been created out of the "cult of personality," since the key to all mysteries is sought therein. The statist myth of socialism is saved by means of this myth.

11. See, for instance, G. Adler-Karlsson's contribution to *Gledišta*, 4/1967, "Funkcionalni socijalizam: Koncept za analizu konvergencije nacionnih privreda" ("Functional Socialism: A Concept for Analyzing the Convergence of National Economies").

12. It is all the more amazing that in the past few years, old illusions about the nature of the Soviet sociopolitical system have been revived. This revival was responsible for the fact that on the occasion of the twentieth anniversary of the Cominform Resolution, nothing was said to Yugoslav youth about Stalinism. After August 21, 1968, the situation changed rapidly in this respect.

13. The examples of Poland and Hungary in 1956 and now Czechoslovakia prove that the same holds true for the intelligentsia in Eastern Europe.

14. Marcuse, under the influence of the events in France, returned to the classical Marxist evaluation of the revolutionary potential of the working class in his paper given at Korčula in 1968. Previously he had been overly impressed by the American situation and on this basis had reached the general conclusion that the Western working class was integrated into the capitalist system, although he did not draw any *reformist* conclusions from this. He placed his *revolutionary* hopes in the "outsiders" to the capitalist system: national and racial minorities, the permanently and hopelessly impoverished, and students and youth in general. [Translator's note: The reference to Korčula concerns the annual conference held there in August sponsored by the editorial board of *Praxis*.]

Authority and Authoritarian Thinking: On the Sense and Senselessness of Subordination

Ljubomir Tadić

The category of authority applies to any social relationship which is based upon superordination and subordination. Since this type of relationship is primarily political, authority has come to be one of the most central concepts of every political (and legal) order. In the authority relation both compulsion and freedom are compressed and unified about the object of authority. And this is why the category of authority is deeply contradictory, its Janus face urgently calling out for more precise definition.

The concept of authority derives from the Latin word *auctoritas*, which has various meanings. *Auctoritas* means conscience, persuasion, recommendation, inducement, source, assurance, confirmation, credibility, importance, reputation, dignity, fame, opinion, and model, but it also means will, decision, order, control, command, and *senatus consulta*. It should immediately be added that these latter meanings (will, decision, order, control, command, and *senatus consulta*) are the most relevant not only to our theme but also to the common understanding of authority.

From a psychological (more accurately, from a psychoanalytic) standpoint, the way in which many people relate to authority reveals special features of their character: some masochistically subordinate

77

themselves to authority, while others stubbornly and defiantly rebel.[1] That is to say, it often happens that an individual may embrace (or reject) authority for its own sake, because *as such*, without any differentiation, it fills him with respect or fury. It is my intention to demonstrate, at least in basic outline, both the contradictory nature of the category of authority, as well as the characteristic features of so-called authoritarian thought, which in all epochs of class society—including prehistorical, legendary socialism—has occupied such a broad terrain.

If at first the meanings of the noun *authority* are not of much help in realizing this intention, then we ought to turn to the clearer and more differentiated adjectival forms, *authoritative* and *authoritarian*. It is obvious that the former is a predominantly positive (or at least neutral) term, while the latter conveys a pejorative sense and sound. Yet the most superficial and, as we shall see below, the most (socially) dangerous notion of authority arises from the idea that authority is a property which individuals have, so to speak, from birth. There is an assumption here of some kind of natural power which drives others who are weaker or less powerful into obedience and subordination. This understanding conceives authority as deeply rooted in the biological, vital sphere of man, and it is understandable that it values and respects massive, crude strength and that it facilely identifies all power with the brutality cultivated in the tradition of the *manus* of the *pater familias*, the "firm hand" and the "strong sword."

Since the behavior of the object of authority involves subordination to alien will, control, order, decision, and command, we must first ask ourselves whether that subordination is always, in every situation, an act of compulsion, or whether, on the contrary, persons who obey an authoritative imperative may agree to such a relationship voluntarily and in their own true interest.

Individual persons, as we have noted earlier, experience authority in different ways: some do so positively, and some in an a priori negative sense. The first living experience with authority comes in the relationship between child and parent. Psychoanalysis, as is well known, has created an entire theory of the transition of the child from the "pleasure principle" to the "reality principle" on the basis of this relationship. It has also fashioned the concept of the "Oedipus complex," with its ambivalent feelings of love and hate toward paternal authority. Nevertheless, it should be noted that the very existence of authority presupposes at least a minimum acceptance of dependence as well as the limitation of personal freedom which this entails.

Here we are confronted with a new, diabolical question: is this loss of freedom a personal or social misfortune in all cases? Does it inevitably signify the enslavement of the object of authority?

To respond to this question we cannot afford to resort to abstract definitions, no matter how successful they may be. Such definitions (as is true, after all, in other cases as well) often lose sight of the social changes which a category may undergo in the course of its development. They are static and usually reduce themselves to superficial generalities. Consider, for example, Max Weber's definition of power (authority): "Power [Macht] is the probability that one actor within a social relationship will be in a position to carry out his own will despite resistence, regardless of the basis on which this probability rests." This definition is an example of abstract modification. And Weber, as if he perceives its inadequacy, a bit later declares that power is a sociologically amorphous concept. To soften its impact, he resorts to the second, more political concept of rule [Herrschaft]: "[Herrschaft] is the probability that a command with a specific content will be obeyed by a given group of persons. 'Discipline' is the probability that by virtue of habituation a command will receive prompt and automatic obedience in stereotyped forms, on the part of a given group of persons."[2]

It is obvious that in both cases, Weber employed less general definitions in order to make the more general ones more concrete, although even the former were still abstract and formal. Moreover, in the same sentence in which he defines the concept of rule [Herrschaft] he also defines the concept of discipline, considering it an obviously constitutive element in the determination of objects of authority. His scheme of power-rule-discipline helps him to add precision to his basic goal (always conceived on the basis of a formal design), which is to attempt to explain the effect of authority on the generation of "uncritical, harmless, *mass* obedience."

Even from this summary survey it becomes evident that Weber understands the concept of authority—albeit from an apparently value-neutral standpoint—in the sense of fate, or at least in the sense of a necessary evil. This implicitly leads him, toward the very end of his analysis in political sociology, to an authoritarian position, as when he defines the state as "the monopoly of the legitimate use of force," thus excluding from his definition every bit of classical content, and when he subsequently, in introducing the concept of charisma, reduces all democracy to common demagogy.[3]

To avoid the dangerous trap of liberalism, in which everything is explained but in reality nothing is explained at all, it is necessary to approach the problem of authority from the standpoint of content, i.e., in a concrete historical sense, linking it with other social concepts and placing it in the framework of a specific social structure.

In a social sense relevant for an understanding of the category of authority, subordination presupposes heteronomy, but it does not always exclude autonomy. Subordination to an alien will can be in the real conscious interest of an individual or social group. Let us consider, once again, the example of the parent whose authority plays an immense role in the proper education of the child. With this example it is possible to demonstrate the blending of the authoritative and authoritarian principles. Roman law, with the despotic image of the *pater familias,* and modern psychoanalysis, with its father-image, both provide us with examples of authoritarian subordination to patriarchal power. If parental authority, however, is used in the real interests of the child, if it helps the child to mature rapidly and contributes to the child's human emancipation, if by deed and example it cultivates the development of the child's creative abilities, if it fosters the development of a free personality, then parental authority should play an extremely beneficial role.

Let us pause for some historical examples. The first example comes from ancient Greece, where the concept of freedom arose. The basic principle of the ancient notion of civil freedom lay in the right of every citizen not to obey another's will, insofar as such obedience was not justified by reason. On the basis of this fundamental principle, from which Anaxagoras' idea that *nus* ("reason") rules the world derived its substance, it was possible to form the first community of free citizens, and it is only in this kind of community in which human freedom is truly possible. If, moreover, the citizen participated in the making of the community's laws, then the heteronomy of *nomos* ("law") did not contradict the citizen's autonomy. The citizen obeyed the laws of his *polis* because war was a "great common undertaking, a great common work" (Marx), the condition of the existence of the *polis* and the individual. And really only in this way can we understand the great authority of the community in the life of every free individual in the Hellenic world. Authority was seen as a kind of generally accepted dependence, which not only quantitatively but qualitatively multiplied human power and corresponded to the personal interests of those who subordinated themselves to it.

Our second example of positive, beneficial authority is furnished by the rise of centralized state power and its bureaucratic hierarchy at the beginning of the modern age, since on the ruins of the particularism of feudal monarchy it built the conditions for the general economic and intellectual regeneration which the young bourgeoisie had brought with itself into the world. The authority of absolute monarchy, however, soon lost its positive significance and assumed a purely authoritarian form. This change in the position of authority is best reflected in the developmental pattern of the age of the Enlightenment.

But before we turn our attention to the Enlightenment as an example of the destruction of old forms of authority and the creation of new ones, we must pause to examine certain elements of the Christian assumptions of the Enlightenment.[4]

It should first be noted that Christianity, in principle, departs from an antiauthoritarian premise. According to Christian teaching, it is impossible to conceive of the individual as free and dependent at the same time without a prior division of the person, the substantive "I," into two different spheres. This dualism, which Marx referred to as the "Christian-Germanic" dogma, consists of two relatively discrete "realms" of freedom and unfreedom as totalities. The "realm of freedom" is reserved for the "inner world" of the divided person, since Christianity conceives of him as a member of the intelligent or divine kingdom (Christ, as the son of God, a "thing in itself," an intelligent being), while the entire "external world," i.e., the individual taken as a member of the natural realm, the world of desire and lust (concupiscence) rejected by God, "man," "appearance," becomes the realm of unfreedom.

Christian dualism, as has been noted above, is relative, for these "realms" do not exist in a relationship of mutual opposition, but rather, in a somewhat paradoxical way, they are reciprocally founded on one another: man can be unfree only to the extent that he is free. Since "true" man—as an intelligent person—is completely free, then as a member of the external world—as a man who is not "man" in the true sense—he must be unfree. For if in this world man were completely free to live in lust, then he would be abandoned to the clutches of diabolical authority: liberated from God, he would be given over to evil.

As a free being, man comes into the world within the framework of a determinate social order. Yet worldly power cannot harm his soul, for the Christian knows that his submission to worldly authority is a "free" act for which he is basically not "guilty," since Christian freedom transcends all worldly authority which is not competent to make decisions concerning the existence or nonexistence of man.

Indeed the Enlightenment itself came into the world in the context of the struggle against authority. With its assault against teleology, the Enlightenment pitted the authority of faith against the authority of reason, intellect, and knowledge. With the exception of the encyclopedists, it attacked teleology not because teleology persisted in affirming the existence of God, but rather because teleology was accepted on the basis of the naked authority of faith. But every rebellion against a dogma which fetters reason simultaneously implies the idea that man must make use of his own spiritual capacities without remaining dependent on authority as such. This principle is evident in Kant's maxim, "Have the courage to use your *own* reason!" It was in this sense that Descartes and Locke had earlier appealed to reason as the supreme judge and guide in all things. Indeed the entire Enlightenment arose in opposition to that laziness of thinking which, as Kant might have said, leads to the minority of man in practical life.

But how can man attain majority in practical life? The liberal Enlightenment responds: through the freedom of publicity and the security of negative freedom. Authority ("higher power"), according to Kant, can, indeed, take away our freedom of speech or writing, but it cannot take away our freedom of thought. In order to think precisely, however, we must think together with others, we must be able to exchange thoughts freely. The main cause for the rise of secret societies occurs in the moment when a higher authority restricts the freedom of publicity, "the public demonstration of truth."[5]

Moreover, in order to submit oneself voluntarily, one must, as an object of authority, have a firm guarantee of at least a certain scope of autonomy.

Enlightenment thought, in contrast to Christian thought, attempted to emancipate the individual within the worldly order of things, in spite of its tacit acknowledgment of new forms of authority in place of the old. While the citizen of the ancient world saw the freedom of the community as the very condition of his existence, in bourgeois society there gradually prevailed a belief in the need for liberation from all bonds of sociability on the basis of the principle of monadology—"each is the master of his fate"—which actually signified the free surrender to fate and chance. In theory, the authority of teleology and political bonds disappeared, but this godless *individuum* was now confronted with the naked reality of life without illusions. The apparently free individual was confronted with the anarchy of production and the injustice of the relations of production. On the one hand it was shown that liberalism is possible without freedom, while on the other the great ideals of the Enlightenment were drowned in the arithmetical economy of "soulless cash payment." Bourgeois relations became "rational, if accidental; objective, if anarchic; necessary, if evil."[6] Individual rationality succeeded in swallowing the rationality of the whole.

The authority of the ancient hero or of the medieval knight derived from the *political* character of the community of the time and from an economic process in which war occupied a central place. A clearly expressed personal character was peculiar to this type of authority.

In bourgeois society, too, authority originates in the labor process. Emancipated from political fetters, however, the object of authority (the worker, the producer) is now subjected to the blind, irrational forces of the market—and in a paradoxical way: in the form of *emancipated labor*. Here, too, the truth appears in a somewhat modified form, as in Christianity: freedom becomes the condition of unfreedom. As a citizen, the worker is free and may venture out onto the "republic of the market" with his own labor power, concluding or dissolving contracts with whatever independent capitalist he may wish. But he cannot avoid subjecting himself to the impersonal authority of the *class* of capitalists and to the despotism of the capitalist factory.

The situation of the worker in bourgeois society is paradigmatic of the general situation of man as an object of authority. Insofar as man, under the influence of Enlightenment ideas and real political changes, lived in the bona fide conviction that the conditions for worldly freedom and happiness had been attained, since all forms of authority which had hindered their advent had been overthrown, he could one day astonishingly assert that those forms of authority were now hidden behind the backdrop of everyday life. Insofar as he accepted this fact with resignation as divine punishment or destiny, he could also accept subordination to the authority of economic, political, or spiritual power as some kind of inexorable natural necessity. Otherwise he would have to rebel against the new authority, for it had been shown that free labor and inner freedom are only limited and partial in their scope.

Thus one of the cornerstones of Marx's historical-materialist critique of bourgeois society was the idea that not only Christianity, but also the Enlightenment, in essence had conceived of the liberation of man exclusively as a spiritual process. Therefore it could happen that human freedom and equality could be achieved only from within, in an abstract manner, as the freedom and equality of a *person* and not as the freedom and equality of concrete people. This abstract liberation manifests itself in all social relationships, in politics as in economics, in the public as in the private sphere. "Man as a member of civil society is identified with *authentic man*, man as distinct from citizen, because he is man in his sensuous, individual and *immediate* existence, whereas *political* man is only abstract, artificial man, man as an *allegorical, moral* person. Thus man as he really is, is seen only in the form of *egoistic* man, and man in his *true* nature only in the form of the *abstract citizen*."[7] This basic idea permeates Marx's work from his early writings through *Capital*. The citizen, the *"personne morale,"* the Christian-Enlightenment "authentic man," lives as a free and equal being both in the "ethereal regions" of political life and as an abstract person, an "economic character mask," in the economic and legal relations of commodity exchange. In opposition to this realm of (imaginary) freedom, there stands the realm of necessity, the sphere of material production, the earthly existence of concrete people. Thus Marx's basic preoccupation lay in moving the domicile of human freedom into this area of practical necessity which had been emptied of both God and people. Marx did not say that the Christian-bourgeois concept of freedom was a naked illusion and deception. Marx only said that this was a partial, incomplete freedom and that complete freedom could be achieved only when concrete, real man reclaims his authenticity from the alienated sphere of political and legal life, when he recognizes and organizes his own powers as social powers. The first condition for the attainment of human liberation is the effort to organize freedom in the sphere of external, material necessity and first of all to overthrow that unjust order whose authority, "the command of capital over labor," is founded on the exploitation of the producers and to establish a new order which, while it surely cannot eliminate the sphere of material necessity in one stroke, can subject it to its own *planned* control, to a new authority which is not and cannot be the product of antagonistic class interests but which instead corresponds to the permanent interests of the *associated producers*. Marx, of course, was aware that true freedom begins only with the conquest of the sphere of material production and that the new order could guarantee only the first condition of that freedom through the shortening of the working day, the expansion of free time which, at a minimum, reduces the fatal crippling of creative human powers imposed by the division of labor.

This brings us to the crucial question: If the victorious proletariat destroys the old order which had been founded on the authority of class rule, what kind of authority should be relied upon so as to subject the sphere of material production to the proletariat's conscious, planned control; and, moreover, what is the nature of that control?

Posing the question in this way, we find ourselves in the midst of the confrontation between revolutionary Marxism and revolutionary anarchism and their controversy over the concept and role of authority.

As is well known, in 1874 Engels published a short essay on authority which he obviously meant to direct against the anarchists. In this essay he attempted to describe the dialectical nature of the categories of authority and autonomy, showing their relatively beneficial and harmful aspects with reference to sociohistorical change. Authority, according to Engels, cannot be avoided either economically or politically. Economically, it cannot be avoided because of the complex nature of industrial production itself, which both in capitalism and after the social revolution presupposes combined action and organization. Thus upon the portals of every factory there is inscribed the despotic principle: *"Lasciate ogni autonomia, voi che entrate!"* This, according to Engels, is the despotism of nature, which avenges itself on man for having subjected it to his authority. Politically as well, authority cannot be avoided, since the very act of revolution and the instilling of reactionaries with fear is the most authoritative thing that can be conceived. The only thing that changes is the nature of this authority, insofar as Engels accepts Saint-Simon's scheme of transforming political functions into purely administrative functions in the area of political economy.[8] As is well known, Engels's position on this matter served Lenin and his followers in the practical realization of Engels's and Marx's idea of the dictatorship of the proletariat.

In his polemic with Kautsky, Lenin appears to have defined the dictatorship of the proletariat in purely authoritarian terms: "The revolutionary dictatorship of the proletariat is rule won and maintained by the use of violence by the proletariat against the bourgeoisie, rule that is unrestricted by any laws."[9] This logic of revolutionary authoritarianism was elaborated upon—without frills or embellishment—by Trotsky in his famous polemic, also against Kautsky, on the nature of revolutionary terror. Here Trotsky drew upon persuasive examples not only from the October Revolution, but also from the great bourgeois revolutions and the American war of secession, when the progressive forces of society defended themselves with revolutionary terror against the forces of counterrevolution. "To make the individual sacred," Trotsky says, "it is necessary to abolish the social regime which has nailed the individual to the cross. And this task can be carried out only with the help of iron and blood."[10]

Here we might enter into a polemic: "*only* with the help of iron and blood"? Yet there can be no doubt about it, for only the worst pedant could attack the right of slaves to rebel against their oppressors as immoral, and the same applies to their right to resist restoration and counterrevolution with every authoritative (*sic*: Ed.) means at their disposal.

The problem, however, is complicated as soon as one faction of the revolutionary class seizes political power, shatters all attempts at counterrevolution aimed at restoring the old order, and attempts with all its strength to transform the people's initial trust, which arose on the basis of the success of revolutionary acts perceived as emancipatory deeds, into an *unlimited mandate* whose authority no longer derives from the interests and needs of the people and is not subject to electoral verification, but rather relies on the "power of history" as a higher metaphysical court of appeal. From time to time, to be sure, the people can be called upon to endorse post factum that which has been done and decided, but this act of acclamation is strictly for decoration and show. Here we are confronted with one of the strangest political permutations of our time: on the one hand, the transformation of revolutionary democracy into a plebiscitarian autocratic regime and, on the other, the metamorphosis of the revolutionary vanguard into a conservative elite.

The concept of a conservative elite as the core of authoritarian rule was first expressed in the modern age in drastic form by the theoreticians of the French counterrevolution (Bonauld, de Maistre, as well as the English conservative Burke), who demanded a privileged, authoritarian position for the old aristocracy as against the "*masse du peuple.*" The "popular mass" here serves as a mere object of authority from which solely "*soumission et croyance*" ("submission and belief") are demanded and which exists merely as a passive complement of the elite. The basic principle of the existence of such elites is founded on uncritical and involuntary obedience, heteronomy without autonomy.

It would seem that the old anarchists—Bakunin, Kropotkin, and their followers—were right when they criticized "authoritarian socialism." For the goal of anarchistic, as opposed to "authoritarian," socialism consisted not only in the abolition of private property and its derivatives, but also in the total destruction of all power, religious as well as political, and even, in a certain sense, intellectual (scientific). This radically antiauthoritarian socialism identified aristocractic and bourgeois power, on the one hand, with the power responsible for the revolutionary authoritarianism of the Jacobins, Blanquists, and Marxists, on the other. For according to authentic anarchism, *any* state— even a revolutionary one—leads by force of logical necessity not only to the reconstitution of private property, but also to the death of the revolution itself, since with the aid of decrees and regulations of all sorts it places the revolution under its own tutelage, creating the preconditions for the enslavement and exploitation of the people by the new quasi-revolutionary aristocracy. It would be wrong to assert, as is most often done in the vulgar interpretation of anarchism, that anarchism is opposed to all order and organization. Its basic reproach against revolutionary socialism consists, instead, in the assertion that the latter's idea of "rational social organization" is implemented "from the top down" rather than "from the bottom up." Thus the ideas of "free associated labor, social property, equality, and justice" in anarchism assume "free associations linked from the bottom to the top, organizations of the unfettered poor, all of liberated mankind" (Bakunin). The anarchist revolution would undergo a long period of preparation in the *"instinctive consciousness* of the popular masses." But here we are confronted with the first of the major problems of anarchist doctrine. If the revolution undergoes a long period of *preparation* even in the instinctive consciousness of the people, the question is: who prepares that revolution, or does it, perhaps, mature of itself in the instinctive sphere of the popular soul? To this question the anarchists respond in an extremely contradictory manner by returning to their point of departure, with embellishments and qualifications: the birth of the anarchist revolution is facilitated by the anarchists themselves, "spreading among the masses an idea which corresponds to their instinct." To be sure, the anarchists do not organize the army of the revolution, for that army is the people itself, but they do organize a kind of revolutionary general staff (*"une sorte d'état-major révolutionnaire"*) to mediate between the revolutionary idea and the popular instinct. Yet perceiving the great danger into which this assumption casts his basic idea, Bakunin quickly adds that for this purpose, about one hundred brave and respected revolutionaries would suffice for all of Europe. And this is not the only contradiction in anarchist doctrine and organization; in the same text, for example, there is expressed the unconditional demand that all members of the organization submit to the dictatorial license and authority of a Committee whose identity is unknown to them.[11]

As is evident, in the final analysis antiauthoritarian anarchism leads to a concept of a revolutionary minority which acts among an unconscious mass, a minority which itself is organized on the principle of strict and absolute doctrine. In this sense, there is no essential difference between anarchism and authoritarian socialism. Moreover, what we see here is an abstract opposition of authorities which, in the end, is nothing but authoritarianism with a reversed sign.

This explicitly (but only illusorily) antiorganizational and anti-centralistic appeal by anarchism to the instinctual, residual sphere of popular and working-class consciousness—an appeal which was not, however, widely accepted in communist anarchism—attained full ex-pression in the later theories of the anarchosyndicalist leader Georges Sorel, who demanded an "unfettered federalized world of proletarian institutions and associations" and who appealed for proletarian coer-cion. Solely the new *"morale de producteurs"* was, according to Sorel, in a position to save society from bourgeois decadence. But what kind of morality of the producers was this and of what did it consist? This was a morality which was created in the factory, in an irrational manner from the process of labor discipline and love of labor (!), from Bergson's *"élan vital,"* from the gross biological-animal sphere of existence, from traditional family upbringing, from "intuition"—in a word, from the entire complex and conglomerate of vulgar materialist psychology which leads directly to the aimless *"action directe"* of the syndicalist myth about the "general strike," to action for the sake of action. It is no wonder that this intuitional orientation toward proletarian class in-stinct instead of proletarian class consciousness glorified the cult of manual labor and accordingly viewed all "theorizing" as fruitless and characteristic of bourgeois intellectuals, just as, to the present day, vulgar materialist and quasi-socialist ideologies defend the privileged position of a conservative elite, denouncing the critical, Marxist intel-ligentsia as an "intellectual elite" and degrading Marxist theories of society to the level of uncritical mass-cultural propaganda and sloganeering. For it is no accident that it was precisely from Sorel that there flowed the notion of the existence of modern conservative elites composed of socially "deserving" persons, which, mediated by Pareto's teaching about residues and derivatives, directly flowed into the move-ment of the "brown shirts" of the former socialist Benito Mussolini, whom, along with Lenin, Sorel sincerely admired.[12]

Only now can we return to the question posed earlier: if freedom in the sphere of material necessity cannot be organized without authority and if that authority is the conscious, planned control of the producers over the processes of production, then what is the nature of that con-trol?

As we have seen, Engels responded to this question á la Saint-Simon: instead of politicobureaucratic leadership, there would be politico-economic administration. The anarchists responded á la Proudhon: federalist associations from the bottom to the top, without the interference of state-legal adjudication and with reliance on prebourgeois forms of municipal-traditional regulation. It must be added that Sorel's anarchosyndicalism shifted the entire sphere of concupiscence from the realm of necessity of material production to the *"concupiscencio dominandi"* of the new proletarian elite. Through the appeal to residual instinct and to the cult of labor and of physical coercion, along with the inflammation of ignorance, prejudice, and *"ressentissement,"* moral sentiments could be diverted to the conscious revolutionary change of the existing state of affairs.

It is in this light that we must regard the two existing models of the organization of material production which were fashioned during the course of, and after, the October Revolution: the model of statist socialism and the model of self-managing socialism. Engels's prediction that state-bureaucratic leadership would disappear if replaced by politicoeconomic administration did not come to pass. Even if it had, however, it would have merely represented a solution within the framework and territory of the political economy of bourgeois society which, instead of government by bureaucrats, brings into being government by the technocratic-managerial type, so characteristic of contemporary "industrial society," which directly leads to the functionalistic rule of an abstract system with abstract individuals and the assignment of "roles" to concrete individuals. Here the power of blind automation of the labor process, rather than disappearing, is only strengthened with the aid of modern technology, with repercussions in all areas of social and political life. The model of workers' self-management would aspire to avoid this pan-bureaucratic alternative. Its strongest weapon is the critique of centralism and state planning, along with the simultaneous stimulation of "free initiative" and competition among commodity producers of the early capitalist type, but without bourgeois intermediaries. But as a consequence of its federalist orientation (in Yugoslavia: Ed.) both in production and in political life, it is not in a position to achieve the level of positive integration which Marx had envisioned for the "association of producers." Since the entire organization of production is based upon the dispersion—through mutual competition—of self-managing collectives oriented solely toward private labor and private need, to the achievement of personal happiness in the exclusive sense of material welfare, the entire public sphere remains outside of those collectives' true domain. While appearing to fall within the domain of "their" authoritarian power as a private possession over which they have no effective control, in fact the public sphere places the self-managing collectives under its own tutelage—or, what amounts to the same thing, calls upon them from time to time so that it may "announce" its decisions to them. Hence it has happened that neither of the principal models of socialism has realized the essential mission of the socialist revolution—the *liberation* of the working class; or to reverse the proposition, the socialist revolution at best has lingered within the framework of the Christian-Enlightenment-bourgeois concept of free labor, by means of which, in the manner of primitive communism, "the category of *laborer* is not done away with, but extended to all men."[13]

The conscious, planned control, of which Marx spoke as a new type of authority in the socialist order, above all presupposes a single subject-object of the authority relation. In order for this to be achieved, however, changes in the very organization of social labor are necessary. The first condition for such organization is the rejection of the compulsory, bureaucratic-centralist unity which leads to a gray authoritarian monolithism and which places the planned control of production in the hands of techno-bureaucrats and their reified organizations. The second condition consists in the rejection of the apparently voluntary, but factually enforced, disaggregation of the producers, which confuses democratization with decentralization and which strongly increases, rather than diminishes, the "pluralism" of authoritarian jurisdictions in the sociopolitical sphere. Both schemes of social organization are contrary to the vital interests of the producers, since both equally lead to domination by alienated authority. Conscious, planned control presupposes the voluntary association of the producers of material and cultural goods from the bottom to the top on the basis of the principle of free election and without any tutelary influence by "higher authorities," since it is the workers themselves who are the subjects and objects of authority and it is from their conscious interest that the rationality of subordination is derived. An approximate empirical model for this kind of organization of freedom in the sphere of "external necessity" is furnished by the (Yugoslav: Ed.) Congress of Workers' Councils as a supreme, elective organ which is subject to recall at any time and whose authority is founded on rational (and always *class*) *consciousness* rather than on irrational *class instinct*, on *class solidarity* rather than on class or national egoism of any kind.

In light of these observations, it is essential to emphasize that the issue of centralism versus democracy is merely a false dilemma for the conceptualization of socialist authority. On the contrary, the real problem is and will remain that of bureaucratic versus democratic centralism—not only in the organization of the socialist political party but in all areas of social and political life. Engels offered a model for this type of centralism within the party—and which, mutatis mutandis, holds for other areas of social organization as well—in a letter to Kautsky four years before his death: "But it is also necessary that people once and for all cease eternally treating party functionaries—their servants—with kid gloves and standing before them, as infallible bureaucrats, obediently instead of critically."[14] This total inversion of the traditional master-slave relationship is the real truth and innovation of Marxist socialism.[15]

Accordingly, conscious, planned control means, in the final analysis, the elimination of the state *as the state*, that is, as an abstract, detached force which stands over society. For class consciousness neither is nor can be reduced to the consciousness of the state. The class consciousness of the proletariat, moreover, cannot attain full expression without the affirmation of the principle of democratic publicity, which alone is capable of creating a climate which facilitates the true transcendence of the dualism of man and citizen and creates a new social order which prevents the perpetuation of class domination.

Here we return to the classical meaning of politics as the activity of practical philosophy by emphasizing, along with the organization of freedom in the sphere of material production, the need for discourse and dialogical thought as necessary weapons for the reconstitution of the principle of democratic and socialist publicity. But neither socialist publicity as the intellectual basis of the new order, nor even that order itself, can exist without a high level of civic consciousness. The principal difference between socialism and every form of authoritarian thought is best expressed in the difference between the status of the *citizen* and that of the *subject*. For only the citizen is a being with the "gift" of free speech. The mentality of the subject, in contrast, is distinguished by *silence* and respect toward higher authority: "Silence, therefore, is the only expedient. *Muta pecora, prona et ventri oboedientia*" ["The crowd is silent, submissive, and obeys its stomach"].[16]

The suppressed *eros* of bourgeois freedom which retreats in the face of repressive authority, as well as limitations on freedom of speech through censorship or police measures—or, what is more commonly the case in modern society, self-limitation and self-censorship—create voids in those of weak natures who have abandoned pride and conviction, voids which become populated with aggressiveness and yearnings for domination as well as the dark, destructive images of *thanatos*. Here, of course, the phenomenon which Adorno called "the authoritarian personality," as the mass basis for authoritarian rule and authoritarian thinking, is not without importance.[17] For it must never be forgotten that, as Marx often emphasized, the agents of bloodthirsty terror of all kinds were *déclassé* elements recruited from the ranks of the lumpen-proletariat. It should be added here that this concept also conveys the existence of a moral void, spiritual poverty, and obscurantism. Such social trash has wormed its way into all great historical movements including the socialist revolutions, where it has sought its golden opportunity. In moments of great political crisis, the forces of internal and external counterrevolution in all ages have been able to recruit their obedient servants from its ranks: hangmen and spiritual murderers, spies and informers of every variety. And it is not difficult to recognize them by the way they wag their tails, by the way they fawn over higher personages, by their readiness to serve anyone "above" them. From the ranks of these weaklings were recruited the Black-Hundred gangs, the Fascist brown-shirts, the Nazi SS and SA detachments, the Chetnik and Ustashi cutthroats, and the police of the Stalinist stamp and brand—in a word, all the "cadres" of political movements which are based on coercion and militarism. If in the workers' movement some of them have succeeded in rising to the summits of party hierarchies, it is easy to recognize them by their telltale identification of authoritarian brutality with revolutionary firmness.

Internal insecurity, intimate doubt in one's own "I," drives weak natures and weak "characters" to admire "charismatic," "powerful" personalities—personalities whose power begins and ends with the specific authority and function which they happen to possess. This is why authoritarian personalities are very well suited for bureaucratic service, for as Marx incisively observed, for bureaucracy "authority is the principle of its knowledge, and the deification of authority is its mentality."[18] As a consequence of a shortcoming in his internal moral equilibrium, the authoritarian weakling grasps for an external environment of political order to serve as his personal refuge. His conformism is his entire moral universe, in which everything is defined in advance, clearly and with distinct boundaries, into good and evil, black and white, beautiful and ugly. This is the source of his instinctual, aggressive hatred toward any critical posture that differs in the slightest from conformism; this is the source of his scowling misanthropic aversion to any sort of innovation.

Let us conclude. Authority is a historical category whose necessity is conditioned by the very nature of social organization and social life. But since social organizations are not eternal, neither are forms of authority relations. In this light, subordination to authority has been reasonable precisely to the extent that the structure of authority has left room for the development of human freedom, happiness, and dignity. And vice versa: as soon as the authority relation becomes void of this human content, subordination becomes senseless, since mere heteronomy as the basis for authoritarian power has no human support and therefore deserves to be wiped from the face of the earth. The sooner the better.

Translated by Gerson S. Sher

NOTES

1. Erich Fromm cites the example of Martin Luther, who entertained a dual relationship to authority: a persistently unfriendly and defiant stance toward one authority and a masochistic subordination to another (see Fromm's contribution to the anthology, *Studien über Autoritet und Familie*, ed. Max Horkheimer [Paris: 1936], p. 132). Marx had similar thoughts about Luther: "Luther, without question, overcame servitude through *devotion* only by substituting servitude through *conviction*. He shattered the faith in authority by restoring the authority of faith. He transformed the priests into laymen by turning laymen into priests. He liberated man from external religiosity by making religiosity the innermost essence of man. He liberated the body from its chains because he fettered the heart with chains" (see Karl Marx, "Critique of Hegel's 'Philosophy of Right': An Introduction," in ed. Robert C. Tucker, *The Marx-Engels Reader* [New York: 1972], p. 18).

2. See Max Weber, *Wirtschaft und Gesellschaft*, ed. J.C.B. Mohr (Tübingen: 1956), pp. 28-29. [Editor's note: Tadić's identification of "power" and "authority" in his discussion of Weber is open to some question. In his authoritative English translation of *Wirtschaft und Gesellschaft*, Talcott Parsons, following N.S. Timasheff, translates *Herrschaft* (which Tadić renders into Serbo-Croatian as *vladavina*—"rule") as "imperative control," noting that *"Herrschaft* has no satisfactory English equivalent. . . . In a majority of cases, however, Weber is concerned with *legitime Herrschaft*, and in these cases 'authority' is both an accurate and a far less awkward translation. *Macht*, as Weber uses it, seems to be quite adequately rendered by 'power.'" See Max Weber, *The Theory of Social and Economic Organization*, trans. I.M. Henderson and Talcott Parsons and ed. Talcott Parsons (New York: 1947), p. 152n. The translations from Weber used in the text have been taken from Henderson and Parsons, pp. 152-53.]

3. See *ibid.*, p. 869. Weber's basic mistake is the identification of democracy with plebiscitarianism—a separate and interesting problem which we cannot go into here. (Editor's note: For a discussion of this issue, see Tadić's "Macht, Eliten, Demokratie," in *Praxis* (International Edition), no. 1-2, 1970, pp. 65ff.)

4. On the links between Christianity and the Enlightenment, see Herbert Marcuse's interesting analysis in the above-cited Horkheimer anthology (pp. 137-39), on which I have partially relied.

5. To an even greater degree than for Kant, the principle of the relationship of reason and authority as the measure of the level of development of the human race holds for Fichte as well. In his discussion of internal freedom, Fichte rejects authority in favor of will with regard to the transformation of the world. In this sense he precedes the ideas of revolutionary anarchism. See also Marcuse, *op. cit.*, pp. 140ff.

6. See Marcuse, *op. cit.*, p. 140.

7. Marx, "On the Jewish Question," in *The Marx-Engels Reader*, p. 44.

8. See Engels, "On Authority," in *The Marx-Engels Reader*, pp. 662-65, esp. 664-65. [Ed.: In view of his earlier insistence on the distinction between the terms *authoritative* and *authoritarian*, it is of interest that Tadić translates Engels as having said that revolution is "the most *authoritative*" (my emphasis) thing that can be conceived. More commonly, however, Engels's famous passage is translated as saying that revolution is "the most *authoritarian*," (again my emphasis) thing that can be conceived: see the translation used by Tucker in *ibid.*, p. 665.]

9. V.I. Lenin, "The Proletarian Revolution and the Renegade Kautsky," in ed. Robert C. Tucker, *The Lenin Anthology* (New York: Norton, 1975), p. 466.

10. See Trotsky in my collection *Partija proletarijata* (Belgrade: Sedma sila, 1966), p. 254. In the same collection, similar thoughts are expressed by Lukács (p. 153).

11. See *Michail Bakunins sozial-politischer Briefwechsel mit Alexander W. Herzen und Ogarjow* (Stuttgart: 1895), pp. 323ff.

12. See Georges Sorel, *Reflections on Violence*, trans. T.E. Hulme and J. Roth (New York: Free Press, 1950; Collier, 1961), as well as another of his works, "The Socialist Future of the Syndicates," in ed. John L. Stanley and trans. John and Charlotte Stanley, *From Georges Sorel* (New York: 1976), pp. 71-93. In his study of Sorel, Gaetan Piron quoted Sorel on Mussolini as follows: "Our Mussolini is not an ordinary socialist. Believe me: you will see him, perhaps, one day at the head of a holy battalion which salutes the Italian flag with the sword. This is an Italian of the XV century, a *condottiere*" (quoted from P. Dreitzel, *Elitebegriff und Sozialstruktur* [Stuttgart: Ferdinand Erke Verlag, 1962]). Sorel also praised Lenin for not having democratized the factories and for leaving the leaders of economic enterprises with absolute, unlimited power (see Dreitzel, p. 37).

13. See Karl Marx, "Private Property and Communism" (from the Economic and Philosophical Manuscripts of 1844), in *The Marx-Engels Reader*, p. 68.

14. Engels to Kautsky, 1891. Engels demonstrates the advantages of democratic centralism over petit-bourgeois, confederative decentralization with the example of Switzerland. Because of their extraordinary contemporary relevance, we quote his observations at length: "The bourgeoisie," says Engels, "through its industry, its commerce and its political institutions, acts everywhere to draw out small, closed localities which live only for themselves from their isolation, to link them together, to merge them into a whole, to broaden their local horizons, to destroy their local customs, dress and concepts, and, from many hitherto independent localities and provinces, to form a great nation with common interests, habits, and attitudes. Even the bourgeoisie is centralized to a significant extent. Only through this centralization, moreover, is the proletariat, far from being handicapped, placed in a position to unify itself, to sense itself as a class, to adopt, in a democratic manner, political concepts that correspond to it, and finally, to conquer the bourgeoisie. Not only does the democratic proletariat need the kind of centralization which the bourgeoisie initiated; it will have to carry it through even more broadly. During the short time when the proletariat in the French Revolution sat at the helm of state, during the rule of the Montagnard party, it carried through centralization with all means, with buckshot and the guillotine. The democratic proletariat, if it now once again should come to power, will have to centralize not only every country individually, but what is more, all civilized countries together, as soon as possible.

"Old Switzerland, in contrast, never did anything but resist centralization. With animal stubbornness it persisted in its separation from the entire rest of the world, in its local customs and dress, in its total local belligerency and isolationism. In its primeval barbarity it lagged behind in the midst of Europe, while all other nations, even including the rest of the Swiss, progressed. With all the hardheadedness of its crude Urgermans, it persisted in its cantonal sovereignty, i.e., on the right to be eternally stupid, bigoted, brutal, belligerent, stubborn, and corruptible to its hearts' content, regardless of whether or not their neighbors suffered as a consequence. As soon as their animal instinct began to speak, they acknowledged no majority, no agreement, no obligation. But in the nineteenth century it is no longer possible that two parts of one and the same country can exist one aside the other without any means of mutual communication and influence." (See Karl Marx and Friedrich Engels, *Werke*, volume 4 [Berlin: 1959], pp. 396-97.)

15. "Only the proletarians," writes Marx of the experiences of the Paris Commune, "inspired by the new social task which had to be fulfilled for all of society, namely the task of eliminating all classes and class rule, were in a position to destroy the instruments of class rule—the State—that centralized and organized state power which assumes to itself the right to be the lord rather than servant of society" (Marx-Engels *Werke*, vol. 17 [Berlin: 1962], p. 542).

16. See Marx to Ruge, May 1843, in ed. and trans. Loyd D. Easton and Kurt H. Guddat, *Writings of the Young Marx on Philosophy and Society* (New York: 1967), p. 210. Centuries of alien domination have imposed on our own soil as well a typically slavish subject-mentality which is expressed in aphorisms such as "The sword doesn't chop off an obedient head;" "Silence is golden"; "Lead your horse where your *pasha* [lord] tells you." Respectable humility toward higher authority is expressed by the aphorism, "Clear water flows from the spring, but the people drink it muddy," which, fortunately, is cancelled out by the jocular but proud words of rebellion, "The fish rots from the head, but it's cleaned from the tail."

17. See Theodor W. Adorno, E. Frenkel-Brunswick, D.J. Levinson and R.N. Sanford, *The Authoritarian Personality* (New York: 1950).

18. See Karl Marx, *Critique of Hegel's "Philosophy of Right,"* ed. Joseph O'Malley and trans. Annette Jolin and Joseph O'Malley (Cambridge: 1970), p. 47.

Part 3

SOCIALISM AS A MOVEMENT

Ethical Antinomies of Revolutionary Existence

Rudi Supek

First Contradiction

If man indeed exists as *total man*, then this is due exclusively to the nature of his consciousness and his ethos. In consciousness the universality of his being is evident: he can apprehend the existence of everything and every being in accordance with *their* own measure. Ethos is the manifestation of man's presence and participation in every being in accordance with *his* own measure, that of man as such, in his strivings and potentials.

Through consciousness man is equally far and near to all things: impartiality, or objectivity, is the virtue of consciousness for itself. Through ethos man is endlessly present in the other and hence in himself: the virtue of ethos is subjectivity, interest, the absence of impartiality. It is true that consciousness clears the path for human inspiration, just as it attains its greatest acuity and depth when it has temporarily been withheld from man. Although ethos is then beset by agony, and even by the danger of disappearing if we turn our backs on man, his removed or distanced consciousness can contribute greater certainty, and sometimes dignity, in relations with other men.

Consciousness enriches itself at the limits of the unknown, and ethos at the limits of the known. Consciousness moves in a space that belongs equally to us as well as to the other beings, their descendents and even beyond, of the cosmos; ethos moves in a space which belongs only to us, even though it might appear to exist nowhere—*u-topos*. Consciousness is exhausted in the existing, and ethos in the possible. Thus the magma of ethos is sympathy, presence which is always participation, experience which is always thought, vision which is always action. In ethos the boundaries between me and thee, between you and us, are dissolved. Man is not only created *in the measure* of each individual; he is also called upon to be *the measure for* the other. He cannot totally avoid being a *witness* of human existence, nor can he neglect being its model. Ethos knows only model witnesses and witnessed models.

Everything that exists has its peculiar laws of motion: ethos moves according to the law of *sympathetic expansion*, according to the law of the unrestrained broadening of human presence from the most proximate toward the most remote persons, leaping across all inherited and imposed boundaries and limitations: family, tribal, national, and racial. Ethos recognizes no closed horizons and likes to measure itself by the blue of the sky.

Let us mention one more difference which distinguishes ethos from objective consciousness or reason. Man can adapt, mobilize, dispose of, or share all his abilities without putting them into question; on the contrary, he thus develops them more fully, for reason will find a "true measure" for them at all times. Ethicality, in this context, is completely nonrational. Each ethical act constitutes an attack on its own nature; it beats according to the law of the human heart—all or nothing.

And however ethos, or sympathetic expansion, might aspire to the universal embrace of reality, in life they are confronted at every step with the boundaries of human existence, with that which negates them. The universality of consciousness does not liberate man from various limitations, illusions, and lies; the universality of ethos does not give him the power to overcome all vestiges of poverty, prejudice, depravity, and inhumanity. But man, as a being of practice, cannot exist without being in inevitable conflict with these obstacles, individual and social, external and internal. And thus he is permanently beset from within by the incompatibility of ethos disappearance and ethos creation, ideal and real human existence, that which is and that whose becoming is desired, for ethos resides more in the possible than in the given. Therefore the ethical consciousness is necessarily and inevitably—*unhappy consciousness*.

The revolutionary will not escape this unhappy consciousness, which penetrates to the depths of his being. He will always scorn the path of the mystic, who sacrifices reality and real people for ideal being and who delights in the bliss of resolved contradictions. His vision of a fictitious, visionary, contemplative picture of a better world will not undermine the force of his involvement in the current of daily life, nor will it remove him from the suffering and aspirations of the ordinary man. Once he has his showdown with life, he will not care about soiling his gown! He will not abandon his conviction that to be a witness and model to others without directly sharing in all their misfortunes is the greatest possible fraud and abuse of ethos. If faithfulness to the ethical vision and its incompatibility with real life is truly the source of unhappy consciousness, then the revolutionary is a person who, instead of mitigating that intimate unhappiness within himself, will only intensify it. He will not allow separate cathedrals to be erected to the ideal in high places, nor will he permit degraded man to be denied access to any shrine that concerns itself with man.

As the mystic's ethical pathos is reconciled in vision, so the revolutionary's ethical pathos is consumed in *action*. Action alone is on the plane of human passion, of true love and hate, for only with its help is the contradiction between the humane and the inhumane resolved in the real conflict of man against man and not-man—for man. In action man is closest to man; he becomes a need which is "consumed," as is every need, through coercion and appropriation, denial and identification.

If action, however, is the sole *real mediator* between the one man's life and another's, if it simultaneously denies and confirms, if it is the negation and affirmation of a specific human relation, is it not then subject to all the limitations to which human existence is subject, and will it not, ultimately, totally subordinate and enslave itself? Will it not inevitably become a victim of group prejudice, of a narrow domain of interest, of the Machiavellian psychology of mass undertakings, of goals which reside in the organization instead of being merely served by the organization? Oriented as it is toward immediate goals, does not action set boundaries to the ethical impulse, and does not man often and inescapably embark upon action *at variance* with his aspirations and ideals? Many view a positive answer to this question as sufficient grounds to condemn all action: yes, at variance, and the more so the more we lose sight of our original motivations or the ultimate goal! But this contradiction does not frighten us, for it becomes fatal to the revolutionary's ethics only when it is surrendered to forgetfulness.

Reality can betray us. Thus Vladimir Ilich (Ed. note: Lenin) understood that the revolutionary proletariat, as the force of mankind's new emancipation, must build equality among people in the management of the state by starting from their direct will—from the workers' councils—thus naturally destroying alienated social power in the form of the state. Yet the excessively thin stratum of the proletariat in revolutionary Russia forced him to retreat from this humane and ethical idea and to rely upon the instrument of human oppression, the state—to be sure, under the control of the revolutionary proletariat, but the state just the same. Today we hardly need to be reminded that this instrumentality can lead to perversion of the spirit of the socialist revolution. Did Lenin thus betray the goal or meaning of the socialist revolution? Should organized force, in the form of the state, have been repudiated at that juncture? Should an ethical demand have prevailed over the real political possibilities of socialist revolution at that moment, with the limitations and negative elements that would have ensued? Surely the revolutionary *can never retreat from the work of the revolution,* and this means that he must believe in the endless paths of historical and human possibilities which bring us closer to it, even in the face of extraordinary impediments. Under one condition: that he never loses sight of the basic goal—the liberation of man.

There is no doubt that Vladimir Ilich found himself in a difficult ethical and political dilemma. He accepted the solution which at the time seemed to be the sole possible one if the *revolution were to continue,* even though this brought him to take a step backward with respect to one of its essential principles. Naturally, knowing this—indeed, having clearly enunciated the revolution's principles—he knew that this retreat ethically *obligated him to the stages to follow.* And that is essential! Every time that the constraints of real human situations compel us to sacrifice something of those principles that directly lead us to the attainment of the ideals for which we struggle, that very ideal must obligate us even further—it must reside in us as an *internal obligation,* so that we may bring it into being as soon as possible.

What guarantee is there that we have not lost sight of the ultimate goal to which we aspire, succumbing to the constraints and attractions of life as it is, full of inequality, coercion, and exploitation? Only our internal obligations, and these can be attested to only by the ethicality, the high ethicality of our personal lives. Thus the dynamic of unhappy consciousness is manifested in ethical postponements, which on the plane of action are manifest as transitory irresolution, while on the plane of consciousness they are imbued with deeper meaning as ideal obligations toward the future and the more immediate presence of the future in the life of the here and now. Summoning the future is the sole basis of redeeming our postponements of the present, for intensifying time and the generations as the fertile womb of action in ourselves! The unhappy consciousness derives its life force from utopia but is never resolved in it.

Isn't utopianism the source of the slackening of human will and action? It is not. To be sure, under one condition: that the presence of the future in the present moment makes us especially keen for all that which is possible, which is capable of development, which is coming into being and which can come into being. If the future remains merely a banner waving outside of us, if it begins to decay within ourselves as nonexistent and impossible, then the ideal itself will begin to crumble within us. Then postponements become a source of the revolutionary's decadence, the cause of his adaptation to the existing state of affairs, a specific style of skepticism which, through cynicism, leads to "real politics."

But here we wish to warn that while internal obligation is something quite special, something unseen that fulfills itself as action only at the eleventh hour, especially in difficult and critical moments, nevertheless it is the greatest strength and quality of the revolutionary. It gives him the stamp of a *silent friend* who, however, always finds the right word. For the forgetful, adaptable, inconstant heroes it is a source of great moral strength and it is on it alone that they can rely on the path, often muddy and untrodden, to the revolutionary goal. It is the true ethical capital which the revolutionary has at his disposal. It is a movement's fortune if such an individual, in addition to the burdens he bears within himself, possesses sufficient spiritual agility to be able to adapt himself to all situations and to find the correct solutions in the confusion of personal and social relations.

The person who has never known how to accept internal obligations in the midst of ethical dilemmas and apparent defeats becomes transformed into an ordinary adventurist, and sooner or later the internal hollowness of his actions, no matter how bold, will become apparent. The person who forgets these internal obligations or who attempts to free himself of them under the pressure of the external influences of power and prestige transforms himself, as we have said, into a "real politician." It is even worse if in the course of this transformation he should remain burdened by "bad conscience"! Then he will come to hate those who have remained true to their internal promises and have resisted external temptations. Then he will try to portray his oblivion and limitations, his partial achievements and transitory successes, as his true success and achievement, as his virtue. He will view himself, naïvely, as an individual who is already at the pinnacle of the ideal which he has yet to attain. He will look upon all those of greater vision and who relate skeptically to the preceding stage as his opponents, enemies, or traitors to the extent that he does not view them as unmenacingly "insane." If these "insane" make themselves dangerous to him, he will attempt to silence and eliminate them as witnesses of his "bad conscience." Like his precursors, he will try to eliminate witnesses of his internal capitulation, and he will sever the head of the prophet whose voice arises from the desert of his ethical oblivion. Fear of this voice may lead to the mass bloodshed of innocents. But here the symbol clothes itself in the bloody body of yet another contradiction.

Second Contradiction

Let us try to be more concrete! This, after all, is not difficult, for each new contradiction binds the revolutionary more tightly to reality itself.

Now we will examine him not merely with respect to the basic relation between him and his ideal—the revolutionary goal. Rather, we will seek him in the true context of revolutionary action, in the militant collective. This collective will be a source of new dilemmas and new ethical contradictions for him. From the collective there radiates strength which fills him with self-confidence, but which can also make it difficult for him clearly to perceive new ethical dilemmas. They will become clear to him, perhaps, only when they will have assumed the form of tragedy.

Is not the giving of oneself and readiness for sacrifice the highest virtue of the man of action? The more devoted one is to the common cause, the less one thinks of oneself. This devotion is an expression of particular highmindedness and is the source of heroism. But it can bear in itself its own negation, leading to the renunciation of one's own personality and thereby to the renunciation of the ideal to which one has sacrificed oneself. The revolutionary may, against his will, become a *false measure* and a *false model*. Let us explain briefly.

In the man of action, devotion to the cause necessarily means devotion to the militant collective, a desire to identify oneself as an individual with them as much as possible. Identification with collective tasks can go so far that one completely forgets one's own personality. And for this, great strength is necessary. Such identification may, however, act as a double-edged sword: every personal attitude, every individual disagreement with the collective opinion or simply with the opinion of whomever at the given moment represents or symbolizes the militant community, can be seen as breaking away and may evoke doubt as to whether a violation of solidarity is at issue. It can mean, as we shall soon see, much worse as well.

Let us suppose that the collective feels endangered and views the very organization as threatened, either through the action of external foes or an internal weakening of solidarity. In such circumstances it is easy to get the idea that he who thinks *differently* and who even has *different* motivations might, perhaps, have different or contrary goals. So long as the original bonds of friendship and solidarity exist among the members of the collective, holding another opinion is not the same as holding a *different* opinion, that is, creating an opportunity for a change in argumentation or the initiation of discussion. But when that solidarity, for whatever reason, wavers and is cast into doubt, then thinking differently draws along with it—as the sun does shade, or as virtue does sin—the question of *different intentions*, of possible betrayal, and discussion immediately turns into investigative procedure. No longer is the thinking, correct or incorrect, of the individual at issue, but his consciousness, his essential orientation, *his very ethos, his personality in its entirety*. Ordinary intellectual discussion has assumed the form of ethical vivisection, and we know from experience that after each vivisection we are left with a carcass or half-carcass. There is, in fact, one half-carcass of formidable vitality, but more about that later!

We do not know who was the first to hit upon the idea that in the interest of organizational unity it would be good for differences in attitudes to be linked with the question of differing intentions, that is, of one's very ethical orientation. Perhaps it was born of factional struggle. In any event the creation of a hierarchical and authoritarian or bureaucratized organization found an exquisite instrument for its own ends in this ethical dilemma. When self-criticism supplemented criticism as the manifestation of one's essential solidarity with the group, when the question of the correctness of thought took the place of the question of the correctness of character, then suspicion and the formal expression of solidarity in the form of self-criticism set off on its destructive course of annihilation of the revolutionary character. Between revolutionary thought and revolutionary ethos there intruded an impenetrable layer of systematic mistrust watched over by the policemen from within and without.

Have you ever been present at one of those examinations when they try to break the subject's ideological stubbornness prior to "self-criticism," when, say, Comrade Filé, equipped with the authority of hierarchy that is based upon the *secret*, says quite calmly: "I have the impression that Comrade Péro could betray his homeland"? This "impression" of the authoritative comrade is enough for Comrade Péro instantaneously to be deprived not only of the purity of his own intentions but even of freedom with respect to the *possibility* of his own development, the right to his own future, that which belongs to each individual, even the worst of us—the freedom to determine one's own future. In this case another person *already determined* this externally, coercively, in one eternal, single word, thereby *depriving him of the possibility of choice* in the company of his comrades, isolating him as with a magic wand in a circle of close acquaintances and casting a curse on him—of excommunication. Yes, with one single word, which is a *mere impression*. To be sure, someone will say, Comrade Filé had the right to do this in the name of the "future," on the assumption that anyone in that circle could become a traitor, and perhaps that he was already someone's tool, in fact a tool of the enemy.

What is to be done in such a situation? To hold one's head high, spit or not spit as the case may be, and abandon this circle, which would mean to admit to "treason"? Or to bend the back, to prostrate oneself, to indict oneself for anything that would suggest dissent, to cry out for solidarity and to promise new proofs of one's loyalty, to search the faces of those assembled for a sign of credence and to plead for favor by offering a merciless self-critique of one's "mistakes," present, past, and future? What, at that moment, is left of one's internal promises to oneself, of the personal virtue which had been cast in with the ideal of a brighter future; what has remained of that silent friend in whom one had such premonitions of indescribable strength after the ordeal of self-criticism? Nothing! Nothing more than that which remains of one's crushed dignity, of buried hopes—empty melancholy, resigned falling-in-step behind those who have already trod the same path, and hope that new actions will wash away the humiliation one has suffered. If one were more resourceful or pugnacious—but ethos is a clumsy sweet old fool in such situations!—one might have retorted, "I have the impression that Comrade Filé could murder me or any one of us without batting an eye!" Yes, if we have a right to "impressions" and if we must make judgments on the basis of impressions . . . .

We shall not dwell upon the much discussed Machiavellianism of the "organizational spirit" and the antinomy of organizational efficiency and personal commitment, the dialectic of the Grand Inquisitor and Christ, the commissar and the yogi, the revolutionary-saint and the revolutionary-demagogue, nor upon the embodiment of ethical dilemmas in various social roles which lift these revolutionaries from their original state of solidarity and transform them into enemies and mutual tormentors. We wish to point out above all how an initial tendency, justified or not, to require evidence or reaffirmation of collective solidarity—even with the aid of means such as the systematic questioning of a member's motives or requiring him to undergo self-criticism for dissident thinking—*led to its actual negation,* to a completely contrary output, to nonsense, precisely in the form of collective or organizational practice. Even if we do not take account of all those intimate wastes that such practices leave behind in the revolutionary's soul, simply as an instrument of the "organizational spirit" they have brought themselves to futility and ineffectiveness, to their true contradiction and negation. How?

All dramas which can be divested of the personal dimension easily become comedy. The same happened with self-criticism. The individual quickly saw that the sincerity or insincerity of self-criticism could not be verified at the moment of testimony, that the verbal expression of solidarity is indeed only verbal, and that even once given it does not hinder the individual from sharing with others how he withheld his true thinking from scrutiny. The responsibility of doubting was quickly transformed into the responsibility of concealing one's true thoughts and even motives. Giving testimony about one's ethical collapse was transformed into a purely formal ritual, into its opposite: from true solidarity to the false testimony of unity; from "closing ranks" to general doubting and disbelief; from "monolithism" to general apathy or even conspiracy, each apostle assuming the role of Judas. The individual who earlier had been tragically torn between his conviction and the ethical demand to identify with the militant collective now has truly become a divided person—one who never states his convictions in their entirety, and one who is content merely to identify, to a reasonable extent, with the thinking of the majority, or, as is much more often the case, with the thinking of collective authority.

Struggling against the bifurcation of bourgeois man, the revolutionary took it upon himself, for the sake of the organization's formal monolithism, to be a divided person. And in the most extreme case he took upon himself the role of being a false measure and a negative model: *the total negation of the very authenticity of the personality* for which he was struggling.

Let us recall, briefly, how this came about. Bukharin was the first to give us an explanation in his last letter, and perhaps in setting forth what was an authentic ethical dilemma paved the way for the events that were to follow, such as the trials against the "tutored traitors." What was the nature of Bukharin's dilemma when, as a revolutionary, he faced the final act which he could execute as a revolutionary? He knew that he had been condemned to death by Stalin, that he was the representative of a defeated faction, and that he could no longer avoid physical liquidation. What more could he contribute to the revolutionary cause? The revolutionary cause now, he reasoned, was in the hands of his enemy who had defeated him and who now represented the majority and therefore the course of the revolution. The course of the revolution, even if represented by people who had condemned him, is *one, indivisible, and absolute,* while any retreat from it is treason, for it will advance more quickly if all march in unison rather than in split ranks. The only thing that is left for me, he thought, is to contribute to that unity and to accelerated progress along that course. I can do this if, in my final statement, I designate myself a traitor and thus, having declared my treason, fill those who have tried to follow me with shock and horror. To be sure, through my confession of treason I will give my opponent the moral right to shoot me and not a single honorable revolutionary will take off his hat at my grave, but what do my personality and its memory matter before the cause of the revolution?

We know that this ethical dilemma combined with the execution of the revolutionary in a state of total humiliation was repeated several times. But once the deception was revealed, all came to agree that one may sacrifice everything for the revolution except one's personal dignity and one's ethos, that one does not have the right voluntarily to assume the role of traitor once one has been a hero of the revolution. The efficiency of the "organizational spirit" in such instances has left behind such a moral void that such "identification" of one's personality with the *organization's interests,* and of the organization with the *revolution's interests,* can no longer be accepted by anyone!

Yet we must keep one thing in mind. This degradation of the revolutionary's ethos did not ensue merely as the consequence of brute coercion, of the systematic breakdown of the physical power of resistance, or of using drugs to break the will. No, it arose as *the consequence of an ethical antinomy,* as the fruit of one of the possibilities of revolutionary action, as a consequence of the erroneous identification of one's own personality with general goals, and thus led to its own negation, to an extreme form of immorality and alienation of the individual from the revolutionary ideal.

There is a lesson to be drawn from this antinomy: while it is true that ethos is verified in action, *ethos cannot become an instrument of action;* while it is true that one's motives are manifested in one's thoughts and deeds, if as a member of a collective one thinks and acts differently, we still do not have a right to doubt his intentions, for an individual is to be judged by his *entire* life even though he may experience failure at a given moment. If we maintain that a man who has devoted his life to the welfare of mankind has no right to be a coward, then surely he has no right to become his own executioner, to accept unfounded accusations and to transform his countenance into a mask of horror which the executioner can raise in front of the terrified eyes of the onlookers—"for their own good."

Third Contradiction

There is no doubt that the desire to identify one's own personality with the collective will is born of a profound ethical impulse and that it can have the ultimate effect of negating and inverting one's true special role. Once, however, it is taken to this extreme, we find that the very same thing occurs, for it is transformed into its opposite—the destruction of the members' belief in real unity, a process which sets in at the level of the collective itself. Thus we have proof that the organization should be built upon whole people rather than on human remains.

Here appears the third contradiction of revolutionary existence. It was enough for the revolutionary to begin to notice how the sacrifice of personality—of his sincere opinions and beliefs—in the name of formal unity (by means of "self-criticism," authoritarian criticism, and similar acts) gradually leads to the retreat of the personality into its own shell, the loss of spontaneity, exaggerated caution, the measuring and disguising of one's words, the suppression of the right to one's convictions or their deferral until "a more favorable moment"—it is enough, to repeat, that he become conscious of how his comrade has become addicted to tactical posturing, hypocrisy, and politicking for him to become sick of "unity" built upon the perpetual trampling of human rectitude. From an initial ethical intention, the desire for unity, there arises an *ethical rebellion*—protest against formal unity and in favor of real unity!

This rebellion finds its justification in many negative phenomena born of formally, bureaucratically, hierarchically imposed unity: universal suspicion and mistrust; the careerism of hypocrites; the rise of moral mediocrities who always adapt better in such conditions, accompanied by the withdrawal of sensitive people into private life; the progressive loss of that real social-critical and self-critical faculty which is achieved through free public opinion; the imposition of false social authorities whose confusion the toadies transform into "genius," not to mention that variety of social insensibility which obtains in a bureaucratic system in which "the lower and higher circles invariably systematically deceive themselves" (Marx) in the false depiction of social reality and of the human condition and human aspirations.

Thus the demand for the authenticity of the personality and for its candid exposure to others at all times has become the central demand of revolutionary society. In the beginning this demand acquires the form of spontaneous, more or less conscious, rebellion which is manifested in *sorties of social nonconformism:* the personality is concerned above all that it demonstrate to others how fully it disposes of its freedom or spontaneity. This nonconformism will first assume a purely *external* form—nonconformism in expression, in the mode of expressing oneself, which is merely one form of clothing one's personality (indeed still a form of "mask-wearing," but a free mask!). This nonconformism in expression, which at first operates merely "unseriously," transforms itself into nonconformism in attitude, which still need not operate much more seriously, but which once placed at the threshold of consciousness demands to go farther—to attain the level of real problems. Such nonconformism, in which the personality first excludes itself from a general current of inauthenticity, necessarily and inevitably leads to its renewed inclusion in real social problems. All this occurs in a period of accelerated social development, but not without a certain drama and intensity; whole generations can remain marked by one stage or another in this development. The revolutionary finds himself faced squarely with new problems and ethical dilemmas. Which ones?

Our revolutionary is not an ordinary rebel. He distinguishes himself from his predecessor by virtue of the fact that he has a very "long memory." He saw the revolution through three phases or, more accurately, sees it entering upon its third phase. Each revolution has its Promethean phase, when it is carried away by great ideals; its imperial phase, when it is carried away with its power and rulers; and its romantic phase, when it sets out in quest of authentic personalities.

The socialist revolution follows the same dynamic, and to judge by the distrust of potentates who have become "commissarized" and "bureaucratized," it is presently entering its romantic phase.

Let's have a look at the revolutionary in action in this phase. What contradictions plague him?

His long memory and experience in action as a revolutionary have led him into a situation where, with a certain amount of authority, he formulates judgments about a dilemma which is becoming increasingly frequent nowadays. It has become so common that it is not at all difficult to describe! The circumstances, in fact, are quite clear: once again a young, more radical element has "butted in" and has placed the "general line," or more accurately the application of that line, into question through its rash declarations. Moreover, it is no longer merely a question of "butting in," for that corresponds to a phase when upholding one's own convictions was viewed as "reasonable behavior." Nor, in the case of this young man, is it so much a question of his adopting a position which does not accord with the thinking of the majority, as it is of his desire precisely to say something that will upset, embarrass, disturb, and perhaps even dumbfound the thinking of the conventional majority. (We are speaking, of course, of formal rather than real public opinion, for one may dumbfound others simply by articulating that which everyone thinks but which no one has dared to voice until that moment.) Fine, the extent to which this declaration was an "offense" is now less important, and the delicacy of the situation does not at all consist in this. The burden falls on the constellation of relations in whose midst the "troublesome word" has fallen. Namely, one immediately finds a clique of those for whom this line is "manna from heaven," for the clique can now demonstrate, through its criticism, accusations, demagogic pathos, or its common fomenting at this "turncoat" who only now can be "evaluated," its own political vigilance and organizational loyalty and its political farsightedness. To be sure, this group, whose moral qualities are well known, elicits an immediate counterreaction in the "rebel," for to the latter its very existence is sufficient reason to sharpen his stance yet further, to generalize his attack, and to lead himself into an even more difficult situation. Not even this, however, can hinder those of a more "sober" or "constructive" frame of mind, who in all such situations try to minimize the damage, at least so as to make the judgments of the fomenter-careerists, as well as the position of the enraged "rebel" himself who is "digging away at the ground beneath his feet," more moderate.

The experienced revolutionary finds this human situation perfectly clear. He cannot help feeling scorn and loathing toward the demagogue-careerists who, like vultures, feed on carrion (of their own ethics rather than of others' bodies), but he cannot deprive them of all their arguments since those arguments consist of total and blind loyalty to the organization and submission to its authority and its alone. Can those who exhibit the greatest loyalty be publicly unmasked? And if he were to make such an incautious gesture, would not these most "zealous" and "ardent" souls try to bury him in revenge? Similarly, he cannot help his feeling of sympathy toward the "rebel," for his hard-headedness and desire for sincerity remind him of his younger days—although in those days much was different and much less complicated! Thus, all he can do for the rebel is to soften the consequences of his own actions; and this will not be very difficult. Have we not always maintained that "one must exert a corrective influence even on the most serious offenders"? This position, sensibly balanced and persuasively presented, is always good for winning over the majority, by nature reserved and uncertain in such circumstances, and to control the "zealots'" aggressiveness. Most often the experienced revolutionary will act in this manner—not only out of sympathy toward the "rebel" but also because of the human common sense which indicates with sufficient clarity where such negative selection of people leads, for with the support of the above-mentioned "technology of the organizational spirit" it has already done such harm to the cause of the revolution!

But let us put these common-sense considerations aside and reflect upon the *meaning* inherent in the revolutionary's ethical dilemma. What is the real meaning of his dilemma?

It is superfluous here to introduce the old antinomy between ethics and power. The problem is more profound than that. The revolt against a social order founded on the exploitation of man by man signified that in that society one person used another *merely as a means* for his own goals; now, we find this phenomenon reappearing in its original form but in a different historical context. For what is it but exploitation—now not so much physical as moral—when one person wishes to make another into a means of his social advancement, depriving him of the right to personal authenticity? The pursuit of authenticity, in these new conditions, would certainly merit punishment for nonconformism. And the offense is easy to verify, even when the pursuit of one's own authenticity can be aborted.

In this new situation, the revolutionary cannot distrust his "revolutionary instinct." He knows all too well that the sole guarantees of real progress and of the community's cohesion are true, totally committed, whole personalities and that when individual backbones begin to bend and melt under the pressure of hypocrisy and coercion, no means of social compulsion (neither police nor military) will salvage the cohesion and reciprocity of the social community.

The contradiction inherent in the revolutionary's ethical commitment has assumed the form of an exquisite paradox: he is compelled to subordinate his inclination and confidence to someone who is rebelling against him, the invested authority of all prior social development, the very opposite of what the rebel is now. But will the revolutionary really flee in fear from such contradictions merely because they are new and unforeseen, merely because they are the vehicles of development and of the accelerated course of history? He will not, for he rediscovers his secret "revolutionary instinct" in the new situation: the individual for whom the other is a profound, true need is always capable of deriving confidence from a rebellious soul. The revolutionary, indeed—always anew, under new and unforeseen conditions—forges solidarity and unity within the militant collective.

Like all dilemmas in which man and his future are in question, these ethical dilemmas, too, are tragic and painful, and their tragedy is the main reason that they are so difficult to conceptualize. Will the philosopher come forth who can conceptualize them in accordance with the measure of historical reason, or the writer who can give them human form? The initial contradictions have, it would seem, arrived at their final consequences, at contradictions whose resolution can enrich us with new meaning and save us from old errors, and which, furthermore, can yield a broad historical horizon and a more humane attitude of man to man. After the tragic fall, the rainbow heralds a wiser future.

Translated by Gerson S. Sher

Not Liberally,
but Democratically

Danko Grlić

When I entitled this discussion "Not Liberally, but Democratically," I did not have in mind either the "liberally" or the "democratically" as they appear in Western European political jargon to denote liberal or democratic political parties. For political parties often bear names which are so far removed from their true orientation (it suffices to recall only the most extreme example of the national-*socialist* party) and which also connote so many different meanings that it would be virtually impossible to characterize either the liberal or the democratic in a political sense in their true, original singularity of meaning within the conglomerate of various ideas and diametrically opposed persuasions of the same name and the programmatic and practical diversity of parties, individual political ambitions, and verbose promises involved in the struggle for power. Besides, in our country neither liberal nor democratic parties have a great political tradition, nor have they made particularly great contributions to liberalism and democracy. Thus in Serbia there existed a Liberal Party founded in the middle of the nineteenth century primarily by intellectuals who had lived in the West and who at first were committed to the creation of a parliamentary system within the framework of specific political and civil rights and complete freedom of trade and commerce. But when that party first came to power

in 1868, it abandoned all the basic demands of its earlier program for
political freedom and thenceforth, directly in the service of political
terror, transformed itself into a mere caricature of its own title. Very
similar things occurred with the majority of various democratic parties,
but to abandon ourselves to an analysis of such political organizations in
our country and in the rest of the world would only serve to confuse
rather than to explain the meanings which these terms hold in their
original form and in modern linguistic usage. After all, the question is
whether, when we speak of political parties, these words of Lenin do not
hold to this very day—to be sure, in a modified form and not equally for
all countries: "Liberals are distinguished from conservatives by virtue
of the fact that they represent the interests of the bourgeoisie, which
requires progress and as normal a juridical order as possible, respect for
legality, a constitution, and the guarantee of a certain degree of political
freedom. But that progressive bourgeoisie fears democracy and mass
movements even more than reaction." This assessment, to be sure,
ought to be applied very carefully to contemporary political conditions,
but all this is not the subject of our discussion.

Let us abstract, then, to the extent that it is possible, from prewar
Yugoslavia or contemporary West European political practice and ask
what precisely these concepts substantively represent, what their significance is today, and how we can justify a negative or positive assessment of the liberal and the democratic in the sense of their direct,
original, real meanings undefiled by their political abuse.

The truth, however, is also that it is very difficult to say anything
philosophically relevant about these concepts, since almost every politician—occasionally even in our country, but certainly in the so-called
socialist camp—thinks that he is a Marxist, and since he is a Marxist
that he is a philosopher, and since he is a philosopher (while he constantly reprimands philosophers and philosophy) that he is the most
competent to say something profound and philosophical about concepts
such as democracy and liberalism. With just a few modifications and a
bit of terminological sophistication, we find ourselves at the highest
philosophical level, one which is unattainable for the so-called professional philosopher because he cannot have such a broad outlook as those
who stand higher up, who therefore can see farther into the distance.
One only need, after all, glance at the *Soviet Philosophical Encyclopedia*
to see how with a change of state power the meritorious "philosophical"
literature on these concepts changes as well. At one time the best
definitions could be furnished only by Stalin; later it was Khrushchev
who had philosophically relevant things to say; and now it is Brezhnev
who is the greatest philosopher. In many such philosophical adventures
of certain politicians from the socialist camp—who, moreover, are slav-
ishly aped by professional, "politically literate" *"staatsphilosophen"*
from the other countries of the camp, working their theses over down to

the finest minutiae—it is as if Hegel's words were being fulfilled: "At the present time, the pettifoggery of caprice has usurped the name of philosophy and succeeded in giving a wide public the opinion that such triflings are philosophy. The result of this is that it has now become almost a disgrace to go on speaking in philosophical terms about the nature of the state, and law-abiding men cannot be blamed if they become impatient as soon as they hear mention of a philosophical science of the state."[1] Let us, therefore, abandon political hairsplitting and its caprice—which can indeed give us cause for impatience—and let us attempt briefly to offer a sensible clarification of the concepts of liberalism and democracy.

One Serbo-Croatian dictionary of foreign terms[2] subsumes all the following concepts under the term *liberalism*: tolerance, indulgence, partiality, lack of principle. Let us set aside, for the time being, the latter two pejorative terms, which probably arose primarily in the context of the political practice of liberals, and ask about the meanings of the words *tolerance* and *indulgence*. Do they not convey positive judgments in this uncompromisedly acrimonious, belligerent world, a world of massacres and intolerance, regardless of the irony implicit in the mild tendencies normally attributed to these terms? In an era of struggle between every feasible conception of East and West, in an era of an unremitting arms race, it certainly is a relief to find a benign, tolerant, indulgent current which desires to dull the swords, to disable the fanatics, and to calm the atmosphere.

But simultaneously—and let us not ask why—liberalization, especially in the socialist countries, has become a compromised concept, irrespective of ascription to any particular political party. When, for instance, certain circles brand certain Yugoslav philosophers and sociologists as liberals (those, that is, who wish to have more room to manipulate and demonstrate their thought freely), these arbiters—who use the expression *liberal* exclusively in the pejorative sense—do not take the trouble of considering in their verdict whether those theoreticians are close to any particular bourgeois liberal party. Those who call us liberals—wrongly and, as we shall try to demonstrate, completely misdirectedly—do so primarily having in mind the fact that there are those among us who long for a somewhat freer atmosphere. These extremely *in*tolerant pseudocritics are, however, profoundly mistaken. For the majority of Yugoslav Marxist philosophers are hardly so benign as to be content with a little bit of liberalization insofar as it may be warranted, for—and this may seem paradoxical at first glance to some— in this way they would negate that which is the most essential and in principle the most significant for the very structure of Yugoslav self-managing socialism. We would have little faith in socialism were we to think that it could and should be put right through liberalization. Or more accurately, if liberalization were called for, that would be a sign that the system was more, rather than less, in need of legitimation. Or more tersely, one could say that in this case we would under no circumstances be able to ascribe to it the name of socialism. Is it not a sign of bad conscience when certain individuals—of whom there are fortunately fewer in our country than in the countries of the "socialist camp"—ascribe to others liberalistic tendencies in relation to themselves? Is it not he who ascribed the very possibility of liberalization to others as an aspiration who thereby acknowledges that he has totalitarian-dictatorial qualities of the sort that others would like to liberalize? For terror is the second incarnation of liberalism. But it is an incarnation without which liberalism cannot survive, since it is meaningless without it. Liberalism lives off terror, but, as we shall try to demonstrate, terror also exists with the aid of liberalism.

In fact, liberalization denotes merely a certain indulgence toward something in itself unyielding, dogmatic, or even terroristic. It has nothing to liberalize if there is no terror. Yet this benign liberality does not affect the structure of that terror but merely modifies it, emancipates it somewhat, and releases its safety valves—not to the extent of completely abandoning the existing relations which have become unbearable, but merely to make them more acceptable and indeed thereby all the stronger. Liberalization, whenever it is radically oriented (if it is not a contradiction in terms to speak of a radical liberal), denotes precisely an apologia for the present—an inhuman present. Liberalization is the quest for favor from the powers that be, for their indulgence and goodwill, an appellation to their kindheartedness, that they show mercy or come to see that it is in their own interest to heed the demand for a somewhat more benign relation toward their subjects. To seek liberalization also means to reconcile oneself almost fatalistically to the basic structure of the system as a given for all eternity, blessed by the sacred authorities, descended from the heavens to the earth, given with the imprimatur of the highest forums, or, as it is the most often expressed in a wonderful turn of speech, "materialistically" shown to be the necessary and inevitable condition of the stage of development of the forces of production. This basic structure, moreover, is not put into question; it is of course not contingent upon us and therefore we cannot change it; what can be questioned from time to time is only its mode of realization, the form in which it will be brought into life, methods of application—in a word, merely the epiphenomenal, the accidental.

Surely today, in the universal grasp of strong, technocratic structures which increasingly press in upon the opportunity for any real negation of the general uniformity, even such liberalizing tendencies may seem amusing, romantically outdated, and scientifically unfounded, although in certain epochs—especially when it is clear that these structures can still be held in check for a while—they are almost always permitted to exist. The perverse aspect of liberalism is precisely that it is always permitted by someone, given, benefacted, as if society were constituted by some higher powers who occasionally survey the unyielding landscape of everyday existence to dispense mercy—letting the reins out a little—to certain favored individuals.

We have said that dictatorial, totalitarian tendencies very often accompany liberalization. As proof of this assertion we could—taking into account only some, but hardly the most essential developments— briefly review those high and ebb tides of liberal tendencies, the south and north winds that have blown in the recent history of the U.S.S.R.

It is well known that the benign south wind, the benign relaxation, began in 1953 with Stalin's death. In 1954 Erenburg published a novel with the characteristic title of *The Thaw*. But even in December 1954 that first, mild period ended, and the north wind was felt, as was apparent at the Writers' Congress where ideological vigilance was called for. In February 1956, beginning with the Twentieth Party Congress, a somewhat warmer wind once again began to blow. Khrushchev wrote a report about Stalin's abuses, Dudintsev published his *Not by Bread Alone,* Sinyavsky published his critical theses on socialist realism. Pasternak published *Doctor Zhivago,* and there were some— mainly posthumous—rehabilitations of Stalin's victims. But that period did not last long, ending in approximately May 1957, when the campaign against writers and intellectuals—and against Pasternak, among others—resumed. In May 1959 there were new signs of liberalization: *Novi Mir* published Dudintsev and Yevtushenko (who is always a good barometer of various climatic conditions) and printed some liberal poems. In July 1960, however, there blew a new north wind with Khrushchev's second speech against writers who, under the influence of the decadent West, were insufficiently party-minded; thus ended the third "southern" period. In that era there were even arrests of those who took the southern winds of the preceding period too seriously. But, happily, in 1962 the wind turned again and blew from the south: Solzhenitsyn published *One Day in the Life of Ivan Denisovich,* Yevtushenko cursed the dead Stalin, and in the journals there were mass publications of materials about the Russian concentration camps. This, however, lasted until 1964, when Brodsky was put on trial, Sinyavsky and Daniel' arrested and sentenced—and then Bachev too, when Solzhenitsyn in vain sent a letter against censorship to the Writers' Congress, and when Aleksandr Ginzburg, Yury Galanskov, Aleksei Dobrovolsky, and Vera Lashkova were arrested for having protested against the sentencing of Sinyavsky and Daniel'. The Central Committee Plenum of April 1968 definitively proclaimed the elimination of all the evil consequences of the cult of personality and demanded strong ideological discipline. This fourth north wind to follow upon the death of Stalin culminated in the occupation of Czechoslovakia and blows with very strong gusts to the present day. Mild, strong, south, north, the police as the final arbiter, the mitigation of police coercion: vodka, then camomile, the "spicy" and then a bit of the brine, *zwei glatt zwei verkehrt!* Thus there is a moment of relaxation—a certain number of people may be let out of the concentration camps, for instance, and permitted for a while even to write about the camps; some irredeemable evildoer may be excluded from the highest positions or even from all public life and some spineless weakling put up to ridicule—not principally because of his evil-doings or cowardice, but because he has become a source of embarrassment to the higher-ups or because he has become so compromised that he is no longer of any use to them. In such cases it is never asked how and in the name of what this evildoer could act so maliciously or climb so fawningly and whether it was not the very system, the very organization—which remains essentially untouched—which gave birth to the political criminal and the toady alike.

Liberalization is very attractive at first glance; everyone, as we have seen in the case of the U.S.S.R., rejoices in it, breathes more freely, is relieved somewhat of their fear, acts openly and points ever more boldly and critically to the mistakes of the past, and thinks less of repression. Thus they lull themselves in the light of that which has been given them through great kindness, no more do they tremble so feeblemindedly before the high and the mighty, no longer do they stand in place peacefully but rather of their own will, they do not believe in the omnipotence of the police, and they are grateful for this ray of light. But can we not ask whether, in their gratefulness, they do not give certain people the right to repression, the right to threaten and intimidate them, to place the citizens ahead of themselves—and not themselves ahead of the citizens—in the eternal position of the potentially accused, so that they are content with their benefactors' goodwill, bigheartedness, tolerance, and their liberal course, and with the fact that, thank God and the leaders, there is no open terror? Thus the atmosphere of a permanent Kafkaesque trial imperceptibly penetrates under people's skin, in a monstrous relationship to which they become accustomed as the normal state of affairs. People become objects—without even being aware of it and, indeed, to their satisfaction—of some absolutely sacred authority whose sanctity they do not dare to question even in their boldest dreams; and that authority is, after all, an unknown quantity. For in power as power there is something irrational, inexplicable, unspeakable, something which can be praised (for after all it is not totally naïvely said that all power derives from God, so why should socialist power be any different?), something that can be appealed to, but not something that can be placed under a question mark. All deformations, moreover, can be attributed to individuals (the case of Beria is characteristic) or even to certain social strata "in general," such as, for instance, the bureaucracy. Bureaucracy, that unknown quantity, always defined abstractly, which as an evil spirit always foils the good intentions of the leaders, which always appears almost as a deus ex machina and not as a legitimate vehicle of the power of specific state structures, can become an object of general uproar and criticism precisely because it always escapes being properly identified for what it is. Bureaucracy as the universal enemy of progress, as that which prohibits complete liberalization, thus unidentified, often remains merely a fiction, an illusion, something that you try to beat against but which your hand simply passes through, a value which can be made to release the angers of all the world over the injustice in it, without it ever being asked what the unknown force is that makes bureaucracy possible and without the rock-strong coordinates within which the bureaucracy *must* always find its highest level ever being subjected to the slightest jolt. If this slavish and obedient spirit is identified with the basis of social relations arising from class structures, and if we reconcile ourselves to those structures as a necessity, then it really becomes irrelevant who serves whom and when. For we are not talking merely about listing the names of individual bureaucrats (for we can always easily find names in that hierarchy, especially those that have been discredited), but about seeing how even those who might most sincerely curse individual bureaucrats and their intolerance (since they wish to liberalize the bureaucracy a bit) create the fundamental prerequisites of bureaucratic life and of ossified forms of power in which someone always gives orders (some more harshly than others), and others servilely obey. For he who gives the orders gives them whether he be tolerant, liberal, rigid, or impatient.

What, then, is there to liberalize? Only, as we have already indicated, that which is in its essence antidemocratic and antisocialist, that which in itself tends toward unfreedom, to which freedom is something external, alien, strange, something to be affixed or added retrospectively, as some sort of decoration or camouflage. Such an independently existing source of power, which is not fundamentally oriented as an organization toward the destruction of its own organism as a state so that it becomes an object of government rather than a subject, can allow itself this liberalization as a decoration which will not fundamentally affect its position by insisting on the basic proposition that power exists not to be served, but to serve—which is to say that in its service there should be no servants.

It is no accident that such totally normal questions and natural assertions have always had a host of compromised designations assigned to them by dogmatists of all colors, in modern times for nearly half a century: anarchy, extremism, utopia, revisionism, left deviationism, ultraism, infantile radicalism, etc. It is from this source that these terrifying designations have arisen and have indeed acquired their terrifying character to an extent that some of these terms have virtually become identified with criminal behavior. Thus it is sufficient merely to assert the existence of a real connection between these designations and an individual for that individual to stand *eo ipso* convicted without a moment's thought as to the fact that by attributing certain of these designations to him he might be receiving an undeserved compliment. Whoever, moreover, attempts to point out the unreality and humor of these concepts must always expect to get himself involved in less humorous and even quite "serious" methods of coming to terms with his defenders. It may seem absurd to some, but it is often precisely those liberals—those modern politicians, greased with all the oils of so-called freethinking liberality, so resourceful and elastic when confronted with new conditions, those eternal ornaments, optimists paid for their grinning countenances—who manage to compromise definitively those radical types who will never become reconciled to the existing state of affairs, persistent "troublemakers" who wish to ingratiate themselves with no one and who thereby make peace between people of good will impossible. In such a world one must always accurately prescribe how much freedom to dispense, to whom, and in what manner. In specific situations it might be possible, for example, to publish a radical work of Kolakowski, but still one must always keep in mind the black list of domestic philosophers who may not be cited by name. We will thus be a little more liberal toward the outside world so we may get something done domestically. Or inversely; but this is not vitally important and always depends on the political requirements of the moment. But to seek more out of a liberalization of the existing state of affairs would mean to seek something that could make someone else angry, thereby creating an opportunity for a renewed imposition of the dictatorial relation. Thus humanist philosophers, for example, are themselves partly responsible for their own unenviable fate. If we seek too much freedom, we will lose what we already have—that is the logic of these liberals—as if freedom is a potato which is being auctioned at the market, as if restricted freedom of expression is any kind of freedom at all, as if this were not a contradiction in terms.

Not, then, liberally. But why democratically? Has not, after all, the word democracy, too, become so tattered and abused that today anyone at all, even Generalissimo Franco, can be called a democrat? Whom does the term bind to anything? Who still gives any thought to the Greek origin, to Aristotle's definition, to the pure and clear interpretation of the word as the rule of the people? Isn't it said often enough in our country, too, that reality is one thing, and ideals and beautiful words another? And in our unified assertion of the meaninglessness of all assertions, it is as if we have reconciled ourselves a little bit to this state of affairs. This is, after all, one of the more ubiquitous forms of the alienation of man and his real needs in words. We are witnessing a phenomenon wherein words bind people to nothing, leaving them without a single source of inspiration. This fact, characteristic of the decay of bourgeois society, of its apologists and ideologues, turns up in socialism as well. For we know that everyone proclaims the advent of socialism—Stalin himself, after all, conceived of one of the freest constitutions in human history at the height of his cruel purges—but we are also familiar with the practice of socialism in a host of countries, which has just as often been a source of resignation. And the astonishment which follows upon that resignation is itself somewhat astonishing. For although the abuse of words in our country has not been as great as in some other socialist countries, still in Yugoslavia—primarily among certain parvenu politicians of the bureaucratic summits of power— there appears a perceived need to placate, to suppress, and to debilitate spontaneous and tangible action for real and fundamental changes through the persistent, pathetic usage of otherwise entirely ordinary words. The transformation of truthful and spontaneous human aspirations into such words, into hypostatized schemes which are adorned and enhanced through the use of creative epithets, often generates a resigned atmosphere in which all ideals are cynically rejected. And this often happens among the young, among those who must become the unselfish and altruistic bearers of the highest human ideals. For if there is no longer belief in anything, then belief will be diverted only to concrete, tangible objects such as money, nice armchairs, objects of comfort, automobiles, the easy life. What good is a book, which is merely full of words, or classes, if we merely need show up at them only to sleep through them?

Let us, nevertheless, restore words to their proper meanings, regardless of the use to which demagogues of all colors have put them for centuries. When we speak of total, direct democracy or even of democracy plain and simple, we are still speaking of a specific new structure and not of a modification of the old. A democratic structure, if it truly merits the name, cannot be content with partial solutions, for it is precisely such partial (i.e., liberal) solutions which are the source of the possibility that someone—from above—may once again decide that there has been enough liberalization, that the time has come for some tightening up, that the freedoms which have been given should now be curtailed. True democratic structure makes it impossible to change course on the basis of any everyday political considerations, to return continually to the old way of doing things, and requires an emancipation and reinvigoration of the entire people in which the powerful will become powerless and helpless whenever they wish to alter the direction of politics against the people's interests. This is a level of developed consciousness and a general climate of interpersonal relations in which no one stands any longer before powerful functionaries—as Marx says—submissively but always critically, in which it is clearly demonstrated that the censor's intellect is lower than his whose text is being censored, and in which censorship—if all have the freedom to engage in critical argument—itself becomes ludicrous. This is a mode of human relations in which careers do not create extollers of the extolled and obedient lip-worshipers and in which a person's value is measured by his real, material, and spiritual creativity and is in no way dependent upon the degree to which he is identified with the state or his function in the bureaucratic apparatus.

When I said that I consider that which can truly be called democratic as part and parcel of a new structure, I was thinking above all of socialism. And not of democratic socialism, for that is a pure tautology (namely, since that which is not democratic has no right to bear the name of socialism), but simply of socialism. One must, that is to say—without any hair-splitting, pseudophilosophical or, what is even more common, pseudosociological analysis, chatter, cryptographic grandiloquence, or circumlocution—assert anew the almost banal fact that Stalinism not only is not socialism but is the greatest enemy of socialism, just as dogmatism not only cannot be Marxism but is the most extreme antithesis of Marxism. Therefore Stalinism may, perhaps, be liberalized to a greater or lesser degree (we have all been witness to such phenomena), but Stalinism can never, under any circumstances, become democracy and therefore cannot become socialism without a radical destruction of everything that made it possible as Stalinism. Thus our country is to be distinguished from the other East European countries not merely by the more liberal course that it may have taken, but—at least in principle—by its fundamental self-managing structure. It is also worth saying that Czechoslovakia after January 1968 was not merely a more liberal version of the Stalinist concept, for in that case—merely because of liberalization, which the occupiers had after all allowed for a time in their own house—August 21, 1968, would never have come to pass.

In this regard I would like to emphasize once again that only democracy—that is, socialism, self-management—can be considered to be the antithesis of Stalinism and the product of its destruction. In their essence, democracy, socialism, and self-management are identical concepts. We cannot, of course, forget that self-management as well as democracy (not to speak of socialism) in their alienated, hence ideological guise, can become a very dangerous means of deception, of spreading false illusions that by the mere "introduction" of self-management and self-government, by enactment or decree, we have earned the right to independent government, thereby negating the need for any sort of rebellion. For in the final analysis if it is we who govern, then there is no one to rebel against nor any reason to do so, and only we—and not anyone at higher levels—can be held at fault for our own misfortunes. We are thus all held to be equally responsible, although—and this is evident from the fact that we can speak of people being situated "above" or "below" others—we do not all equally share in the making of decisions. Self-management in its deformed guise can represent a surrender of power or a sharing of the power of the great gods by a host of smaller gods who, sprinkled with this blessing from on high, multiply like mushrooms after the rain. Thus professional politicians are no longer chosen in such great numbers, but they have been replaced—and we wonder at this somewhat naïvely—mainly by the directors.

But not even the best ideas, it will be said, can always be implemented perfectly and to the letter. Thus when they approximate reality, they become degraded in a certain sense, even though this is the only way of making their contact with reality at all possible. Self-management, too, cannot remain an idea unspoiled and unsoiled by the contradictions of reality, pure in its ideal form; it, too, must yield itself to the weaknesses and primitivism of individual human beings and to the undeveloped and backward character of society. In a word, compromises are necessary, extreme stances are only harmful. But in this regard it is often overlooked that such "extreme" stances may seem extreme to some precisely because they are regarded from opportunistically compromised positions, from a servilely conciliatory, soft-hearted, peacemaking niche. A person who views everything consequential and radical as exaggerated, identifies himself with the objectively existing state of affairs and finds everything to be too idealistic, abstract, quixotic, unrealistic, and always fallacious with respect to "our reality" (but never with respect to himself as an otherwise famous and widely acknowledged progressive champion). Thus many, many people, and most often those who might have most contributed to the changing of reality, constantly appeal to reality, to the obstacles it imposes, failing to see that it is often precisely they, with their fallacious sense of reality, with their *realpolitik,* who *are* the obstacles and the reality to which they appeal so plaintively.

Nevertheless it is worth asserting—without enumerating all the real correlates and perversions, which can lead to the absurd—that self-management is the true alternative to all forms of totalitarianism, to all forms of government in the name of the people but against their real interests, or to all forms of terrorism whether they appear in the severest forms of concentration camps and the annexation of sovereign states, or in the somewhat more liberal form of criticism from above which is a priori right (and whose rightness increases with the rank of the position from which it is spoken). If self-management—its truly important economic aspect aside—does not also encompass this aspect—that those "below" can have equal rights in ideological and material matters regardless of what those "above" may think of it—then self-management is merely the most common demagoguery, an ideological facade by means of which responsibility—and thereby not a small amount of power as well—may be withheld. Or, more radically stated, so long as there exist those "above" and those "below" as two separate spheres of society, we can speak only of liberalization, but not of a system of self-management.

Beyond this, self-management is not, nor can be, a state, but rather a permanent revolutionary process of the emancipation of all potential forces in a democratic society which precisely by virtue of its real rather than illusory democratic nature, and not even necessarily by its industrial output, is ahead of, rather than behind, bourgeois society. While we will not catch up with certain Western countries in the near future (which does not, of course, mean that we should not try), where socialism (conceived as democracy)—that is, self-management—has a world- historical opportunity is precisely in the sphere of free interpersonal relations, relations not determined (as they often are in the West) by any sort of money hierarchy, acquired or inherited politicoeconomic circumstances, dividends, property, or dependence upon more or less oligarchic power structures. In comparing socialism with the Western world, one must not, however, forget that Marx's critical analysis of capitalist production was based on the assumption that capitalist society had already emancipated the individual, that people enter into the process of production with, for example, the elementary equal right to choose their place of work, which did not exist for long afterwards in socialism and which still does not exist to this day in many countries of the socialist camp. This means that they (and not only in such nonessential matters) are *behind* not only contemporary capitalism, but even the capitalism of Marx's time. And it is precisely in this respect, in the relations of production, in society in general, in the freedom and right to work, that socialism as self-management can and must be indisputably ahead of capitalism. In order for there to be self-management there must be a process—not only a process which can never show signs of regression and abandonment of what has already been achieved, but one which does not even allow itself to stagnate. For in that process even stagnation is a falling back, hypostasis, and thus sterilization, just as the stagnation and numbing of life is not merely marching in time but rather the road to death if not death itself. The possibility of ideologization—which is often accompanied by verbal apologia for self-management, fixing it at the status quo—is therefore not merely a threat to the future development of self-management, but a very real possibility that it may be turned into its opposite, into the death of those forms which we dare not leave anchored in their present state but which must unceasingly grow if they are to live at all.

But in this process it will not do merely to liberalize all the old structures; rather, they must be completely burst open and shattered in a revolutionary manner. No verbal epithets, no vows or entreaties will help to achieve a democratic, socialist, self-managing social system. Through the revolutionary changing of real relations we change society so that continuous change may become the basis of permanent transformation. In this changing of the real world, however, one must never forget the fundamental importance of criticism. Indeed it can be stated that there is no longer any sense in criticizing Stalinism, for Stalinism is beneath the level of criticism; we have outgrown that particular kind of perversion and along with it the critique of these perversions. We must build the new rather than basing ourselves on the historically obsolete. To be sure, the critique of statism and Stalinism is not merely criticism of the past, as the Czechoslovak example so well illustrates. Besides, not even criticism of that which is beneath the level of criticism is always without its useful aspects. In his "Critique of Hegel's 'Philosophy of Right,'" Marx clearly stated this truth for his time: "But war upon the conditions in Germany! By all means! They are beneath the level of history, beneath all criticism; yet they remain an object of criticism just as the criminal who is beneath the level of humanity remains an object of the executioner. In its struggle against them criticism is no passion of the brain, but is rather the brain of passion."[3] Criticism which, according to the ever heretical Marx, has become the brain, the interpreter of our passions, is oriented toward total, direct, self-managing democracy. Again, there are some who may reproach us for being overly abstract. For such democracy exists nowhere yet in reality. This, however, does not at all mean that the struggle for it is any less real than everything which exists as real, for it is if anything more adequately attuned to the real historical moment and the historical possibilities which exist in our country. Thus, it may be that Don Quixote is more real than Sancho Panza.

Translated by Gerson S. Sher

NOTES

1. G. W. F. Hegel, *Philosophy of Right*, trans. T. M. Knox (Oxford: 1952), p. 7.
2. Bratoljub Klaić, *Rječnik stranih riječi, izraza i kratica* (Zagreb: 1958).
3. Karl Marx, "A Contribution to the Critique of Hegel's 'Philosophy of Right': Introduction," in *Critique of Hegel's 'Philosophy of Right'*, ed. Joseph O'Malley (Cambridge: 1970), p. 133.

Part 4

SOCIALISM AND IDEOLOGY

Ideology as a Form and Mode of Human Existence

Milan Kangrga

The basic question in defining the concept of ideology, as it derives from Marx's science, is precisely the question of the *possibility* of such a definition. This question raises a simultaneous question about the *standpoint* from which the concept of ideology is possible at all. What is the nature of a position about which something may be regarded, identified, and called ideological? Or even more precisely, if we are talking about the ideologicity of the existing or of the given world which, as such, imposes itself upon our critical faculty of inquiry, can that existing ideological world as such be at all approached from, or within, the very horizon of the existing? The question is, furthermore, vis-à-vis what or in relation to what does the ideological (consciousness) exist? Only from these points of departure is it really possible to offer a definition of so-called ideological consciousness as the very root, sense, meaning, and character of the ideological.

The traditionally understood and accepted concept of ideology as "false consciousness" *(falsches Bewusstsein)* contains an implicit meaning which, in all its possible definitions and connotations, necessarily leads away from Marx's primary and essential standpoint. This is easily and immediately seen as soon as we examine the *criterion of falseness* of this ideological consciousness as we seek to trace the various attempts that have been made to define it.

This question is always posed as soon as we try to identify and affirm the *opposite* of this ideological (i.e., false) consciousness, since it is precisely this opposite which assumes the role of the criterion of falseness—of the ideologicity of consciousness (or knowledge). It is obvious that the first criterion of false consciousness (in other words, the antithesis of false consciousness) will be sought in the *true,* which is after all the natural thing to do. But the matter is not so simple as it might appear at first glance. For that which is true requires, in turn, a criterion of its own truth. Thus, how we understand the concept of truth depends, as we have seen, upon the definition of the true and the false—and in this case, of the ideological.

At this point, however, we must stress a point that is crucial to the entire argument. Namely, so long as the ideological is exhausted merely *within the sphere* of consciousness as such and consciousness reserves to itself the entire definition of the ideological, it cannot be expected but that the entire question is posed and perceived in a *gnoseological* framework (i.e., the theory of knowledge) and that its resolution is sought therein. Insofar as the concept of the true and the false—and consequently the concept of the ideological—acquires a gnoseological character, then the very concept of truth and truthfulness appears as a subject of investigation and definition for the theory of knowledge. But this is the primary, basic, and greatest error in the very approach to the matter of defining, explaining, and understanding the concept (Marx's concept, that is) of the ideological. From this point there follows the entire traditional gnoseological mode of argument required by this position, which not only concludes but even starts out with purely positivistic assumptions. Yet with such assumptions the ideological is inconceivable.

In the gnoseological mode of argument, the criterion of the truthfulness and, consequently, of the falsity of ideological consciousness is sought in concepts such as the adequacy, correspondence, coherence, accurate reflection—and so forth—of consciousness and the object (the subject and object of knowledge), while truth is defined purely in terms of the theory of knowledge as a property of judgment about the object, in which case the entire matter is posed and pursued and left within the theoretical sphere of perception. This school of thought does not put the object itself into question, since it comprehends the object as a purely external thing which—contrary to Marx—is "immediately given from eternity," and it consequently views the basic task of consciousness as that of accurately or correctly reflecting or perceiving that independently existing or (objectively) true given for what it is. This relationship of consciousness is then termed the truth about the object.

For this theoretical position, likewise, the question does not arise (precisely because it cannot arise) of whether, perhaps, it is not dealing with an *alienated object* with which it wishes to establish total identity, or the question of whether such a relationship of consciousness toward an object so understood is not precisely an alienated relationship. As a theory it is incapable of posing this kind of question, which is to say that in this manner it remains within the framework of the present, indeed within the standpoint of existing reality, which serves precisely as its ultimate and sole criterion, since neither the object nor its own relation to it may appear in the form of alienation. For the simple or immediate given (for consciousness) can only be and remain what it is, and within this theoretical-contemplative framework there is no alienation. Alienation cannot be perceived from the sphere of alienation itself. That which is comprehended and accepted merely as a given cannot be alienated, cannot be wrong or false, and accordingly not ideological, for it is precisely that given which is left only to itself as its own criterion. Had Marx adopted this point of view, he would never have arrived, for instance, at the concept of the commodity ("the fetishistic character of the commodity"), for he would not have been able to perceive in the commodity a social, historical, and human *relation*. He would instead have always had before him merely a simple *thing* as an ordinary *fact*, as an immediate material object of theoretical consciousness standing before him in its given form and not as a "sensible-sensuous" thing. Marx was not, however, a mere theoretician, and his attitude toward theory *as* theory is well known, as is his critique of philosophy, which was unable to resolve the crucial question of theory precisely because it is not a task of knowledge but of living, while philosophy comprehends it *only* as a theoretical task.

With regard to the above-mentioned relationship of consciousness toward its object as conceived in theory, which is of fundamental importance to our discussion, we shall cite Marx's well-known passage:

> But man is not merely a natural being: he is a *human* natural being. That is to say, he is a being for himself. Therefore he is a *species being,* and has to confirm and manifest himself as such both in his being and in his knowing. Therefore, *human* objects are not natural objects as they immediately present themselves, and neither is *human sense* as it immediately *is*—as it is objectively—*human* sensibility, human objectivity. Neither nature objectively nor nature subjectively is directly given in a form adequate to the *human* being.[1]

If, moreover, on the one hand the object never presents itself immediately to human sense and human consciousness—for in this case it would be neither human sensibility nor human objectivity (it would, that is, be no objectivity at all, for only man can relate to an object)—and on the other hand if consciousness, thought, and knowledge are not and cannot be the exclusive object of theoretical discussion, then it also follows that the resolution of the problem of so-called false consciousness (thinking and knowing) cannot be sought in the framework of a single theory, in this case the theory of knowledge. Therefore neither the definition of the ideological nor the problem of ideology is a subject for gnoseology. The question now is: What does all this mean?

We must first keep one more important thing in mind, however. Namely, since, according to Marx, "consciousness can never be anything other than conscious being" or the consciousness of being (*Bewusstsein = bewusstes sein*) then in both meaning and orientation and indeed on the basis of the essential assumptions underlying Marx's philosophical thought, consciousness can be either the consciousness of true being or the consciousness of untrue being. At this point it is necessary to stress that indeed only this manner of posing the question, in order for it to be possible at all, points to the necessity of surpassing and transcending the existing world and existing reality, for within them this question could not even be posed. If, moreover, being determines consciousness, then true consciousness corresponds to true being while untrue consciousness corresponds to untrue being. But the being of people is their sociohistorical process, in which and by virtue of which they become what they are. In the first instance we would be left with an a priori truth of existence, as an idea, an ideal, or an abstractly presupposed harmony in an eschatological sense. But if, in contrast, untrue consciousness *corresponds* to untrue being, then it represents the *accuracy* of that untrue being, which is to say that it is *adequate* to that being, it is its measure, it coincides with it and is the accurate, correct consciousness of untrue being. We thus have before us an untrue or false conscious being (but not false consciousness as such), in the form of its separation into an autonomous realm of material existence (which moves in accordance with its own laws), independent of an equally autonomous and, in this sense, abstract realm of consciousness, which reflects it (that existence) as it is for itself and in itself. *Only thus,* that is, on the assumption of the division of conscious being into the autonomous and independent movement and unfolding of alienated material existence (for which the equally abstract categories of necessity, chance, determinism, etc., are then valid) on the one hand, and into consciousness opposed to being which now moves in accordance with its own (gnoseological, logical, theoretical, scientific, etc.) laws on the other—only thus does consciousness become ideological consciousness. But this is precisely an ideological position; it is precisely the correct definition of the ideological.

In this relation of being and consciousness (being and thought), which in their separateness are always in unity, there is nevertheless a third possibility as well, namely, that consciousness does not correspond to untrue being (in this case to specific historicosocial facticity), that it is not adequate to it, but that it opposes that being and impedes it since it is born of a desire to change it. It can do so because it always derives from the primary unity of being and needing, being and thinking, which is its real source and root. This is the standpoint of that which is not yet but which can and should be, the standpoint of that which is different from what already (as the untrue) *is;* the possibility of freedom as the epochal-critical standpoint of revolution, the true instrument of history. And this is precisely Marx's standpoint and what makes it all possible for him to regard the existing state of affairs, that which is (being) as untrue, false, illusory, alienated, and in that sense as ideological. This is, moreover, the standpoint of the future, of that which is not yet, and existing (sociohistorical) reality cannot play the role of the criterion of falseness or untruthfulness here because it is always cast into question anew so it may be something that is humanly real, relevant, and meaningful, so it may *become* on the basis of the conscious-free and purposeful active relation of subjectivity which produces it and changes it in a specific direction.

In his critique of Hegel's philosophy, Marx offered an exquisite formulation of the ideological character of philosophy, and thereby a crucial definition of all forms of ideology:

> Therefore, that which constitutes the *essence* of philosophy—*the alienation of man in his knowing of himself,* or *alienated* science *thinking itself*—Hegel grasps as its [true] essence . . .[2]

This passage makes explicit the essence of philosophy as ideology. Therefore we might, paraphrasing Marx, say as follows: That which constitutes the essence of ideology (i.e., philosophy, politics, morality, art, religion, the state, law, as well as political economy, sociology, the natural sciences, etc.)—the alienation of man in his recognition or knowing of himself in these forms, or alienated knowledge thinking itself—is viewed from an ideological standpoint as natural, normal, self-evident, and moreover true to the essence of man, his world, and his life. In this way his alienated or illusory being, identified with material existence, becomes "true" in its ideological aspects merely by virtue of its being adequately recognized or reflected as such. Consequently ideology *is not false consciousness* (about some presupposed object which exists in itself, or which is neutral toward that consciousness, or which is even true as such) but is rather accurate consciousness, adequate knowing, knowledge in the measure of alienated (untrue) being (and existence), which moreover coincides with the illusoriness of human life; or more precisely, ideology is its *existential* untruth. Ideology thus corresponds to alienated human existence as its own self-knowledge within alienation, as the knowledge of one's own alienated condition which poses, regards, acknowledges, accepts, and reflects that condition as one's true being, as one's true human determination, as real life, as the sole possible sense and form of human existence. It appropriates and adopts the existential lie about the adequacy between untrue consciousness and untrue (alienated, illusory) being as its own truth.

What is, moreover, decisive here for the very definition of the ideological is that it *remains within the framework of the present*. The ideological is precisely the theoretical and practical affirmation of that which has been and that which simply is (in the form of the "given object") as its sole spiritual, intellectual, and existential field of vision and action, in which case the present appears as the real basis, the sole possibility, and the true perspective of human activity. This is the real horizon of the ideological manner of living, thinking, and knowing, a horizon which as such becomes visible and problematical only once it is genuinely—practically and historically—transcended and once one is situated in the standpoint of the future, which casts a true light on the present as alienated and ideological and as in essence untrue. Since, moreover, it is the present that is the medium of the ideological, the fundamental definition of ideology consists in *the self-affirmation of one's own alienated condition as the essence of true being*. Ideology, consequently, is a form and mode of human existence which is thought, lived, and experienced on the basis of the assumptions and within the essential confines of the present as such, on the bases of the Old World.

If, moreover, ideology is existential untruth—i.e., if it is essentially an existential question and not a special question for the theory of knowledge—then neither a definition nor a resolution of the problem of ideology can be sought, for it is not to be found here in the area of consciousness and knowledge itself or even in the critique of consciousness as such, since as we have seen, ideology never appears in this form but only as conscious being. Nor, therefore, can the solution be contained within the framework of specific philosophical or scientific disciplines that would, in view of their concerns, regard this (ideological) consciousness as a cognitive act, such as, for example, gnoseology, sociology, psychology, the sociology of knowledge, psychoanalysis, social psychology, and so on. This is the only sense and meaning which Marx's Second Thesis on Feuerbach can have:

> The question whether objective truth can be attributed to human thinking is not a question of theory but is a *practical* question. Man must prove the truth, that is, the reality and power, the this-sidedness of his thinking in practice. The dispute over the reality or non-reality of thinking which is isolated from practice is a purely *scholastic* question.[3]

Gnoseology, the dominant type of philosophizing in the modern age (from Descartes and Bacon to the present day), itself is both an index and a result of the specific alienation of the modern world from its historical eternity (praxis). Remaining exclusively within the predetermined confines of the problem of the coincidence of the subject-object (on the basis of the traditional *adaequatio rei et intellectus*), that is, in the framework of the question of the extent to which thought (consciousness, knowledge) accords with its external object, it does not come to terms with the historically structured nature of the object, its character and its origin, nor indeed with its objectivity. Thus it does not come to terms with the very possibility of the object, which remains for it "something given." It must exclude from its field of vision the question of its own perspective and therefore does not see that it is dealing with objects that are *products of labor,* that is, products of *alienated* human activity, and accordingly that it always deals with alienated objects (and moreover with an alienated subject-object action relation from which the object derives merely as a defined thing) and with empty assertions about the adequacy of an alienated subject and an alienated object. Thus the sole and highest level which gnoseology can attain is that of *accuracy in alienation* or, in other words, the confirmation of the correctness of its own alienation and bewilderment in the midst of objects as things that exist for their own sake and in reification as an essential untruth. It cannot, moreover, hold truth as its object when it is itself reified knowledge, for its basic assumption and point of departure and sole perspective (alienated being) is untrue. The gnoseological position is at base an ideological position, from which it cannot define or recognize something as ideological. Thus it is itself subject not only to critical investigation but above all to a radical change of the historical and social conditions that facilitate and produce it.

In this sense it must be stated that within the realm of Marx's thought, gnoseology is not even possible, nor would Marx have been able to fabricate such a theory from his philosophical position, which consists precisely in the *realization of philosophy.* This is why Marx criticizes precisely those aspects of Hegel which still permit a gnoseological approach to the problem of truth, since Hegel himself still adheres to the assumptions of the traditional concept of truth as adequacy. Criticizing Hegel for his *"false* positivism" and his "merely *apparent* criticism," Marx does so precisely when he addresses himself to the ideological nature of Hegel's perspective. His remarks pertain just as well to every future positivism and neopositivism to the present day as well as to the ideological standpoint as such. For in this connection Marx critically observes, commenting on Hegel:

> The man who has recognized that he is leading an alienated life in politics, law, etc., is leading his true human life in this alienated life as such. Self-affirmation, in contradiction with itself—*in contradiction* both with the knowledge of and with the essential being of the object—is thus true *knowledge* and *life.*[4]

This means that instead of genuinely casting off and transcending the foundations of these alienated, hence ideological, forms of human existence, gnoseology merely accurately and correctly recognizes, reflects, or knows as such, being left only with a "right" knowledge of the present, revealing itself for this very reason as typically ideological. It reveals itself to be ideological for Marx because its perspective is confined to that which is rather than that which is not yet, in which case any philosophy as a theory—and especially any individual science—has no ground to stand on since it has lost sight of the primary unity of being and need or, in other words, of being and thought, insisting exclusively on their abstract difference, that is, on the separation of theory and practice.

Since, moreover, the question of ideology is simultaneously or even primarily a question of the truth of being, that is, of true human practice, the problem of truth and the problem of ideology cannot be viewed exclusively as a question of *true or false consciousness and knowledge* nor as a question of the truthfulness, correctness, or accuracy of judgments about the object or of coincidence with the given object. Rather, the question of truth is a question about true human existence. Man lives, acts, relates—in a word, exists and becomes—either as a true or as an ideological and thus alienated being, and therefore the question of truth and thus of ideology penetrates to the marrow of existing reality itself and continually places that reality in question anew. That question can be posed, as we have seen, solely from the standpoint of that which is not yet but which can and must be, from the standpoint of the active future, of action as possibility—that is, from the standpoint of historical practice itself. Therefore the real surpassing or transcendence of the present simultaneously through thought and action represents the essential historical-revolutionary precondition not only for the elimination of the ideological but also for the very definition of the ideological, which implies the very possibility of regarding something as ideological. Otherwise both the assumption and possibility of critical thought itself would be absent, with the inevitable result of remaining within the framework of simple positivism. And this would represent the essence of the standpoint which Marx opposed when he posed the question and problem of ideology.

Translated by Gerson S. Sher

NOTES

1. Karl Marx, "Critique of the Hegelian Dialectic and Philosophy as a Whole," in ed. Robert C. Tucker, *The Marx-Engels Reader* (New York: 1972), p. 94.
2. *Ibid.*, p. 90.
3. *Ibid.*, p. 108.
4. *Ibid.*, p. 96.

Ideology and Values

Miladin Životić

All existing positive values which we experience live and function in the context of specific general totalities. Science, technology, morality, law, politics, and religion are only a part of a broader totality—human cultures.

Basic cultural structures as the totality of all values have heretofore had the character of *ideologies*.

Ideology is an expression for the class structure of the total system of cultural values.

I

When in 1947 UNESCO issued a resolution to organize a "philosophical analysis of contemporary ideological conflicts in the world" in order to create the theoretical preconditions for transcending these conflicts, a group of philosophers was charged with compiling a "dictionary of technical terms" which would be needed to interpret the information to be obtained about them.

In this work of interpreting basic concepts, the most difficult task, according to one of the participants—the Norwegian philosopher Arne Naess—was in defining the meaning of the term *ideology*.[1] Today, several different meanings are attributed to this term. In the *Socio-logical Dictionary* we read that ideology is the "collection of ideas, beliefs and modes of thought characteristic of a specific group such as a nation, class, caste, profession, religious sect, political party, et al."[2]

Theodor Adorno defines ideology as "an organization of opinions, attitudes and values—a way of thinking about man and society." Ideology, according to Adorno, is also "a highly developed system of a social organization's official beliefs and attitudes."[3]

According to Karl Mannheim, ideology embraces "the characteristics and composition of the total structure of the mind" of a specific epoch or social group.[4]

According to Lasswell and Kaplan, ideology is a "political myth functioning to preserve the social structure."[5]

Ideology is also seen as a system of belief which presents value judgments as empirical truth with the goal of justifying, consciously or unconsciously, particular group interests. This definition of ideology is given by Theodor Geiger.[6]

The term *ideology,* which is such common parlance nowadays, does not have a single clear meaning. Nevertheless, in the context of all the foregoing definitions and separating out those that only appear to be the same, one finds that the term *ideology* is used to denote a class consciousness which expresses specific social interests. Indeed the analysis of this type of social consciousness comprises a vast literature which has acquired a designation of its own—the science of ideology *(Ideologielehre).*

II

The first time this term was used was in the works of Condillac and Destutt de Tracy in discussing the science of ideas.

But after Napoleon, the term acquired a narrower definition. Napoleon accused a group of philosophers among his subjects of losing themselves in the idle play of intellect far from reality, emphasizing that his own political activity ought to become the subject of theoretical study. Disdainfully, he called these philosophers, who involved themselves in abstractions far removed from political practice, ideologues.

As a result of political propaganda, after Napoleon this term entered scientific terminology with this value-negative sense, denoting consciousness as error, as inaccurate knowledge of reality. The word *ideology* signified untruthful consciousness of reality. What kind of untruthful consciousness? Not just any untruthful description of reality, such as conscious deceit for the purpose of concealing specific particular interests. In the age of the Enlightenment it had been a widely shared conception that any inaccurate description of reality was a conscious deceit caused by the need to masquerade selfish group interests. In the age of Enlightenment rationalism there had reigned a belief in the unlimited power of reason, and from the standpoint of that belief any inaccurate consciousness of reality was interpreted as conscious deceit of others. Thus the French *philosophes* of the eighteenth century explained religious consciousness as an intentional lie created by a privileged estate.

The historiscist temperament which developed during the nineteenth century caused philosophy and the social sciences to turn their attention to seeking the objective causes for the phenomena of human error. Only individual judgments, conclusions, or individual systems of reaching conclusions could be false, but not the entire system of ideas of an epoch, the mode of thought or value system of an age. When a specific conclusion of attitude was asserted to be conscious deceit (false), it was implicit that the truth of the object of that assertion had been attained, known, capable of being arrived at by anyone, and was merely being concealed by design. The entire ideational structure of an age could not be proclaimed as an intentionally created false consciousness.

Rationalist philosophy, with its faith in the unlimited power of reason to know the absolute truth about the world and man, with its assessment of the social consciousness of feudalism as a conscious lie fabricated by the ruling estate for the purpose of defending its selfish interests before the people, itself represented a limited and inaccurate consciousness about the world and man.

III

Karl Marx understood ideology to signify the class structure of social consciousness, a "production of ideas" in which the product becomes an end in itself, an authoritarian force which reduces man to a means. In this "production of ideas" man reflects his objective dependence upon material social forces and represents that dependence as the essence of the world in which he lives, as his own essence. Ideological consciousness is an accurate reflex of untruthful human existence. The ideological products of consciousness are the only possible products for a specific historical epoch, for they express the historically necessary boundaries of human development, the fact of man's dependence upon the products of his labor and upon the social forces that objectively control him.

There are two fundamental characteristics of ideological consciousness:

1. For Marx, ideological consciousness is above all that consciousness which distorts and "turns on its head" the *essential* relation between man and the world. In it, man is presented not as the creature of

that world. The essential relation of man to the world as creator is itself objectively distorted, "turned on its head," making ideology the accurate expression of empirical human existence.

2. Ideological consciousness is partialized, fragmented consciousness; it "tendentiously" represents that which is merely a *part* of the world and man as the *whole*. In ideological consciousness this "tendentiousness" is an expression of the objective fragmentation of man into the religious, moral, legal, political, and laboring modes of being, into spheres which exist in a state of mutual conflict.

Ideological consciousness is inaccurate consciousness of a particular kind—it is a reflection of factuality and a mystification of essence, an affirmation of the objectively alienated world, and a denial of the openness of man to new possibilities; it is guidance for action in the framework of the present and man's illusion about the future.

Ideological consciousness is a reflection of partial social interests embodied as historically necessary forms of satisfying general social interests. In the past, this consciousness has been revolutionary when it has expressed class interests in development and reactionary when it has expressed class interests which conceal the prospects for new human possibilities in the context of given social reality.

Rationalist philosophy, as a teaching of the unlimited power of reason to know the world, is an ideological theory that is especially effective in opening perspectives for the development of scientific knowledge. Today, this Enlightenment rationalism is preserved in positivist illusions that all human problems are capable of being solved *immediately* merely by applying the methods of the individual sciences. Reason is man's power as a being of labor, the power of objectification, the power of controlling nature. This is how reason was understood in the context of Enlightenment philosophy. That philosophy was an ideological preparation for the development of science and industry. Today the belief in the unlimited power of science and technology (scientism and technicism) is an ideological fetter on man's consciousness about himself, for it shuts off the perspectives for new human potentials. This ideological fetter derives from objective social technocratic structures, not the conscious deceit of others. Today it is only in the most reactionary political sophistry that social consciousness is presented as intentionally false, as consciousness intentionally propagated by the ruling strata. Ideology is always man's self-deception about himself.

In *The Republic*, Plato developed the theory of the "noble lie," of the right of the rulers to lay the foundations for distributive justice—for justice on the basis of which each would receive that which is his right—through the myth of natural human inequality, of differences in the nature of people. Plato elaborated in detail a theory according to which the wise ought to rule in a society in which some work, others wage war, and yet others provide leadership. Of those who work it could be said that they were fashioned from bronze, the warriors from silver, and the rulers from gold. Social inequality must be presented, through a "noble lie," as natural inequality.[7]

Elements of this kind of *conscious* lie also exist in modern ideologies. But ideology is not reducible to them alone. Stalinism elaborated Marx's teaching on ideology from the position of a vulgar "theory of interests" and from the standpoint of this theory engaged in a "skirmish" with contemporary bourgeois culture. Philosophy, social theories, political doctrines, and even the art of bourgeois society were shown to be forms which were consciously made to serve bourgeois interests, conscious deceptions in the service of those interests. Stalinism transposed the motives of crude political propaganda into its assessment of all forms of modern ideological consciousness.

The ideological consciousness of modern man is not such a crude expression of his class existence.

IV

The class basis of modern man is manifest in different ways in specific areas of value—in science, in morality, politics, philosophy, etc. The basic characteristics of modern ideological consciousness appear in the form of scientism, technicism, moralism, political cults of charismatic leaders, in the form of political pragmatism, in modernizing (demythologizing) tendencies in religion, which ought to help man to endure in this world but which always conceal from him the true sources of his human aspirations, and so forth. The ideological character of modern social consciousness makes itself evident above all in the inclination to present individual, particular, partial spheres of value as the sole sources of value. The ideological consciousness is that consciousness in which the permanent and—in the framework of bourgeois society—unresolvable conflict between values unfolds. This conflict occurs through the confrontation of manifestations of partial consciousness which are presented as consciousness of the whole.

Marx wrote, in this regard, "the nature of alienation implies that each sphere applies a different and contradictory norm, that morality does not apply the same norm as political economy, etc., because each of them is a particular alienation of man; each is concentrated upon a specific area of alienated activity and is itself alienated from the other."[8] In class society man cannot be an integrated personality since he is not a free personality, since he does not live in a society which views the free personality as an end in itself; thus in bourgeois society man is a legal personality, a political being, a moral person, a scientific specialist, a religious being, and so forth. And in each particular sphere he is in contradiction with the other spheres. Man lives in a state of constant collisions among values, in conflicts which are an expression of his objective fragmentation. He cannot achieve integrity as a legal being harmonizing his relations with morality, religion, science, art, etc.; nor can he achieve integrity as a moral person living in a society governed by political-legal norms; and so on.

Man achieves integrity when he transcends this partialization in its entirety. In the context of a society in which there are positive value systems with their specific norms—the legal norm of justice, the moral criterion of good and evil, technical criteria of efficiency, and so forth—there are constant conflicts of value.

These value conflicts exist separately in the context of each positive value sphere as well as in the mutual relationships among these spheres. We live in situations in which our norms of courage and wisdom, obligation and happiness, general good and personal good, etc., come into conflict. Each positive value sphere has its own partial norm of value. Thus law and morality, politics and art, science and politics, science and art, technology and art, and so forth, are often in conflict. Man appears as *homo scientificus*—a being who measures everything by norms of scientific value, *homo technicus*—a being who measures everything by technical norms, *homo moralis, homo politicus, homo juridicus, homo religiosus, homo metaphysicus,* etc. Each of these spheres in its partiality aspires to comprise the whole man.

This fragmentation of human consciousness is merely the objective reflex of the real dismemberment of man's social being, in which man directs his activity into a particular profession, into work in the context of the objective division of his being into the general social and private spheres.

Since society as a whole lives in spheres separated from one another, individual consciousness must be fragmented into as many spheres as society is objectively fragmented.

Philosophical theories have themselves been an expression of this fragmentation. From time to time there arise philosophical doctrines which attempt to conceive and define man integrally, but only in the framework of individual, particular spheres of positive value. Kant and Fichte are panethicists, viewing human essence as consisting in man's moral being. Modern positivists view the essence of man solely in the sphere of his specifically scientific activity. The Stalinist teaching of *partiinost* (party-mindedness) presents a conception wherein man is above all a political being, a member of a specific political organization to which he must subordinate his total activity.

Philosophy has heretofore been more a reflex of the division and fragmentation of human consciousness than it has been the clear consciousness of the sources of that division and the possibilities of transcending it. In the context of modern philosophy a severe conflict is unfolding between philosophical panrationalism and philosophical irrationalism. The former holds only the analytical-instrumental, scientific consciousness to be the sole sphere of knowledge, depriving affect, passion, emotion, and desire of any claim to knowledge. Irrationalism completely excludes analytical reason from its definition of authentic human essence and reduces the essence of man to irrational will or emotion. Each of these philosophies is only a partial, ideological consciousness of man, the expression of the objective conflict of analytical reason, objectified in technology, with human *personal experience* of the world.

A philosophy which views analytical reason as basic human consciousness, excluding the other spheres of the human spirit, can never grasp the essence of art, morality, religion, and so on. Thus Hegel, from the standpoint of panrationalism, interpreted the artistic merely as the rational idea given in the form of sensuality. From the standpoint of such a rationalist definition of art, the primary consideration is the rational *idea* as the presupposition of artistic creation. This panlogism is one of the constitutive elements of socialist realism as the ideological theory of art of the Stalinist epoch: the artist must have a clear, rational idea of creativity in order to be able to create. What this has led to is rather well known.

Irrationalist philosophies are most often inadequate as critiques of science, technology, and reason in general.

The basic form of value conflict is that between heteronomous and autonomous values. All previous positive values have been, as we have shown elsewhere,[9] primarily heteronomous, since they are the expression of social universality alienated from the individual. We have also analyzed previous forms of positive morality as a sphere of heteronomy, since alienated social universality does not cease to be heteronomous merely by virtue of its "internalization."

A conflict between legal autonomous values with heteronomy occurs and lives only in those movements which struggle for the social personality in a free, self-governing human community.

In the context of these value conflicts, it is above all religion which assumes the role of the integrative medium. Its function has been, and remains, that of compensating for true integrality.

It has been, and remains, "the general theory of this world, its encyclopedic compendium, its logic in popular form, its spiritual *point d'honneur*, its enthusiasm, its moral sanction, its solemn complement, its general basis of consolation and justification."[10]

Religiosity can assume quite different forms, but its essence is the same—the search for the integral totality of life, the realization of essence, the realization of hope, the realization of one's own personality with the aid of faith in "that which is beyond this world." That which is beyond may acquire the form of demythologized religion, but the essence of this faith in the "higher wisdom" remains—the ideological distortion of real relations and their being turned on their head. The ideological consciousness is that consciousness which fails to penetrate through to the reasons why man turns toward the sphere of the otherworldly, but it is also that consciousness which has always contained the objective causes, the objective sources of that turning.

V

The age of the end of ideals or the end of ideology? Let us review the fate of the two basic ideals of our time—the ideals of *liberalism* and *communism.* Liberalism and communism, as ideals and ideally based social consciousnesses and theories about society and man, are the two great visions of the world which have played an immense role in the formation of the intellectual climate and traditions of our time.

The ideals of liberalism trace their roots to the bourgeois revolutions, particularly the French Revolution and its "Declaration of the Rights of Man and Citizen," to concepts of the individual citizen whose freedom is the basis of social freedom, the citizen whose aspiration for development in equal conditions leads to the organization of society in the form of the state. In liberal theory, individuals who have agreed on a contractual basis to enter into the framework of state structure do not do so to place their freedom at the disposition, at the feet, of some higher power, but rather for the sake of their own welfare and prosperity. John Locke, Benjamin Constant, Wilhelm von Humboldt, John Stuart Mill, Herbert Spencer, and the other spokesmen of the basic ideas of liberalism also built on the basis of the ideals exalted by the French Revolution, the ideals of liberty, equality, and fraternity. It was John Stuart Mill who gave expression to these ideals in the most complete manner. In his *On Liberty,* he writes: "That principle is, that the sole end for which mankind are warranted, individually or collectively, in interfering with the liberty of any of their number, is self protection. That the only purpose for which power can be rightfully exercised over any member of a civilized community, against his will, is to prevent harm to others."[11] In that which merely concerns himself, each person is independent and legally unrestricted. "Over himself, over his own body and mind, the individual is sovereign." "This, then," Mill continues, "is the appropriate region of human liberty. It comprises, first, the inward domain of consciousness; demanding liberty of conscience, in the most comprehensive sense; liberty of thought and feeling; absolute freedom of opinion on all subjects, practical or speculative, scientific, moral, or theological."[12] Individual freedom, the freedom of private initiative, is for liberals the basis of a rationally organized society. Society cannot interfere with the individual's private initiative when he establishes goals which relate only to himself. The individual knows more and better about himself than does the state; he is in a position to make better judgments about that which is good and profitable for him, to make better judgments than others—and in this no one may hinder him. "The only freedom which deserves the name, is that of pursuing our own good in our own way, so long as we do not attempt to deprive others of theirs, or impede their efforts to obtain it. . . . Mankind are greater gainers by suffering each other to live as seems good to themselves, than by compelling each to live as seems good to the rest."[13]

The basic forms of freedom are the freedom of thought, of speech, of the press, of association, of behavior in accordance with one's own beliefs, and the freedom of private economic initiative.

Liberalism particularly insists on the freedom of thought and the freedom of private initiative. "If all mankind minus one," says Mill, "were of one opinion, and only one person were of the contrary opinion, mankind would be no more justified in silencing that one person, than he, if he had the power, would be justified in silencing mankind." Freedom of thought is impossible without the freedom to doubt and to express one's personal opinion. No one has the right to claim infallibility for himself. Each has the duty to follow his own intellect, regardless of the conclusions to which he may come. Each has the right to completely free discussion of the bases of every thought and every opinion. "If even the Newtonian philosophy were not permitted to be questioned, mankind could not feel as complete assurance of its truth as they now do."[14]

Social education without this freedom can be nothing but tyranny. The freedom of judgment, critical thought, and personal expression is the precondition for the development of the individual's social character. Man sharpens his powers, say the liberals, by distinguishing between good and evil, and he cultivates his moral virtues only when he can choose freely. The state cannot be a moral policeman, overextending its competence to interfere in the freedom of conscience, thought, and individual choice. The state may limit individual freedom only when the individual's behavior harms others, when it restricts the freedom of others.

The ideals of liberalism are theoretically grounded in a utilitarian philosophy according to which the general social interest is constructed from the sum of individual interests of *rational* individuals.

Utilitarianism and liberalism are expressions of the age of the rise of capitalism and of the reigning belief of that time that individual self-initiative is the basis of social development. This was an age in which there were no visible tendencies in social development toward the bureaucratic social system. The liberals spoke out against the strengthening of the power of state officials, against bureaucracy—even when composed of the ablest men—for bureaucracy tends to appropriate freedom from the people.

Mill's *On Liberty,* the classical work of liberalism, concludes with these words: "A State which dwarfs its men, in order that they may be more docile instruments in its hands even for beneficial purposes—will find ... that the perfection of machinery to which it has sacrificed everything, will in the end avail it nothing, for want of the vital power which, in order that the machine might work more smoothly, it has preferred to banish."[15] Only free private initiative and the free development of each individual can ensure social progress, "for with its help we obtain as many centers of improvement as there are individuals."[16] Something happened, however, which classical liberalism did not foresee: the state of laissez faire capitalism, of the unhindered self-initiative of private persons, transformed itself into an authoritarian bureaucratic force.

Liberalism demanded that state institutions act toward the individual in accordance with rational principles deriving from the individual's free consciousness and activity. Bureaucratic society has destroyed that brand of rationalism and created another—technological rationality. Utilitarian-liberal doctrine takes the individual of bourgeois society as the measure of all things: all social institutions must be evaluated in accordance with the interests of the normal and rational private citizen. In the context of this doctrine, this normal individual is seen as a natural egoist whose rationality consists in his respecting the interests of other individuals in his own personal interest. If maximum personal happiness is desired, it can be achieved, according to utilitarianism, only if it promotes, rather than impedes, the happiness of others. Social justice is founded on an equilibrium of one's personal interests and those of others. The general good is expressed through the general will, but the general will is not some self-sufficient substance with its roots in spheres divorced from individual consciousness, activity, and interest. It does not derive from mystical entities such as, for example, the spirit of the people *(Volksgeist)* or *Staatsraison,* but rather from the rational goals of individual wills.

Liberalist rationalism is opposed to the division and contraposition of social vs. individual interest. Utilitarian doctrine stubbornly defended and elaborated the basic position of social contract theory that all people are by nature equal, that of all qualities reason is best distributed among people, and that reason, grounded in individual experience, is the basis for resolving all social relations and problems.

No rationality apart from individual reason is possible.

Herbert Spencer asserted that "the limitation of state-functions is one outcome of that process of specialization of functions which accompanies organic and super-organic evolution at large."[17] Spencer predicted that the state, as a power above society, would perform increasingly fewer functions because the development of knowledge and skill would enable individuals to organize themselves into increasingly harmonious social relations. This prediction was belied by subsequent social development. The rationalization of social relations was accomplished beyond, and independently of, the realm of individual behavior. In the context of this rationalization, under the impact of the technological revolution of the twentieth century, social institutions have not lost their control over individual behavior but have strengthened it instead. The state has ceased to be a "night watchman" for the individual's interests and has become an instrument in the hands of a separate, highly developed social stratum—the bureaucracy.

Thus, subsequent social development had the effect of weakening liberalism's influence. The liberal political parties gradually became a negligible adjunct to the political systems of the West.

Classical liberalism was unable to become a doctrine that could satisfy the interests of the *working class*. Liberalism conceptualizes equality only within the framework of bourgeois legal perspectives in the sense of equal rights, but not in the sense of equal social conditions.

Thus the ideal of equality, in the context of liberalism, beyond its legal aspect, acquires a religious, illusory complement. While utilitarianism and liberalism are the heirs of the Enlightenment critique of religion and Enlightenment rationalism (the liberals fought for the separation of church and state), they left it to religion to rationalize real inequalities. Faith in God before whom all are equal, faith in the Creator who created all people equal, and faith in the Savior who died for everyone, has the role of ideological rationalization for real inequality. Real equality is surrendered to the wisdom and goodness of the Creator and to the belief that it will be realized sometime in the distant future.

Liberal democracy was unable to be democracy for all. "What meaning," writes Maurice Duverger, "did freedom of thought, freedom of the press, freedom of public meeting and association have for workers in the basements of Lille ... locked in for at least fourteen hours a day, overcome with work, almost totally impoverished and deprived not only of culture but also of the most elementary education, who barely succeeded in staying alive?"[18]

But the *fate of the ideal* of liberalism was not resolved through the appearance of socialist and communist ideals and political parties which were to have appropriated the rational kernel of liberalism and its demand for individual freedom as the condition for social freedom. The development of socialism did not transcend liberalism, but rather rejected it. The fate of the ideals of liberalism was resolved through the appearance of technology and bureaucracy—a social phenomenon in which bureaucracy serves the ends of technological rationality, created in the scientific revolution of the twentieth century, in order to introduce new forms of authoritarian control and manipulation over the individual. Socialism has not transcended the bourgeois-legal conceptual perspective with regard to human freedom. Its development has discarded even those freedoms which bourgeois society had already achieved. This is the source of an extremely significant characteristic of our time—the hunger for bourgeois values. This is the source of liberalism's obsession for a number of the great minds of our age. For there have arisen social orders in both East and West which have not only failed to develop the basic human values stressed by liberalism—the freedom of thought, speech, conviction, association, etc.—but have smothered and crippled them instead.

Classical liberalism assumed the existence of small states and small state machineries. But in the meantime there have arisen two great superpowers which have divided the world into blocs, and along with them powerful state bureaucratic machines. Classical liberalism assumed the existence of private capitalists, private entrepreneurs, but in the meantime there has arisen the powerful system of state capitalism. Classical liberalism assumed an increasingly large role for the individual and his consciousness of his reason, but the locus of rationality in the regulation of social relations has shifted from the individual to impersonal bureaucratic institutions. This movement has taken place in the context of a process in which social institutions have become increasingly alienated from the individual.

Classical liberalism believed that more knowledge and education makes the individual freer and enhances his social power. For the representatives of classical liberalism, knowledge is the basis of the rational ordering of social relations. But in our time there has arisen a society in which the power elite is not, as C. Wright Mills properly asserts, a cultural elite. Those who govern society are not individuals of knowledge and culture. People of knowledge become merely hired professionals. A society has arisen in the context of which liberalism cannot function and can no longer give answers to questions about the directions, basic values, and goals of social development—not because liberalism has become obsolete, but because it has simply been discarded.

In these conditions, liberalism is experiencing a twofold fate. First, it remains merely an ideal of a small number of the intellectual elite whose survival is dependent upon its own total reification and institutionalization within the framework of bureaucratic systems.

The ideals of liberalism today serve above all as a touchstone of resistance for a small stratum of the Western intelligentsia against their transformation into the hired help and servants of the bureaucratic state. But that intellectual elite which, with its liberal ideals, relies upon its own total reification increasingly lives in a state of exile, powerless to influence the course of social life and the solution of practical social problems.

At the same time, the ideals of liberalism are undergoing a bureaucratic-ideological transformation. They are becoming rhetorical phrases, decorative elements of the vocabulary of politicians through whom and by whom the process of the bureaucratization of society is being carried out. In a society in which the state machinery is growing stronger and is assuming all social functions—political, economic, educational, and the like—in a society in which individual life is increasingly deprived of its independence by virtue of its adaptation to the institutional context of social life, the invocation of the ideals of liberalism can only be ideological and mystifying in character.

In practical social life the conflict between liberal and conservative political parties has virtually ceased. Liberal ideals today serve as an instrument for the moralistic embellishment of reality; they live only in the rhetorical phrases of modern political pragmatists, phrases which do not alter the present but instead struggle for its perpetuation. In this context, invocation of the freedom and right of personal expression is merely an ideological embellishment in conditions of the ever advancing authoritarian institutionalization of society, in the framework of social life in which practice devoid of liberal values is nothing more than ideological exploitation of those values.

The ideological character of this appeal to liberal values consists in the fact that they are used to distort the relationship of man to reality. Instead of serving the end of critical knowledge of human potentials and the boundaries of the present, they are used for the mystification of the present and thereby the strengthening of man's dependence upon the present, for manipulation to the end of confining the individual within the bounds of society as it is.

This chasm between liberal phraseology and authoritarian social practice is growing ever wider in modern Western society. This is increasingly a "democracy without the people," in the felicitous phrase of Maurice Duverger. The democratic freedoms are the property of an increasingly small power elite. The freedom of choice is being eroded by the authoritarian programming of individual consciousness and the restriction of electoral alternatives. It is virtually impossible to distinguish between the programs of opposition parties and parties in power. The Gallup poll can successfully predict electoral outcomes in Western "democracies" because the individual is programmed and manipulated. Prediction is reduced to mere calculation, taking into account the volume and level of preelection ideological indoctrination, indoctrination which stands at the disposal of powerful mass communication media. The public has become a mass—a receptor of political ideology which lacks the ability to resist ideological indoctrination.

Thus the ideals of liberalism live in ever greater dissonance with reality. They help a small number of people from being overcome, but these people most often are possessed of a pessimistic sense of the dissonance between freedom and reality, an awareness of their powerlessness to transcend it. As a means of ideological indoctrination, the ideals of liberalism serve to create illusions of freedom, to contribute to the pseudorationalization of reality, to cancel out the critical consciousness of existing reality. Invocation of liberalism's ideals in these conditions serves not to open the way to new possibilities, but to perpetuate the status quo.

The ideals of liberalism are most commonly exploited to compromise socialism and communism, to create a false dilemma between communism of the Stalinist variety and the liberalism of bourgeois society. The goal of this ideological manipulation of liberalism's ideals is to narrow the consciousness of the possibilities among which man can and must choose in finding his way out of the present. This exploitation of ideals creates a dual mystification: the first identifies communism with Stalinism, while the second identifies liberalism with the existing structures of bourgeois society. Conflicts of interest between the two bureaucratic supersystems are presented as conflicts between liberalism and communism. This sort of ideological exploitation of liberalism's ideals will continue in every greater measure to be oriented toward the goal of concealing the true meaning of communist ideals while blunting direct attacks on Stalinism.

For the objective movement of society is yielding increasing similarity between the structures of Western societies (especially the U.S.A.) and that of the Soviet system. The social order in both systems is founded on the growing power of bureaucracy. That power is being strengthened by the development of technology. Technological development in both systems is being transformed into an end, rather than a means of human liberation. This perversion of means into ends, as with all perversions of the end-means relationship, is supported by specific particular interests: as an end in itself, technological development is a powerful weapon of bureaucratic control over people, and in both systems technology is increasingly an instrument of human control rather than one of human liberation. The similarity of these two systems is most evident if their social structures are viewed from the standpoint correctly suggested by Max Weber. If, says Weber, one wishes to evaluate any social order, one must ask what type of person it gives optimal conditions to become dominant. C. Wright Mills has this in mind when he writes: "The most important questions that must be asked about any area of society are: What kinds of people do they tend to create? What personal life styles do they stimulate and cultivate?" From this standpoint, Mills accurately asserts of the relationship between Soviet and American society: "In the American white-collar hierarchies and in the ... Soviet 'intelligentsia'—in quite differing ways but with often frightening convergence—there is coming about the rise of the cheerful robot, of the technological idiot, of the crackpot realist. All these types embody a common ethos: rationality without reason. The fate of these types and this ethos, what is done about them and what they do—that is the real, even the ultimate, showdown on 'socialism' in our time. For it is a showdown on what kinds of human beings and what kinds of culture are going to become the models of the immediate future, the commanding models of human aspiration."[19]

In the Soviet Union today, there has developed a powerful bureaucratic society, in which there reigns the holy trinity of political bureaucracy, technocracy, and military bureaucracy. Soviet society has not dissolved the basic contradiction of bourgeois society, the contradiction between private individual and social power alienated from him. It has reinforced that contradiction and developed it in a new manner. As in the West, there has been a strong development of the state and its institutions, which deprive the working class of the possibility of the direct control of society.

Marx's ideals of communist freedom have, in this society, experienced a fate similar to that of the ideals of liberalism in the Western "democracies without the people."

What is the relationship between Marx's ideal of a communist human community and the ideals of liberalism? Both theories of freedom view reason and freedom as coterminous; greater rationality is the basis of freedom and vice versa—greater individual freedom is the basis of greater social rationality. Both doctrines view freedom as the essential condition of authentic human life. Both theories consider that there is no freedom where the individual is not free, that freedom can only exist through the freedom of the individual. Both theories include, above all, the freedom of choice and the freedom of the autonomous determination of personal goals in the concept of freedom. Both theories consider that social universality must be founded upon the self-activity of the individual. And so forth.

The differences are essential. But these differences are not differences between two mutually exclusive value systems, as is maintained by both pseudoliberal bourgeois politicians and Stalinists alike.

Liberalism's ideals can be fully realized only if they are transcended, and not abolished, by the communist ideal of freedom. Liberalism aspires to the freedom of the private citizen, the freedom of the individual who is unable to transcend the state as an alienated general force which persistently tries to frustrate his aspirations to independence in the name of private interest. Today it is quite obvious how illusory this freedom of the private individual is. The individual in bourgeois society is a person who has not yet attained his true sociability, living in the breach of ceaseless conflict between private and general social interests. Liberalism aspires to rationality as the equilibrium of limited private interests. Marxism seeks a new type of rationality as the basis and expression of freedom.

Bourgeois society, through the sphere of private interest, has also established and strengthened the sphere of "abstract, dumb" authoritarian social universality and alienated political institutions. Freedom is possible only when both types of contradiction are transcended. So long as this division of man into a private being and a subject of the authoritarian social totality is not overcome, there will be no true freedom nor true rationality, which consists in man's ability to govern society without the aid of external forces, to be a self-manager. Communism is the demand to create a society in which social institutions will be a means, an instrument of individual self-organization and self-management, rather than a force above the individual. Rational freedom as the ability to regulate private interests in a society of alienated universality is impossible. It has been shown that under these circumstances the only possibility is the mode of technological rationality, which is primarily exploited as a form of manipulation by the power elite over the other members of society.

The freedom of private initiative is in decline, while the authoritarian censorship of personal behavior is on the rise.

Marx's vision of the new rationality and freedom is linked with the appearance of the free, self-managing human community, which arises only when both the egoistic individual and the alienated institutionalization of society are negated, when, in Marx's words, *political* society is negated, that is, a society in which there exist political institutions as instruments of power over man. Man cannot organize his own powers in the context of the *political* community but only in the process of the withering away of the state and its political institutions. Either socialism is the process of that negation, or it is not socialism. Socialism is not a new type of statist-political control but a *process* of abolishing all institutions which would close society within the framework of a *fixed political* system.

Social revolution, Marx wrote, is the individual's protest against his isolation from the social community. It is revolution which seeks the free community as the essence of individual man. Any society in which the common interest is fixed beyond the interests of liberated, self-active individuals is not a free human community in Marx's sense, but rather a specific type of political class society.

Marx demands an upheaval in the relationship between the individual and society in which alone the truly free individual and the true unity of freedom and intelligent rationality are possible: the negation of all forms of authoritarian social totality, as well as an individual who autonomously bears his social being in himself as his need and his power. In this process the role of the proletariat is not to establish its power in a political system, i.e., a fixed system with institutions of power over the other members of society. For the proletariat's essential, true interests, this is a contradiction in terms. Whenever a fixed political system of power is established in the name of the proletariat, its name is used falsely. The true interests of the proletariat, as the bearer of universal human emancipation, are given only in the process of the negation of that social stratum whose function is to control people. Only through this negation can the free human community come into being. And in it, the proletariat, too, is negated and transcended as a class. The proletariat has no objective, particular interests which require it to defend any eternally fixed political social system.

Marx's ideal of the free, self-managing community has experienced a fate similar to that of liberalism. It is the touchstone of resistance to bureaucratic societies which call themselves socialist, but today it suffers from a massive ideological, mystificatory transformation. The basic goal of that transformation is to purge its doctrines of their role of revolutionary critical negation and leadership of the process of transcending all forms of political (alienated) society. When these negativistic critical connotations are expunged, they become their opposite— apologetic instruments for political practice which strengthens the political system of the rule of man by man, instruments for the rationalization of particular bureaucratic interests which are presented as the sole possible general social interests.

These are some forms of ideological deformation which Marx's ideal of the free, self-managing community has suffered under Stalinism:

1. One of the most vital ideological mystifications is the idolatry of work and of the working class *as a class*. Soviet society is characterized by a state economy. The worker in that society is a wage laborer in the service of the state bureaucracy. He is not free to dispose of the means of production and control over the distribution of his surplus labor. In these conditions, Marx's teaching about the working class as the bearer of the process of universal human emancipation is transformed into its opposite. For this ideology wants the working class to remain a class, and by means of this ideology of the working class, its true human future of transcending itself as a class is concealed from its view. Not a single interest of the working class as a class can be

realized in conditions in which its historical potential of transcending itself as a class and of creating a society of true equality is denied it. In this ideology, man as worker becomes the ethical ideal for all to follow. The characteristics of a creative being are attributed to the worker: "Work plays the main role in forming the esthetic views and interests of the Soviet worker. On the other hand, the development of his ethical views enables the worker to understand the beauty of work more profoundly and to transform work into his primary vital need."[20]

The development of individual sociability, in the framework of this ideology, is interpreted as a process of internalization of social norms: "The moral code of the builder of communism views collectivism as one of the most important capacities of Soviet man."[21] Collectivism, or the subordination of the individual to the collective, is for this ideology the condition of individual freedom; freedom is interpreted as a form of subordination to the needs of society and to the laws of the external world.

2. This idolatry of work and the working class parallels other forms of idolatry, of which the most important is the idolatry of the charismatic leader (i.e., the cult of personality). The phenomenon of the cult of the charismatic leader is the most complete reflex of the social being of bureaucratic society which calls itself socialist. In every society in which there exists class inequality and the rule of man by man, this cult of power must appear. It is the most general expression of the dependence of the individual upon a power standing above him and controlling him.

The cult of personality is a new form of religion, which no class society can do without. Contemporary Soviet ideology is being used to carry out a strident educational critique of religion, yet that ideology itself has adopted the basic concerns and functions characteristic of the religious consciousness throughout the ages: to give expression to the individual's dependence upon social forces and to present this state as the essence of human life and the sole possible form of human existence. The death of the heavenly God has given rise to earthly gods. The earthly ruler in whom control and social power are concentrated becomes the object of adoration. He is the most complete embodiment of universal interests. Everyone must await his sage voice as the word of law. Without him there would be chaos. He is the incarnation of rationality and freedom. Compared to him, all others seem to be creatures incapable of making the slightest decision or taking the slightest risk. After him, there will be chaos. His capricious voluntarism is seen as a form of the fulfillment of the historical process. He lives beyond responsibility, but he is therefore a watchful father who judges and punishes severely but justly. He is unchangeable and irreplaceable, the basis of the unity of party, people, class, state, and so forth. All these religious elements of the cult of personality are incomprehensible if not understood as accurate reflections of a real state of autocracy, a real usurpation of power, bureaucratic power which has smothered social development, a real sensation of dependence on the part of every member of society upon an autocratic center of usurped power. As with every ideology, this cult, by presenting man's dependence upon powers which control him as his essence and the sole possible form of reality, conceals the possibility and perspectives of true human freedom.

The idolatry of charismatic power goes hand in hand with the authoritarian representation of the practical political goals of the given society as ideals, along with the identification of existing reality's macrostructures with socialism as a living reality. Thus the ideals of socialism have come to be an instrument of tyranny, exploited to require behavior which is consonant with the global structure of the existing "socialist" society, or rather with the interests of those who govern that structure. Communism's ideals have been transformed into an ideology which conceals the contradictions of the "socialist" system and which identifies socialism with the social order of bureaucratic control.

Not even the communist parties beyond the boundaries of the "socialist" countries have overcome this transformation of Marx's ideals of the free human community into an ideology which justifies and mystifies a bureaucratic social system. This has had a profound consequence, for the absence of a critical relationship toward the "socialist" countries on the part of the Western communist parties has been intimately linked with the loss of critical touch with Western society itself. The Western communist parties have increasingly lost their claim to be the bearers of Marx's ideals of socialist humanism. They have tolerated strong influences and ideological indoctrination from the fraternal parties of the socialist countries and have therefore surrendered their revolutionary critical vantage point for an adequate critique of bourgeois society as well as losing touch with the true interests of their working class constituencies.

The values of Marx's humanism have ceased to guide the practice of the majority of the Western communist parties. In their worldview, in their theory, in their interpretation of Marxism, and in their tactics of political struggle, they have increasingly come to resemble social democracy and its *realpolitik,* which rejected the revolutionary struggle to change the class structure of modern society.

3. Invocation of the ideals of socialist humanism has a dual function in the context of Stalinist social systems—first, to mystify the present by identifying the given order of things with socialism; and second, to serve as a moralistic, decorative supplement where mysti-

fication is insufficient and unsuccessful. When the bureaucratic system displays its inherent brutality of human inequality and unfreedom, there arise epidemics of moralistic eloquence, campaigns to commemorate still unrealized ideals, short-lived periods of moralistic sermonizing, moralistic demands for equality, declarations, and emanations from the seat of political power, so that after the recovery of the given political system of bureaucratic control, all might be surrendered anew to the waters of forgetfulness.

When it does become necessary to speak, for instance, of socialist equality as an ideal, this is done in the form of moral sermons which change nothing of existing structures. Ideals thus become instruments of embellishing social structures that are inherently unequal and socially unjust.

4. The ideals of Marx's socialist humanism undergo an interesting transformation in the ideology of Stalinism when the latter undertakes to *evaluate the past*. In Marxism these ideals are the basis not only for critical knowledge of the present, but also for the critical evaluation of the past. For only by means of a critical, rather than an apologetic, relationship toward history—especially toward the history of the communist movement—can we know and discover true possibilities and the true future. In Stalinist ideology, by contrast, the relationship toward and evaluation of the past is oriented above all toward the goal of strengthening the meritocratic base of bureaucratic power.

The power of modern "socialist" bureaucracy is meritocratic, the rule of the meritorious. The majority of people who seized power after the socialist revolution were revolutionaries. But their accomplishments—their merit—have become subjects of ideological indoctrination. Their struggle for the free human community, for the freedom of all, has been transformed into a new form of power over people.

When the bureaucratically controlled society emerged, various ideological myths about the past began to appear in it. The past as well as the present became a medium in which only the infallible and brilliant thought and action of the charismatic leader were seen. Charismatic personalities became the demiurges of history. The working class was seen as a plastic material to which these personalities gave form and shape. The charismatic leader was ubiquitous: wherever he was, the crucial battles were fought and the fate of the revolution decided. A critical relationship toward the past emerged occasionally, but only when bureaucrats were coming to terms with each other. And then history would be abbreviated and pages in the history books describing the merits of the loser would be excised and discarded. If a new person rose to the pinnacle of the hierarchy, history would undertake to change itself from its beginnings. (When Khrushchev was in power, there was not a single history of World War II that did not stress his contributions above all others.) Since the struggle for ascendancy in the power elite is a feature of all bureaucratic systems, the heroes of the past—those whose names have been given to villages, cities, streets, factories, and schools—slowly fade away, while history be comes ever more abbreviated. The greater the concentration of power, the shorter history becomes.

This kind of history, moreover, always becomes treated as a paradigm. Historical manuscripts become pedagogical treatises. Their goal is to establish a model for the behavior of future generations. Thus bureaucracy enslaves the past, present, and future. By means of this idolatry it attempts to deprive new generations of the ability to offer their own judgments about their predecessors and to choose on the basis of their own visions of the future. The sole goal of the meritocratic stylization of the past is to reinforce the influence of the present agents of bureaucratic power. Thus, although this ideology appeals to Marx's materialist understanding of history, it abandons that teaching and presents history as the work of heroes. The role of the working class and the popular masses is emphasized here not as a matter of principle, but as a phrase with no palpable effect on the mode of historical interpretation.

5. We have already spoken of the relationship of Stalinist ideology toward theoretical thought. Here, we will discuss only the changes that are taking place in this respect in the current context.

Ideology in the contemporary "socialist countries" significantly differs in certain respects from Stalinism as it existed during Stalin's lifetime. Several new characteristics oblige us to speak of neo-Stalinism. In Stalin's time, the voluntarism of charismatic power was the *ultima ratio* of theory and practice. Only that which emanated from that capricious voluntarism was viewed as objective. The basis of theoretical discourse was a coerced acceptance of coarse ideological mystifications imposed by that voluntarism and presented as the framework of "freedom." Today, we have the struggle for technological rationality in social practice and theory. This is well illustrated by what is happening in philosophy and other theoretical fields in the Soviet Union, for the state of theory is a reflex of what has transpired in that society since the Twentieth Party Congress. In philosophy and the social sciences a struggle is unfolding between the Stalinist old guard and the new generation, which is pointing philosophy and the social sciences toward operationalism and functionalism and which opposes sectarian, dogmatic attitudes toward the results of modern science. Political voluntarism, in the harsh, direct form of ideological intervention, is less frequently imposed as the supreme arbiter in the resolution of theoretical problems. The time has passed when the Party's Central Committee issued directives even in the area of genetics. Today, politicians seek the help of philosophy and the social sciences in creating the most efficacious methodology possible for the political practice of the present. The results of science and positivistic Western philosophical orientations are increasingly being exploited for the development of technological rationality and efficient day-to-day politics. In the Soviet Union, works in functionalistic sociology, symbolic logic, the theory of meaning, cybernetics, and so forth, are being translated en masse. The basic goal of all this activity is to bring theory and practice into conformity with the results of the modern technological revolution.

What has changed in this picture? The demand for the rejection of all critical attitudes toward the totality of social life has remained the same. Since this critical attitude toward totality is lacking in modern positivism as well, the methodology of these orientations can be applied very successfully to the efficient manipulation of existing facts and relations. A critical attitude, a dogmatically intolerant strain of criticism, is reserved only for Western humanistic philosophy and theory, for the philosophy of existence, phenomenology, and, above all, for the representatives of the Marxist critique of modern society. Self-censorship remains the condition for one's involvement in theory. Excommunication and political anathematization are applied only to those who desire to know and speak the truth about the totality and to relate critically to it, but no longer to those who dabble in value-neutral areas.

The acceptance of the existing structure as the sole possible reality remains the framework for all theoretical thought. Within this framework efforts are made only to make the voluntarism of bureaucratic rule more methodical, to exploit the opportunity for anesthetized manipulation attained through the use of modern technology, and to transcend the cruder forms of censorship and torture. Theory presents us with a new image of the spirit of officialdom—the official who puts science into his service in order to endow politics with a methodology for the use of technology in the solution of partial problems in the context of the present. "Situational logics" and methodologies for efficient social management are fabricated in various spheres of present-day social life. The theoreticians' bureaucratic conformism acquires new forms. Communism, social equality, socialist democracy, the freedom of personality, the self-activity of the proletariat, self-management, and the other values of socialist humanism drop out of the theoretician's technological dictionary one by one. The Stalinist old guard regards the loss of these decorative values as part of a process of de-ideologization and opposes this process from the standpoint of its demand for the old forms of *partiinost'*, i.e., for the direct subordination of theory to political voluntarism. The new guard struggles for the technological rationalization of political voluntarism.

This new tendency reduces the humanistic problematic to the demand to construct a new system of ethics whose goal is to socialize the individual within the context of the existing totality and to adapt him to present social structures in an optimally functional manner. The basic characteristic of neo-Stalinist ideology is a technocratic, scientistic attitude toward science and the theory of society and man. Advocacy of the current view that science is the sole instrument, measure, and form of knowledge fits very nicely into the irrationality of the whole. For science thus becomes an instrument of the teleological rationalization of the present instead of an instrument of critical knowledge and change of the present. Instrumentalism and functionalism in theory, by virtue of their basic epistemological orientation, are becoming virtually indistinguishable from modern Western positivism. The tasks of humanism are reduced to the fabrication of moral guidelines for the individual in society as given, to the development of a methodology for the introjection of an authoritarian totality into individual consciousness and behavior. Thus do technocratism and moralism enter into a dualistic union characteristic of modern bourgeois ideology in general. In this way there is created mass conformism in individual consciousness and behavior; this conformism is quite evident particularly today, when that system has exhibited the full extent of its cruelty in the occupation of Czechoslovakia and only a small number of people were found to raise their voices in protest.

VI

Today we read of the end of ideology.

There is Daniel Bell's book by that name—*The End of Ideology.* Raymond Aron has written a study on the end of ideology, *La fin de l'age idéologique.* Theodor Geiger also speaks of the end of ideology in his *Ideology and Truth.*

"As ideological," writes Geiger, "ought to be designated those expressions which, in linguistic form and in the content expressed through that form, present statements about reality as theoretical but which contain atheoretical elements which do not belong to objective-cognitive reality."[22] Ideology, according to Geiger, is a collection of value statements that are not scientific, cognitive statements, statements that cannot be empirically verified. The category of value statements includes philosophical, esthetic, ethical, and political statements, based upon "primary value judgments" *(primär bewertungen Werturteile)*—on judgments of sensual taste. It is meaningless to speak of such judgments as true or false. Ideological statements arise when it is desired to express a biased judgment as objective scientific truth. The task of science is to eliminate from knowledge all "existential factors," all subjective bias. There is commencing, according to Geiger, an era of science that is replacing ideology based on "biased judgments." Will this era of science bring an end to the distorted, mystified consciousness of man about himself and his relationship toward the world?

The modern world of science and technology has led to the total adaptation of all values to the present, to a negation of those values that govern the practice of criticism—the negation and transcendence of the present. The antagonism between values and reality has all but disappeared. But in this way, as Herbert Marcuse has shown,[23] there is created a new ideology, an ideology with no oppositional elements, with no resistance, with no ideals. Ideals, as critical projections of a new totality, yield to the functionalistic, structuralistic, and behavioristic identification of totality with the existing whole.

When Daniel Bell speaks of the age of the end of ideology, what he really has in mind is the age of the end of ideals. He writes:

> World-wide economic depression and sharp class struggles; the rise of fascism and racial imperialism in a country that had stood at an advanced stage of human culture; the tragic self-immolation of a revolutionary generation that had proclaimed the finer ideals of man; destructive war of a breadth and scale hitherto unknown; the bureaucratized murder of millions in concentration camps and death chambers . . . all this has meant an end to chiliastic hopes, to millenarianism, to apocalyptic thinking—and to ideology. For ideology, which was once a road to action, has come to a dead end . . . . The driving forces of the old ideologies were social equality and, in the largest sense, freedom. The impulsions of the new ideologies are economic development and national power.[24]

We are entering an age of professionals and engineers, of a technical intelligentsia and political bureaucracy devoid of ideals. Philosophers are becoming social engineers, while artists are being called upon to be, in Stalin's words, "engineers of the human soul." Theory is assuming the form of parcelized practical-technical knowledge which asks merely *how* to solve concrete problematical situations in the context of the present rather than asking about the nature of the present itself. The sacrifice of intellect is becoming a condition for the pursuit of theory. This sacrifice is no longer demanded merely in the name of the Party, the Revolution, Class, and General Interests, but in the name of Science itself. The aspiration for personal verification and pursuit of the truth has yielded to the demand for responsibility toward the present. We are entering an age of technology and mass culture which offers us leisure devoid of content as the sole form in which one may keep oneself company in one's free time. Mass culture is becoming the new opiate of the masses, a powerful means of divorcing consciousness from the basic problems and difficulties of life with which man lives from day to day. The individual and society are reconciled by means of the total absorption of the individual into the "collective," into existing structures. In public affairs the sole actor is the organization man, the man who thinks, acts, and feels as he is required to by a specific organization—i.e., by those who control him.

We are entering an age in which being a unique personality is often the same as being a private persona, isolated from the public sphere of society. Those who control public life are increasingly evading social control and are creating a situation of growing irresponsibility.

The revolution's symbols and ideals are becoming instruments of manipulation and decorative embellishment, weapons for the defense of bureaucratic interests. "The power of the mind (today)," as Theodor Adorno rightly maintains, "is the blind mind of today's potentates."[25] Our time is one of a vacuum of ideals, of the disaggregation of ideals, but also of new sources of resistance. We stand before the following possible alternatives. The first is sketched out by the Soviet academician A. D. Sakharov in his manifesto on "Progress, Coexistence, and Intellectual Freedom." This alternative is grounded in a technocratic vision of the future founded on a belief in the unlimited power of science and in the development of technology, which will gradually reconcile the ideological differences between the two world superpowers who will undertake an organized struggle for "geohygiene," a higher standard of living, solution of the problem of hunger, etc., and gradually resolve their differences through mutual assistance. An affluent society might result, but in the framework of existing bureaucratic structures, it would be a society devoid of personal freedoms.

A second perspective is provided by the contemporary resistance of the younger generation to the affluent society and the authoritarian manipulation of people. But the younger generation has a better idea of what it does not want and is more unified with respect to why it does not want it than it knows, with a unified sense of purpose, what is needed with regard to the formation of new ideas. This situation was accurately described by Ernst Bloch at the time of the student disorders [Editor's note: of the late 1960s]. "There no longer reigns," Bloch said, "the state of affairs formulated by Brecht as, 'I see the goal clearly before my eyes, only I don't know how to approach it.' Rather, it seems that one knows how to approach the goal before it is seen. But if the anticipation of the distant goal does not exist in the present, neither can there be more proximate goals to correspond to it."

Translated by Gerson S. Sher

NOTES

1. Arne Naess, *Democracy, Ideology, and Objectivity* (Oslo: 1956).
2. *The Sociological Dictionary* (New York: 1944); definition by Maurice Parmelee.
3. Theodor Adorno, et al., *The Authoritarian Personality* (New York: 1950), pp. 2, 162.
4. Karl Mannheim, *Ideology and Utopia,* trans. Louis Werth and Edward Shils (New York: n.d. [1936]), p. 53.
5. Harold D. Lasswell and Abraham Kaplan, *Power and Society* (London: 1952), p. 123.
6. Theodor Geiger, *Ideologie und Wahrheit: Eine Soziologische Kritik des Denkens* (Vienna: 1953), p. 66.
7. See Book III of Plato's *Republic.*
8. Karl Marx, "Economic and Philosophical Manuscripts," in ed. and trans. T. B. Bottomore, *Early Writings* (New York: 1963), p. 173.
9. Editor's note: see Miladin Životić, *Čovek i vrednosti* (Man and Values) (Belgrade: 1969), from which this essay is taken.
10. Karl Marx, "Contribution to the Critique of Hegel's *Philosophy of Right:* Introduction," in *Early Writings,* p. 43.
11. John Stuart Mill, *On Liberty* (New York: 1947), p. 9.
12. *Ibid.,* pp. 10, 12.
13. *Ibid.,* pp. 12–13.
14. *Ibid.,* pp. 16, 20–21.
15. *Ibid.,* pp. 117–18.
16. *Ibid.,* end of Chapter IV.
17. Herbert Spencer, *The Principles of Sociology* (New York: 1895), vol. 2, p. 659.
18. Maurice Duverger, *La Démocratie sans le peuple* (Paris: 1967), pp. 109–10.
19. C. Wright Mills, *Power, Politics and People* (New York: 1963), p. 393.
20. *O chertakh lichnosti novogo rabochego* [On the Features of the Personality of the New Worker] (Moscow: 1963), p. 198.
21. *Ibid.,* p. 137.
22. Geiger, p. 66.
23. Herbert Marcuse, *One-Dimensional Man* (Boston: 1964).
24. Daniel Bell, *The End of Ideology* (New York: 1960), pp. 369–70, 373.
25. Theodor Adorno, in Kurt Lenk's anthology, *Ideologie* (Berlin: 1968), p. 326.

Conclusion

SOCIALISM AND HUMAN RIGHTS

The Marxist and Stalinist Critiques of Right*

Ljubomir Tadić

It is helpful to draw a distinction between the positivist, or historicist, *via facti, rightist* critique of natural right and law—which first appeared after Thermidor and in more general terms in the period when the bourgeoisie was transformed into a conservative and reactionary class—and the historical and dialectical critique of natural-right and natural-law philosophy.

We come across the first form of the latter in Vico, who places history at the center of his legal philosophy in attempting to contrast the Cartesian method with Aristotelian practical philosophy and in so doing to transcend the sharp distinction between that which is general and absolute and that which is concrete and individual. History is the point of convergence of the true and the artificial. In the area of law, Vico attempted to reconcile the rational with the authoritative, natural law

---

*Editor's note: Throughout this essay, Tadić uses the Serbo-Croatian *pravo*, the equivalent of the German *Recht*, to denote both "law" and "right." In view of the lack of an exact English equivalent, I have taken the liberty of using either *law* or *right* depending upon the context. This linguistic asymmetry, however, introduces serious problems of interpretation for the English-speaking reader for whom *right* and *law* are both conceptually and terminologically distinct. Where, therefore, it appears that neither English term will satisfy Tadić's intended meaning, I have given both (e.g., "right and law").

with positive law, and on that basis to avoid positing a rigid opposition between them.

Hegel made a second attempt in this direction in his critique and rejection of the dogmatically established identity of nature and spirit in natural-law and natural-right philosophy brought about by the fact that this philosophy has no clear conception of their points of opposition. If we keep in mind that "spirit," in Hegelian philosophy, is another name for history, then it becomes clear why Hegel definitively rejects the introduction of "dumb nature" into the sphere of lawfulness. In a similar manner he rejects the formalism of Kant and Fichte and upholds a material definition of morality *(Sittlichkeit)* and the situating of lawfulness in that sphere of morality. While the fact that Hegel saw this "moral totality," by means of which the formalism of natural-law constructions is transcended, as residing only with the "people" does not diminish the theoretical significance of his critique. Hegel himself remained a prisoner of legal formalism in many respects. The great contribution of Hegel's critique of natural law and natural right is that instead of referring to the hypothetical freedom of the "state of nature," Hegel pointed to the principles of self-determination and freedom of personality, with which law and right become situated in the context of society and history. In this manner Hegel gave specificity and substance to the seminal idea of German idealism and facilitated the appearance of the dialectical critique of law in Marx's materialist conception of history. The most important stimuli for the Marxist critique of bourgeois law and right were already incorporated into Hegel's critical analyses of bourgeois society.

But while Hegel, in introducing the concept of the "people" into the philosophy of law and right, stood halfway between historicism and rationalism, Marx from the very outset subjected to criticism the historical critique of natural law which derived from Hugo and from Savigny, the founder, or at least the main theoretician, of the "historical school of law." "Hugo," says Marx, "*misinterprets* the master *Kant* in saying that since we cannot know what is *true,* we consequently let pass as *entirely valid* what is *untrue* if it merely *exists* . . . . If what is *positive* is to be *valid because* it is *positive,* then I must *prove* that what is *positive* is *not* valid *since* it is *rational.* And how can I prove this better than by showing that the non-rational is positive and the positive is non-rational, by showing what is positive does not exist *through* reason, but *in spite of* it? If *reason* were the *norm of what is positive,* then *what is positive* would not be *the norm of reason.*"[1]

The positivism of the historical school of law signifies a justification and defense of feudal relations, not with an appeal to their *truth* but with an appeal to the *factuality* of this existence, or rather of their permanence in the *past* on which real history has already turned its back. History as the *past,* in Marx's understanding of history (and law), can no longer be rationally justified, for the *historical untruthfulness* of social relations can no longer be supported on the basis of the fact that those relations existed or still exist. Only those elements in existing reality—because they are historically truthful—are justified which represent the germ of revolution and the *future*. In relation to feudal society and feudal law, the future belongs to bourgeois society and natural law.[2]

But natural-law and natural-right philosophy express the dualism of is *(Sein)* and ought *(Sollen)*, of reality and ideal. From the standpoint of ideals, of that which ought to be, they criticize existing, positive law and right. This dualism is also expressed in the opposition between reason and reality (in the sense of the present). Ideal or absolute law [*pravo*], as *justice,* becomes a critical measure by which the positivity of current law may be judged.

In contrast to natural-law philosophy, which conceives the ideal as a suprahistorical, abstract hypostasis, or in the sense of "endless progress"—as, for example, in the case of *pre*-Hegelian German idealism—Marx, like Hegel, rejected the *abstract-utopian* conception of ideals.[3] In place of the "norm" *(Sollen)*, he echoes Hegel's concept of "existence" *(Werden)*, or identifies "norm" with "existence."[4] In this manner the ideal is understood as the *development,* the *infusion with direction and meaning,* and the *articulation* of *internal social forces* whose movement is empirically evident and can be empirically proved. The ideal does not come into the world by *transcending* theory; rather, it is derived from the *immanence* of the very historical process, from existing, real trends, conflicts, and struggles. In all this the ideal is expressed not as some sort of subjective judgment, desire, or mere demand which can be relativistically embraced or rejected, but as the *objective* expression of the interests and knowledge of specific social forces which represent *historical truthfulness* or, what comes down to the same thing, forces to which the future belongs: the truth *is* not; it *becomes.* Thus in place of the concept of "natural necessity," there appears in Marxism the category of "historical necessity," which operates not only through the technological element of the productive forces, but which also always takes account of the *human* element as the motive force and creator of history.[5] Rejecting the conservative and reactionary understanding of history which relies on the past as the organon of historical occurrence, Marx also rejects that conception of the future which is supported by "this or that reformer of the world."[6] The *changing of the world* is not, for Marx, synonymous with the *reforming of the world,* because revolution, as the true changing of the world, cannot be satisfied with any reforms of that which, of historical necessity, is destined to fail. The reform of the present means only the hindrance and disruption of the necessary working of history, which, bearing within itself the principle of freedom, rebellion, and the urge for objectification, like Hegel's "spirit" burrows like a mole beneath the earth and accomplishes its end. *Reality* is not synonymous with existing *givenness*. History, as the constant approximation of reality, is not complete and never can be, for "every solution poses a new problem, every positive determination contains its negation and thereby the motor for a new positive determination."[7]

Marx does not understand nature, much less human nature, as something forever given and immutable. Such "nature" is merely an abstraction. History, on the contrary, links the endless mutability of nature and human nature through the medium of labor and praxis, a mutability which can be reconstructed from the development of social relations. Change, in this context, does not mean mere change which establishes one order of things in place of another. Revolutionary change is only that change in which a new order arises from the *negativity* of the old. The new positivity is born of a process of overcoming the resistance of the old world, analogous to the process in which, with the application of labor, the resistance of natural matter is overcome and a new product created. *The revolutionary act is a special form of objectification which abolishes reification.* Marx does not prescribe the perfection or ideal of nature, much less its naturalistic form of the "state of nature," as a remedy for the defects of human relations.

Analogously, Marx does not resort to appeals to morality, right, or justice in order to justify the historical necessity of socialism or to discredit the bourgeois system of rule. Marx is not guided by the ideal of some natural right of the proletariat when he subjects capitalist relations of exploitation and bourgeois law to criticism, despite the fact that certain modern theorists are inclined to ascribe to him an absolute concept of justice which, it is true, is *ontologically* rather than ethically relevant.[8] Marx does not, however, view the liberation of the proletariat from relations of capitalist exploitation through the prism of *class* emancipation, but rather exclusively in the perspective of *human liberation* from *all* relations of servitude. It is for precisely this reason that the working class, in its struggle, claims "no *particular right* because the wrong which is done to it is not a *particular wrong* but *wrong in general,* which can claim no *historical* title, but only a *human* title."[9] The liberation of the proletariat is possible, moreover, only as *universal* (human), and not partial (merely class) liberation, since any partial liberation presupposes that one part of the people will remain unfree.

Socialism, as a historical necessity, follows from the very essence of class relations and class struggle in capitalism whose tendency is articulated in revolutionary social theory.

We have shown elsewhere that natural right, at a specific historical moment, spills over into the realm of political economy. Hence in Marx's theory the critique of bourgeois right is most intimately linked to the critique of political economy. Thus the focal categories of the philosophy of natural right—freedom and equality—are viewed by Marx as "idealized forms of exchange and exchange value."

Historically, capitalism is impossible in principle without the abolition of slavery and the dependency relations of serfdom. In practice, this means that the rise of capitalism presupposes the creation of *political freedom* and *legal equality* on the bases of which the *freedom of labor*[10] and the *contracting of labor* are founded. Vital changes, moreover, had to take place in the "master-slave" relationship. The capitalist mode of production—the transformation of money into capital as a social relation—is inconceivable without free labor and the legal subjectivity of the worker,[11] that is to say, without the prior condition of the existence of a worker who, like *every* bourgeois individual, brings to the market a *commodity* of which he disposes; yet he disposes *only* of his labor force or labor capacity. But the political freedom and legal equality of the worker, enabling him to conclude legal contracts for his labor, go hand in hand with his *economic bondage*.[12] Precisely because of the twofold character of this freedom, or the *equivocation* in the bourgeois concept of freedom, Marx, in a paradoxical expression, calls bourgeois society "emancipated slavery."[13]

A closer analysis of the relations of production—that is to say, of bourgeois private property—demonstrates the economic, political, and legal consequences of the labor process and the division of labor in capitalism. In property relations themselves it was inevitable that fundamental changes would take place to generate the "absolute divorce, *separation* of property . . . from labor capacity."[14] In other words, the objective conditions of labor must become so indifferent and alien to living labor power that *objectified, dead labor* imposes itself upon living labor as a ruling force. In the capitalist mode of production the inherent property of labor to be objectified is transformed into *reification,* that is, into a relation in which *things rule people* and the *product rules the producer*.[15] In this manner, the politically free and juridically equal worker (the producer) simultaneously creates his own slavery as well as an alien power and authority. Thus Marx links the rise of *state,* as well, to the process of the *separation, alienation,* and *emancipation* of the product from the producer.[16]

In subsequent analysis, Marx points out that bourgeois property is a historical product. Prior to the formation of the capitalist mode of production, in which exchange value *(Tauschwert)* dominates, property signified no more than man's relationship to the natural conditions of his production as conditions belonging to him, as the "natural presuppositions" and "extended body" of man.[17] This is precisely why Marx, comparing the old forms of production and property with *pure* private property of the bourgeois type, affirms that in these forms it is not *wealth* but *man* himself who appears as the goal of production and hence that the old view was more high-minded than that of the modern world, for which, in contrast, wealth is the goal of production, and production the goal of man. In comparison with the "emptying-out" and "total alienation" of the bourgeois world, the "childish world of antiquity," Marx concludes, appears "loftier."[18]

What are the legal consequences of bourgeois property relations? In the process of exchange both capitalist and worker enter the market as *persons* and exchange their commodities in accordance with the principles of the free exchange of equivalents. In the course of the labor process, however, in spite of the contract between juridically equal subjects, there is created value which is not compensated in wages. The labor contract, and thus law itself, *conceals* the real relation of exploitation and subjugation of the worker. Thus the relation of the exchange of equivalents is transformed into a *"pure semblance"*[19] of equality. The consequence of the bourgeois law of private property is a severe, class-based divorce of right and duty: the *right* of the capitalist to appropriate alien labor without equivalent, and the *duty* of the worker to relate to his labor and to the product of his labor as to alien property.

But from the (private-)*legal* perspective all is in good order. "The circumstance, that on the one hand the daily sustenance of labour power costs only half a day's labour, while on the other hand the very same labour-power can work during a whole day, that consequently value which its use during one day creates, is double what he pays for that use, this circumstance is, without doubt, a piece of good luck for the buyer, but by no means an injury to the seller."[20]

Thus the problems generated by capitalist exploitation and the antagonistic nature of class society cannot, according to Marx, be solved by appealing to right and justice. Where justice is not decisive, force is; bourgeois society can be abolished solely by means of a "despotic encroachment" in property relations, the "expropriation of the expropriators." Marx was left with this conclusion because in bourgeois law the *ideas* of freedom and equality degenerate into a *semblance*, that is, into an *ideology* of freedom and equality.

In the *Critique of the Gotha Program* Marx reaffirmed this conviction. For him *"equal right"* (in the "transition period" as well) "is still in principle—*bourgeois right*, although principle and practice [idea and ideology: L. T.] are no longer at loggerheads . . . ."[21] Bourgeois right "without the bourgeoisie" reigns in the transition period as well since "what we have to deal with here is a communist society, not as it has *developed* on its own foundations, but, on the contrary, just as it *emerges* from capitalist society; which is thus in every respect, economically, morally and intellectually, still stamped with the birthmarks of the old society from whose womb it emerges."[22]

The *equal standard*, moreover, is *labor*. Therefore "this *equal* right is an unequal right for unequal labor. It recognises no class differences . . . but it tacitly recognises unequal individual endowment and thus productive capacity as natural privileges. *It is, therefore, a right of inequality, in its content, like every right.*"[23]

And in the *Critique of the Gotha Program* Marx rejects the independent character of right, which, instead, shares its fate with the economic structure of society and the cultural development conditioned by that structure. So long as labor is a "means of life" but not "life's prime want" for man, so long as the individual is subordinated to the division of labor, he remains in the power of "the narrow horizon of bourgeois right," that is, in a horizon in which labor prevails as the standard of equality. True equality is inconceivable without the abolition of classes. It is possible only in a social order in which the motto is realized: *From each according to his abilities, to each according to his needs.*[24]

If we follow carefully the course of Marx's critique of bourgeois right, then we are left with the conclusion that the focus of his concern was with *private right* or that right whose fundamental category is private property, from the nature of which are derived the concepts of freedom and equality. If it were to be concluded from this that Marx rejects private right on the basis of state or *public right*, then his critique of the state as an alienated force ruling over people—a force which, precisely according to Marx, is merely the *consequence* of the rule of products over the producers—would be senseless. State socialism, however, pits liberal private-right ideology, founded upon an apologia for private property and the freedom based upon it, against a *Staatsrecht* ideology, that is, an apologia for *state property* as socialist property. Yet the historical result of this confrontation has been that the state has replaced the private capitalists as a *collective capitalist*, in which case the producers' relation to the objective conditions of labor is not changed *in principle*. Property has altered its form, but exploitation is not abolished nor is the circumstance that "total human enslavement is involved in the relation of the worker to production." Therefore not the "socialist state," but the free *"association of the producers"* is the form of community in which, according to Marx, human emancipation can be realized and the forms of enslavement deriving from alienation and reification in the labor process abolished. The goal of this association is to create the practical preconditions for the free and multifaceted development of the individual, a society in which these individuals will not *collide* with each other but will rather *relate* as truly free subjects and people.

Only in this association do the postulates of *rational natural right* to *human self-determination* and *self-realization* deriving from German idealism become objectively possible, for the realization of philosophy and the elimination of the proletariat are mutually conditioning factors.[25] It is precisely in these postulates that there is expressed natural right's greatest idea, that of *human dignity,* an idea in which there inheres the demand for the emancipation of human beings from the status of things, i.e., of the objects of right, an idea which cuts across the narrow horizon of bourgeois right. The legal subjectivity of bourgeois right, according to Marx, still does not eliminate, but rather presupposes, the enslavement of man by things.[26] But from this, as we have seen, it does not follow that Marx views political freedom and legal equality as trivial results of bourgeois society. They are merely *inadequate,* although they represent the highest forms of emancipation that can be achieved *within* that society. Thus Marx's critique of the French and American declarations of the rights of man and citizen consists in indicating that in them, in the final analysis, it was not so much an issue of the liberation of *man* as it was of the liberation of the *bourgeois,* the bourgeois "egoistic individual," who is simply passed off as man in general. In those declarations private property, indeed, triumphed over freedom; property was the *boundary* of human rights, that "narrow horizon" which the bourgeois revolutions, in all their *practical* accomplishments, did not succeed in surpassing, although in their *ideal* demands those declarations propounded the universal society. From Marx's critique of private property and its consequences for human freedom, however, it does not at all follow that Marx underestimated or even rejected bourgeois freedom as mere "bourgeois hypocrisy."[27] He criticizes private property insofar as it is an *obstacle* to the realization of *even greater freedom,* i.e., of human self-determination and self-realization in ever greater sociability in which others are not limits to my freedom but rather the guarantee of its realization.

Ernst Bloch is profoundly correct when he says that "everything which qualifies itself as anti-persona, antiliberal is not socialism."[28] The Marxist critique of bourgeois personification and liberalism must be distinguished from the rightest and indeed Nazi-Fascist critique. Yet it must also be distinguished from the pseudoleftist, pseudo-Marxist critique, which not only attacks bourgeois private right but discredits *subjective right* as well. This critique views *subjective public rights* in particular as merely bourgeois and as incompatible with socialist democracy. It is correct that Marx criticized the bourgeois *Rechtsstaat,* but he never considered, nor did it even occur to him to do so, that an absolutist state would be better than a liberal one. Where legislation and jurisprudence serve the ends only of *order and organization,* we are no longer dealing with laws of right but really only (as Bloch says) with mathematical-physical laws which "act without resistance and without exception."[29] Thus the ideal of all authoritarian legislation is the prevalence of duty over right, of sanction over freedom.

The reappearance of "Justinianism"—the imperial-statist concept of right in socialism and the reduction of right and law into a mere technical instrument in the hands of the "socialist state"—has its roots in the fetishization of "objective laws," that is, in a vulgar materialist, mechanistic, and scientistic interpretation of Marxism and socialism. It was precisely this fetishism of the "objective laws" of socialism that created an ideological pretext and justification for the unlimited *voluntarism* of state power. Statist, "socialist" power is legitimized as the executive organ of a suprahistorical and suprahuman lawlike regularity which acts independently of human will,[30] while the "masses" are present to act merely as the mechanical, "extended arms" or even as the passive material of that power or regularity. The "association of the producers" has no place, of course, in a state organization so conceived and realized, for in such a social order there is no place for any organization founded upon the self-determination and self-initiative of the citizens or producers. Planning—through which capitalist reification was to be transcended—rather than being the affair of free associations, is the business of technobureaucratic structures of the state organization and their arbitrariness, while the fulfillment of ministerially imposed (from *above*) plans excludes even the slightest self-activity of the producers and reduces them to the passive objects of a force alien to them which, to repeat, can be overcome only by force as well.

In statist socialism, certain of the negative aspects of capitalism are transformed almost magically into positive qualities of socialism. What Marx and Engels judged to be the vices of capitalist society become the virtues of socialist society. In socialism, too—according to the reigning doctrine—social relations exist independently of human will and consciousness and, so it is claimed, to an even greater degree than in capitalism. The "objective laws" of *socialism* act as *natural necessity* and natural laws, and they are founded, as Engels said of the laws of *capitalist* economies, on the "lack of consciousness of the participants." Marx compared these laws to the law of gravity, for they have the same fateful consequences as "when a house falls about our ears."[31]

The undialectical critique of natural law and right changes into "socialist" legal positivism with the conservative function of stabilizing the existing system of relations. Thus the Marxist critique of bourgeois right loses its emancipatory, dialectical function, while "socialist" legal theory, under the name of "the theory of state and law," is nothing but "legal positivism clothed in Marxist terminology."[32]

The history of this paradoxical and, from the standpoint of human emancipation, fateful transformation can be traced from the "Marxism" of the Second International, itself later to be inherited by Bolshevism. Kautsky's "Marxism" and the similar interpretation of law to be found in the works of Karl Renner[33] continued, despite all the reservations they generated, to play an active role among early Soviet legal theorists such as Stuchka, Raisner, Razumovsky, and Pashukanis.[34] In the works of Soviet theorists, bourgeois law and right are negated by "revolutionary suitability," the determination of this suitability later being transferred to the exclusive competence of the "socialist state" formed on the basis of "socialist" state law and right. State law attained a privileged position in statist socialism and became one of the most important factors in "socialist construction."[35] Thus did "objective lawfulness" become the basis of "juristic" idealism and voluntarism. Juridical laws, as in the sociotechnical *application* of the "objective laws" of social movement, were to safeguard the construction of socialist society by legalizing the "will of the ruling (working) class" through their coercive power. Economic plans, as acts of command, were imposed in the form of laws with criminal sanctions. From the time of the Moscow trials all socialist alternatives to the Stalinist course of the "strengthening of the state" were proscribed and persecuted as the most grievous offense "against the people and the state," while *criminal law* and sophistically interpreted "class law" assumed a place of honor in the system of all-encompassing state law. From this time forward, the path to the enforced slave labor of the concentration camps and the martyrdom of citizens and producers was thrown wide open and justified and sanctioned on the basis of "objective necessity."

Translated by Gerson S. Sher

NOTES

1. See Karl Marx, "The Philosophical Manifesto of the Historical School of Law," in *Writings of the Young Marx on Philosophy and Society,* ed. and trans. by Loyd D. Easton and Kurt H. Guddat (Garden City, N.Y.: 1967), p. 98. In this short essay Marx calls Kant's philosophy "the *German theory* of the French Revolution," and "*Hugo's natural law* . . . the *German theory* of the French Ancien Régime" (*Ibid.,* p. 100). In Hugo's philosophy of law, of course, the expression "natural law" is retained solely in name and without content.

   In his "Contribution to the Critique of Hegel's 'Philosophy of Right': Introduction," Marx calls attention more pointedly to the archaic nature of the ideas of the historical school of law: "A school of thought, which justifies the infamy of today by that of yesterday, which regards every cry from the serf under the knout as a cry of rebellion . . ., a school for which history shows only its *a posteriori* as the God of Israel did for his servant Moses—the *Historical school of law*— might be supposed to have invented German history, if it were not in fact itself an invention of German history." See the *Marx-Engels Reader,* ed. Robert C. Tucker (New York: 1972), p. 13.

   On Marx's attitude toward his professor of law, Savigny, see Hasso Jaeger,

"Savigny et Marx," in *Archives de philosophie du droit* (Paris), vol. XII,1967, pp. 65–89; and Wolf Paul, "Der aktuelle Begriff marxistischer Rechtstheorie," in *Probleme der marxistischen Rechtstheorie*, ed. Hubert Rottleuthner (Frankfurt a/M.: 1975), pp. 79ff.

2. On the concept of the future as a *historical* category, see the exceptional analyses in Milan Kangrga, *Čovjek i svijet: Povijesni svijet i njegova mogućnost* (Zagreb: 1975), pp. 11ff.

3. For more detail, see Ernst Bloch, *Naturrecht und menschliche Würde* (Frankfurt a/M.: 1961), pp. 225ff. See also Ernst Bloch, "Ideale ohne Idealismus," in *Philosophische Aufsätze* (Frankfurt a/M.: 1969), pp. 26–31.

4. "Reason has always existed, only not always in reasonable form. The critic can therefore start out by taking any form of theoretical and practical consciousness and develop from the *unique* forms of existing reality as its norm and final goal" (Karl Marx to Arnold Ruge, September 1843, in *The Marx-Engels Reader*, p. 9). In *The German Ideology,* Marx and Engels call communism the energetic principle of the future, but assert: "Communism is for us not a stable state which is to be established, an *ideal* to which reality will have to adjust itself. We call communism the *real* movement which abolishes the present state of things. The conditions of this movement result from the premises now in existence" (Karl Marx and Friedrich Engels, *The German Ideology* [New York: 1947], p. 26). In *The Civil War in France*, it is asserted, in the same spirit: "The working class . . . [has] no ready-made utopias to introduce *par decret du peuple* . . . . They have no ideals to realize, but to set free the elements of the new society with which old collapsing bourgeois society itself is pregnant" (see *The Marx-Engels Reader,* p. 558). See the critical remarks directed toward Marx's and Engels's "normative abstinence" in Hubert Rottleuthner, "Marxistische und analitische Rechtstheorie," in ed. Rottleuthner, *Probleme der marxistischen Rechtstheorie,* pp. 280–81.

5. In that sense, Marx, as is well known, saw in the *revolutionary class* the most important productive force, i.e., the motive force of history.

6. Marx and Engels, *Werke*, vol. 4 (Berlin: 1974), p. 475.

7. See Ernst Bloch, *Naturrecht und menschliche Würde*, pp. 150–51.

8. See, for example, Ralf Dahrendorf, *Marx in Perspektive* (Hannover: 1952), p. 164.

9. See Marx, "Critique of Hegel's 'Philosophy of Right': Introduction," in *The Marx-Engels Reader*, p. 22. [Editor's note: The translation of the foregoing passage is rendered somewhat differently here than in the cited edition.] "Human right" *(menschlicher Titel)*, "human emancipation," and "human society" appear in Marx in dialectical contrast to "historical right," "political emancipation," and "bourgeois society." Thus, for instance, Marx writes: "From the relationship of estranged labour to private property it further follows that the emancipation of society from private property, etc., from servitude, is expressed in the *political* form of the *emancipation of the workers;* not that *their* emancipation alone was at stake but because the emancipation of the workers contains universal human emancipation—and it contains this, because the whole of human servitude is involved in the relation of the worker to production, and every relation of servitude is but a modification and consequence of this relation" ("Economic and Philosophic Manuscripts of 1844," in *ibid.*, p. 66). Or: "*Political* emancipation certainly represents a great progress. It is not, indeed, the final form of human emancipation, but it is the final form of human emancipation *within* the framework of the prevailing social order ("On the Jewish Question," in *ibid.*, p. 33). Or, finally: "The standpoint of the old materialism is '*civil*' society; the standpoint of the new is *human* society, or socialized humanity" ("Theses on Feuerbach," in *ibid.*, p. 109).

All these passages testify to Marx's insight that in bourgeois society and bourgeois law, only the right and freedom of the *bourgeois individual,* and not of *man,* are possible. Human rights and human freedoms are possible only in a humane society, or in a society *without classes.* But this society is likewise impossible with-out the entire wealth of previous historical development.

10. "The slave, together with his labour power, is sold once and for all to his owner . . . . He is *himself* a commodity, but the labour power is not *his* commodity. The *serf* sells only a part of his labour power. He does not receive a wage from the landowner; rather, the landowner receives a tribute from him . . . . The *free labourer,* on the other hand, sells himself and, indeed, sells himself piecemeal." "Labour power was not always a *commodity. Labour* was not always wage labour, that is, *free labour*" (Karl Marx, "Wage Labour and Capital," in *The Marx-Engels Reader,* p. 171).

11. "For the conversion of his money into capital, therefore, the owner of money must meet in the market with the free labourer, free in the double sense, that as a free man he can dispose of his labour-power as his own commodity, and that on the other hand he has no other commodity for sale, is short of everything necessary for the realisation of his labour-power" (Karl Marx, *Capital* [New York: 1967], vol. I, p. 169. Marx accounted for the possibility of this meeting with the worker on the labor market by referring to the history of the "primary accumulation of capital," particu-larly in England.

12. "The worker leaves the capitalist to whom he hires himself whenever he likes . . . . But the worker, whose sole source of livelihood is the sale of his labour power, cannot leave the *whole . . . capitalist class,* without renouncing his existence. He belongs not to this or that capitalist but to the *capitalist class*" (Marx, "Wage Labour and Capital," in *The Marx-Engels Reader,* p. 171).

13. See Karl Marx and Friedrich Engels, *Werke,* vol. 2 (Berlin: 1959), p. 129.

14. Karl Marx, *Grundrisse,* trans. Martin Nicolaus (New York: 1973), p. 452.

15. Marx calls this consequence of the capitalist mode of production the "personification of objects" and the "representation of persons by things" (*Capital,* vol. I, p. 114). Elsewhere (*Grundrisse,* p. 157), Marx says in this connection: "The social character of activity, as well as the social form of the product, and the share of individuals in production here appear as something alien and objective, confronting the individ-uals, not as their relation to one another, but as their subordination to relations which subsist independently of them and which arise out of collisions between mutually indifferent individuals. The general exchange of activities and products, which has become a vital condition for each individual—their mutual interconnec-tion—here appears as something alien to them, autonomous, as a thing. In exchange value, the social connection between persons is transformed into a social relation between things; personal capacity into objective wealth."

16. "This crystallization of social activity, this consolidation of what we ourselves pro-duce into an objective power above us, growing out of our control, thwarting our expectations, bringing into naught our calculations, is one of the chief factors in historical development up till now. And out of this very contradiction between the interest of the individual and that of the community the latter takes an independent form as the *state,* divorced from the real interests of individual and community, and at the same time as an illusory communal life . . ." (Marx, *German Ideology,* pp. 22–23).

17. Marx, *Grundrisse,* p. 491.

18. *Ibid.,* p. 489.

19. *Ibid.,* p. 458.

20. Karl Marx, *Capital* (New York: 1967), vol. I, p. 194. What is at issue here is not only the semblance of equality, but the illusion of freedom on the basis of *free competition:* "The assertion that free competition = the ultimate form of the development of the forces of production and hence of human freedom means nothing other than that middle-class rule is the culmination of world history—certainly an agreeable thought for the parvenus of the day before yesterday" (Marx, *Grundrisse,* p. 652).

21. Karl Marx, "Critique of the Gotha Program," in *The Marx-Engels Reader,* p. 387.

22. *Ibid.*, p. 386.
23. *Ibid.*, p. 387.
24. *Ibid.*, p. 388. In his famous letters to J. Bloch, Starkenburg, and Mehring, Engels attempted to stress the relative independence of right and law (and of the rest of the superstructure), emphasizing that Marx and he had neglected this in their works.
25. Marx's radically formulated "categorical imperative" reads: "... *to overthrow all those conditions* in which man is an abased, enslaved, abandoned, contemptible being ..." (Marx, "Contribution to the Critique of Hegel's 'Philosophy of Right': Introduction," in *The Marx-Engels Reader*, p. 18). In the "association of the producers" public power loses its political character, casting off its "political shell."
26. "Reification in modern society is the price of personification"—Eric Weil, *Philosophie politique* (Paris: 1956), p. 37.
27. Otherwise, Marx would never have written his brilliant works devoted to the critique of German *jurisprudence*, particularly those in which he attacked *press censorship*. Note, for instance, these words: "We are to act within the legal boundaries of and with respect for the law, but at the same time we are to obey institutions that make us lawless and replace law with arbitrariness." (Karl Marx, "Comments on the Latest Prussian Censorship Instruction," in Easton and Guddatt, p. 82). Or: "in a society in which *one* organ thinks of itself as the only, exclusive possessor of reason and morality on the state level, a government that in principle opposes the people and assumes that *their subversive attitude* is universal and normal, the civil conscience of a faction—such a government invents tendentious laws, *laws of revenge*, against an attitude existing only in the members of the government themselves" (*ibid.*, p. 80). Or, furthermore: "Laws that make the *sentiment* of the acting person the main criterion, and not the *act as such*, are nothing but *positive sanctions of lawlessness*" (*ibid.*, p. 79). Marx concluded this essay with a famous sentence from Tacitus, "*Rara temporum felicitas, ubiquae vilis sentire et quae sentias dicere licet*" (How rare the fortunate times in which you can think what you wish and say what you wish) (*ibid.*, p. 92). And finally, a footnote concerning Engels's attitude toward right and freedom: "... that same English law is the only one which has preserved through the ages, and transmitted to America and the Colonies, the best part of that old Germanic personal freedom, local self-government and independence from all interference but that of the law courts—which on the Continent has been lost during the period of absolute monarchy, and has nowhere been as yet fully recovered" (Engels, Special Introduction to the English Edition of 1892 of "Socialism: Utopian and Scientific," in Karl Marx and Frederick Engels, *Selected Works* (New York: 1968), p. 392.
28. Bloch, *Naturrecht und menschliche Würde*, p. 214.
29. "Where there solely or predominantly reigns only command on the one hand and subordination on the other, as in a company or in a Jesuitic order, norms are not legal [Editor's note: norms of right]" (*ibid.*, p. 242).
30. Confirming this fact, Joachim Perels accurately observes: "Objective laws, in Marx, possess no suprahistorical character; they are the externally enforced laws of the capitalist mode of production, to which individuals are subordinated as objects of exchange. In socialism these laws, according to Marx and Engels, are abolished and, through the rational planning of the production process, are replaced by the associated producers who work with socialized means of production" ("Der staatlich verordnete Sozialismus," in the above-cited Rottleuthner volume, p. 350).
31. Marx, *Capital*, vol. I, p. 75. See also Perels, p. 352.
32. Oskar Negt, "10 Thesen zur marxistischen Rechtstheorie," in the Rottleuthner volume *(op. cit.)*, p. 33.
33. See Karl Renner, *The Institutions of Private Law and Their Social Functions*, ed. O. Kahn-Freund and trans. Agnes Schwarzschild (London: 1949).
34. See my "Sovjetska teorija prava u periodu od Oktobarske revolucije do 1928.

godine," *Pregled* (Sarajevo), no. 11–12, 1957; and "Teorija J. B. Pašukanisa i neki problemi marksističke teorije prava," an introduction to my translation of Pashukanis's *Opšta teorija prava i marksizma* (The General Theory of Law and Marxism) (Sarajevo: 1958). In the recent literature concerned with the problem we refer to the above-cited work of Oskar Negt (especially pp. 46ff.); Norbert Reich, *Marxistische Rechtstheorie, Historische und aktuelle Diskussionen und Tendezen* (Tübingen: 1973); Umberto Cerroni, *Marx e il diritto moderno* (Rome: 1962); as well as the above-cited *Archives de philosophie du droit* (Paris), vol. XII, 1967, which is wholly dedicated to the theme, "Marx et le droit moderne."

35. In the name of legal "radicalism" Vyshinsky and Yudin accused Pashukanis and other Soviet theorists of "legal nihilism" merely because they were disturbed by any theory of the withering away of the state and law. Thus, for example, in an article on "Socialism and Law" (*Bolshevik*, no. 17, 1 September 1937, p. 35), Yudin drew a "difference in principle" between Soviet and bourgeois legal forms, which did not hinder him from defining law *(pravo) abstractly* as the "totality of laws issued and propagated by the state," as "the actively expressed will of the ruling class which consecrates and immortalizes the ruling class's economic and political interests" (p. 33). In the same article (p. 42) Yudin concludes: "It is necessary to liberate ourselves once and for all from *hostile* theories [my emphasis: L. T.] which attempt to demonstrate the necessity of the withering away of the state at the present stage." The senselessness of this demand for "liberation" follows from the fact that Yudin, on the one hand, sophistically interprets the *withering away* of the state as a mere act of *abolishing* the state. On the other hand, however, this demand is in pragmatic accord with Stalin's theory of the *strengthening of the state* and the continual sharpening of "class struggle" in the process of the construction of socialism.

Self-Realization, Equality, and Freedom

Zagorka Golubović

I

The first and fundamental condition for the achievement of freedom—freedom for *all*, not merely for some members of society—is the achievement of social equality among people or, to invert the proposition, the *abolition of social inequalities* which, for those members of society who belong to the unprivileged classes, serve as a chain of objective impediments and restraints not only upon the development and fulfillment of their human potentialities, but upon their very ability to ensure themselves the minimum conditions of human existence. To speak, therefore, about freedom in societies where the principle of social inequality prevails is to accept as normal a distinction between "free" and "unfree" people, for in such societies the freedom exists as a *privilege* of certain classes and individuals.

The essential difference between bourgeois and socialist society consists precisely in the fact that in socialism, these two principles—*equality* and *freedom*—must go hand in hand, qualitatively changing the very meaning of freedom. Then freedom no longer has a narrowly legal and political meaning (freedom as the right to speak, write, and associate freely and to be subject to the law as a citizen of the state[1]); it

175

acquires a much broader and more profound meaning, transforming itself into the possibility and demand for *human self-realization.*

Bourgeois society can accept and proclaim freedom only in the former, political sense since such freedom does not imply the social equality of all citizens at any cost but is instead content with equal rights within the framework of the elite strata of society, i.e., those to whom bourgeois culture (newspapers, journals, science, artistic works, and so forth) is accessible. It is incapable of even verbally embracing freedom in the latter, *human* sense since this would contradict several basic principles upon which bourgeois society is founded (the principle of free competition and defense of private property, along with the closely connected assumption that people are "by nature" unequal and that this determines who will occupy what place in the social hierarchy).

The principle of human self-realization presupposes social equality and social conditions in which this demand can be realized not only for *some* but for *all* members of society. A socialist system which articulates this principle is the antithesis of societies which tolerate the existence of privileged and unprivileged social strata. Thus the question of social equality is the touchstone of socialist society and, it may be said, its principal aspiration.

There are, however, two interpretive variants of social equality—or rather, two types of demands for abolishing social inequality. Both represent a modification of the radical demand for the achievement of social equality.[2]

The first variant modifies the principle of equality by "proving" that there is "natural inequality" among people; the second, by justifying inequality which arises from the results of labor. In the first case "biological proofs" are invoked and in the second, "social interests," but in fact in both cases these "proofs" are taken as a priori truths without examining their nature and the problems inherent to them.

What, then, is the status of these "proofs" which are to persuade us that the radical demand for social equality is a utopian illusion?

Let us begin with "natural inequality." It is a familiar fact that people are differentiated not only by virtue of their external qualities, but also by virtue of their abilities, temperaments, and pursuits. In this sense people are not equal—that is, *they are not uniform.* But to assert this is completely different from "proving" that people are by nature unequal, that some are born with natural ability and others without— which further implies that some are predetermined to be leaders, the elite, while others are to be the led, the mass, and so on. (We could go even further, deriving all that follows from this line of reasoning and which is quite well known in the annals of social theory and social relations.)

To be sure, some people are born with higher intelligence quotients, with more distinct abilities for effective action and creativity than others; some acquire dispositions at birth which—under suitable conditions—make them passive and disinterested in active participation in social and cultural processes; others come into the world with significantly diminished abilities to understand what is occurring around them and—under suitable conditions—this dulls their intellects and stunts their potentials. All this can of course be proved by empirical analysis. But any substantive analysis must pose the question of the *causes* of the "natural inequality" of individuals, abandoning pure description and bringing into question the innateness of such fundamental differences.

Modern psychology, which devotes a great deal of attention to problems of early socialization and on this basis attempts to explain individual personality structure, can offer counterproofs to the thesis that unequal fundamental abilities among individuals are the result of the "unequal biological nature of man" in the sense of innate, unalterable properties. The problem of biological and "social" heredity is intimately connected with this, for it is demonstrated that many so-called natural inequalities among people arise as a result of the transmission of certain socially reinforced dispositions and as a function of the sociocultural conditions into which children are born and in which, even more likely, their parents (and often earlier ancestors) lived as well. The social conditions of children and parents depend above all upon the social class to which they belong and the social and cultural opportunities which are at its disposition. In this web of factors the parents represent a channel of socially "inherited" qualities and abilities (or disabilities), since on the one hand they reflect the social circumstances under which they themselves were formed, while on the other they pass on to their children certain confirmed qualities, habits, and inclinations as definite potentials for their own personalities and in that manner offer them a primary framework within which their children's dispositions will be stimulated or suppressed.

When this process is viewed across a succession of generations, it could be asserted that essential differences among people—such as, for instance, the distinct creative abilities of some individuals and the absence of all creativity among others or a high level of independence and commitment to act in accordance with one's own principles as opposed to a complete absence of independence and commitment to formulate a distinct "I"—arise historically, as the result of the quite different social and cultural circumstances in which individuals are formed, constrained as they are to live in determinate conditions. For how can it be otherwise explained that there has always been a far greater number of able, intelligent, creative individuals among the elite strata of society, while in the lower strata such people have been the exception—except if we accept the standpoint that elitism is something innate, threatening us with the danger of biologizing society and social divisions, which modern science has long since rejected.

In other words, inherited differences in essential human qualities can be explained by differences which have arisen in historical circumstances which impose upon people different conditions of life which, subsequently, accumulate over a series of generations and ultimately appear as the "inherited" qualities of the descendents. The fact that individuals belong to different classes implies that some find their positive potential stimulated while others find it pemanently frustrated. In a historical perspective, this yields the result of an accumulation of a greater number of abilities in the ranks of the privileged strata and, conversely, an accumulation of limited abilities among the unprivileged. In this manner, social inequality accumulates and is transmitted to posterity as "natural inequality." It needs no proof that children reared in an environment in which their ancestors belonged for generations to the higher cultural strata will bring into the world a richer degree of human potential than children whose ancestors belonged to a long historical line of exclusively manual laborers, deprived of even an elementary degree of culture.[3] Accordingly, what we call "natural inequalities"—which, in an empirical sense, cannot be denied—are ultimately the result of the protracted action of social inequality and can be resolved, moreover, only through the abolition of the source from which they arise. This is not to assert that all differences among people will be eliminated, not even in the sense of differences of degree with respect to the development of certain abilities, but only to say that the elimination of social inequality will be accompanied by the elimination of the division of people into the able and the inept, since favorable sociocultural conditions for all members of society can stimulate specific abilities in *every* member of society to a certain degree. And a world in which there will live people of different abilities will surely look quite different from the present world, in which some are born able while others must accept the position of the "less highly valued" as a "natural" law.

What are the social implications of this interpretation of "natural inequality" among people? This conception presupposes that with fundamentally altered social conditions—if all social and cultural values are made accessible to all members of society—and without privileges and rights to greater participation in the distribution of social and cultural goods whether by virtue of inherited title or the achievement of high social position, "natural inequality" will be transformed into natural differences in characteristics, inclinations, and the possession of various abilities without classifying a single individual a priori in the number of the inferior (except for mentally undeveloped and disturbed persons, who, also, must be treated as medical cases and not as less valuable in a social sense).

Thus, the genuinely radical demand for the elimination of social inequality can solve both the problem of "natural inequality" as well as make the self-realization of man an operative principle of socialism. And vice versa, the "proof" of "natural inequality," which is utilized as an argument against radicalization of the demand for the elimination of social inequality, is merely a sophism which begs the question, for it fails to verify its initial assumption and to identify the causes of the phenomenon which it seeks to explain.

Justification of social inequality on the basis of the results of labor is also linked to a deliberate avoidance of posing the question of how and *why* there come to be different results of labor, on the basis of which very important forms of social inequality are founded: unequal distribution of material goods, unequal opportunities for participation in culture (above all, in the process of education), and unequal conditions for the achievement of certain social positions (even in the bourgeois sense, in the form of social mobility). One of the causes of the differential labor contributions of individuals is what we have discussed above, i.e., the reproduction of social inequality through accumulated "natural inequalities," in which individuals born into favorable social circumstances have significantly greater opportunities to prepare themselves better for their activities and professions and to achieve superior labor results. Another cause, however, is of an entirely different order and derives from the voluntaristic evaluation of labor value, not as the real results of an individual's work but as types of work in which human activity is hierarchically classified and evaluated—not on the basis of their *social* importance (for every society's existence depends much more on production workers than on politicians!), but on the basis of the social *position* which a specific type of work implies. Thus, according to this principle, the higher the social position associated with a specific type of labor, the more highly the "labor result"—which is evaluated abstractly, independently of the real and concrete result which is actually achieved[4]—is valued.

And, finally, the self-reproduction of social strata, which for the mass of peasant and worker children predetermines that the majority will remain within the boundaries of those strata and will be able at the most to train for certain professions (usually those near the bottom of the hierarchical ladder), perpetuates social inequality as well as the limited framework in which individuals from these strata will be able to develop their abilities, to broaden their education, and to prepare themselves more successfully for advancement up the social ladder of the professions and social status.

If, therefore, one attempts to get to the root significance of social differences which arise "on the basis of the results of labor," one must confront these implications. And since in socialism, too, it is individuals from the peasant and worker strata who are mainly affected by these differences, historically generated "natural inequalities" come to be set in concrete, and the circle is closed.

It is evident that so long as there is social inequality among people and strata, freedom remains a privilege—be it of specific classes, groups, or energetic individuals who succeed in earning it. Under these circumstances it still has not become a general and fundamental condition for humane living.

II

Freedom understood in the broad human (and not the narrow political) sense of the term is linked to the principle of the self-realization of the personality and the creation of humane conditions of life. Indeed this very definition of freedom implies that at issue is not merely the freedom of certain exceptional individuals,[5] but rather freedom as a way of life for each individual. It might be said that the concept of freedom here is taken in the sense of "freedom for," rather than in the limited sense of "freedom from" (as Fromm makes the distinction).

In this understanding of freedom as a principle of human community there is a qualitative distinction between bourgeois, civil society and bourgeois democracy, on the one hand, and socialist society and social self-management, on the other.

In bourgeois society, freedom is understood above all as the right to be guaranteed due process and freedom from coercion and repression, to defend civil rights in the sense of the autonomy of the citizen. In other words, bourgeois society can go no further than to guarantee the individual's right not to be persecuted for his thought expressed in written or verbal form and to defend the individual from state arbitrariness within the boundaries in which the individual *as a citizen* must be free so as to be able to participate in bourgeois society.[6] Bourgeois society, however, stops here, for the bourgeois revolution proclaims the *freedom of the citizen* but not the complete human emancipation of the individual. Nor does bourgeois society create the basic preconditions for a more complete human emancipation, since it is founded upon the economic (and, accordingly, the broader social) inequality of individuals and classes and upon exploitation and antagonistic class interests. Thus bourgeois society is incapable of stimulating freedom in a deeper human sense—freedom for people to create the conditions of their own lives and to make sovereign decisions about them.[7]

Freedom, conceived in the sense of the individual's ability to develop unhindered as a human being and to emancipate his entire human potential—in social and cultural conditions which stimulate this process rather than obstruct it—is a qualitatively new definition of freedom. It is the goal of socialist society, in the name of which the socialist revolution was fought and in the name of which socialist ideas and movements continue to appeal to this very day, despite contrary experiences in terms of practical results in countries with socialist political systems.

Any socialist society which embraces the principle of *self-management* cannot renounce two vital preconditions for the realization of a self-managing society: social equality and freedom conceived in the above sense. (Naturally, the realization of freedom in the sense of the guaranteeing of the basic bourgeois rights is the first step toward the achievement of freedom more broadly conceived.)

Among the paradoxes confronted by socialist societies—which had not been preceded by well-developed bourgeois institutions and the tradition of bourgeois democracy—was the paradox of the nonachievement of bourgeois rights side by side with socialist demands for the achievement of those human rights which far surpass bourgeois society. Thus it has happened that the fundamental principle of communist society, "the freedom of the individual as the condition for the freedom of all," has been inverted into the principle of the freedom of the impersonal collective and the "sacrifice of individual interests for the sake of the social interest." In this context all bourgeois rights are denounced as bourgeois preconceptions, and instead of departing from the achievement of these rights to build a bridge to more complete human emancipation, they are rejected in their entirety and with them the right of the individual to fight for his freedom. This is why the question of bourgeois rights continues to be so urgent for socialist societies today, and when it is posed it is not so that the struggle for human emancipation may be concluded, but because without it the struggle *cannot even be begun.*

Yet one finds that the refusal to recognize elementary bourgeois rights, without which there is no freedom even in the most limited sense of the term, is replaced by the thesis about the refusal to remain bound by the legacy of bourgeois society. This is evident when it is said that bourgeois democracy cannot be the goal of socialism—which is correct; but it is forgotten that without elementary bourgeois democracy as a basic medium it is impossible to create even the foundations of self-management, for, first of all, bourgeois democracy guarantees basic human security, enabling people in this way to participate in self- management, and second, it builds institutions in which at least the basic principles of democracy must be respected, which is also a good "primary school" in which people learn to utilize their freedom. Conversely, it is often proclaimed that support for the guaranteeing of elementary bourgeois rights—which is the condition for free participation in a self-managing society—represents reconciliation to bourgeois society. Probably this inversion is necessary for the justification of individual reprisals, for it is in principle impossible to explain why the development of self-management requires intensified repression.

Simultaneously, *truth* as the social expression of the human right to equality and freedom has come to be replaced increasingly often by the notion of *legality,* since the criterion of law (forgetting that law is an essential aspect of the state and that the state is an inevitable institution of class society) serves as the basis for evaluating what is socially permissable and what is not, instead of the law being merely a means for the increasingly successful approximation of social justice.

Since the law—as the juridical expression of the power of the ruling class and of the state as its institution—is in essential opposition to freedom as a human attribute (the law may defend only specific rights which come under the concept of "granted rights" from the standpoint of the state), insistence on legality implies that this principle must ultimately come into conflict with several essential principles of socialism, such as those of equality and freedom which have already been discussed in this essay. Thus to address ourselves merely to a few terms which are in current use, one may hear of legal and illegal enrichment, the restriction of people's rights as citizens "in the interest of state security," and so forth.

This does not mean that freedom tolerates only anarchy in the layman's sense of the term. But it is overlooked that between anarchy and law as the instrument of the state there exists a wide range of much more suitable social behavior and control, such as, for instance, the free and responsible decision making of subjects of organized associations, which presupposes the preservation of a much broader latitude for individual and group initiative and freedom than when assessments of "the possible" are made by one or several bureaucratic centers. In this manner "organized freedom" in responsible associations might present an alternative to the classical and less-than-classical forms of coercion in which freedom as an attribute of the life of each member of society disappears and remains only in its most narrow and restricted forms—always the privilege of the few.

In discussing freedom it is vital to emphasize these different meanings in order to comprehend what is meant when individual societies assert that they respect freedom as a mode of behavior for their members, which in itself need not be a false assertion but may denote very different things. Therefore, so long as we do not consider *for whom* a society guarantees freedom and *what kind* of freedom it permits, we cannot make judgments about the degree of humaneness which that society has achieved.

Translated by Gerson S. Sher

NOTES

1. By saying this I do not wish to underestimate this aspect of freedom—insofar as not even this degree of freedom has yet been achieved in socialist systems—but only to point to the limited significance of freedom so conceived, which remains within the framework of specific *political rights of man as a citizen.*

2. It is common nowadays to treat the radicalization of this demand in a pejorative manner—as "equality in poverty," or as *"uravnilovka,"* which is fundamentally inconsistent with the principle of the self-realization of individual potentials since the principle of self-realization of individuals is replaced exclusively by the principle of the interest of the collective.

3. Here is where an answer is to be sought to the question of the self-reproduction of social strata (including the intelligentsia), for children from the lower strata compete with children from the higher strata and are handicapped at the very outset, since they are deprived of that positive "social heredity" which enables the latter to achieve better results with less effort in the process of schooling. But here also lies the touchstone of socialism, which must contribute toward overcoming this social injustice through social measures and commitment of resources.

4. For how is it otherwise to be explained that an enterprise director is remunerated independently of the losses suffered by the workers' collective, even though the workers receive a diminished income? [Editor's note: In Yugoslav factories, following the principle of self-management but also that of commercial incentive, workers' wages are allocated directly from profits and thus vary with the fortunes of the enterprise. The director's salary, however, is determined by the workers' council at a fixed level.] The same analogy could be raised in the area of politics as well, in which the bill for failures is paid not by those who are at the helm but by those who had no share in the "political mistakes" which have been made.

5. Intellectuals, too, often take an interest in their own freedom, postulating the demand for free cultural creativity; I feel, however, that the first demand of any true intellectual must be the achievement of freedom as a condition of humane living and of respect for the human dignity of each person, which is much more general and fundamental than the freedom of cultural creativity since it relates to *all* members of society and not only to those who have the privilege of being the creators of culture. In the absence of this more general demand it is possible for intellectuals merely to parade the freedom of creativity for all those who are not among the creators of culture.

6. Of course, this is a great legacy of bourgeois society which should not be underestimated, nor is it the intention of the present discussion to do so.

7. This is why [Editor's note: in bourgeois societies] the demand for self-management as a community of free people is transformed into a demand for "participation in management," which fails to go beyond the framework of the bourgeois conception of freedom since it does not disturb the basic heritage of bourgeois society but rather coincides with it, as some adherents of the Left emphasize, in a program of integration into the existing system.